AMERICA THROUGH EUROPEAN EYES

A NARRATIVE OF A JOURNEY
THROUGH THE
EASTERN & WESTERN STATES
OF
AMERICA

Sketches of America

A

NARRATIVE

OF A JOURNEY

OF FIVE THOUSAND MILES THROUGH THE

EASTERN AND WESTERN STATES

OF

AMERICA

WITH REMARKS ON

MR. BIRKBECK'S "NOTES" AND "LETTERS"

BY

HENRY BRADSHAW FEARON

[1818]

AUGUSTUS M. KELLEY · PUBLISHERS

NEW YORK 1970

First Edition 1818

Second Edition 1818

(London: *Printed for* Longman, Hurst, Rees, Orme & Brown, *Paternoster-Row*, 1818)

Reprinted 1970 by

AUGUSTUS M. KELLEY · PUBLISHERS

REPRINTS OF ECONOMIC CLASSICS

New York New York 10001

. . . .

S B N 678 00584 2

L C N 70 100124

. . . .

PRINTED IN THE UNITED STATES OF AMERICA

by SENTRY PRESS, NEW YORK, N. Y. 10019

Sketches of America.

A

NARRATIVE OF A JOURNEY

OF FIVE THOUSAND MILES

THROUGH

THE EASTERN AND WESTERN STATES

OF

AMERICA;

CONTAINED IN EIGHT REPORTS

ADDRESSED TO THE

THIRTY-NINE ENGLISH FAMILIES

BY WHOM THE AUTHOR WAS DEPUTED, IN JUNE 1817, TO ASCERTAIN WHETHER ANY, AND WHAT PART OF THE UNITED STATES WOULD BE SUITABLE FOR THEIR RESIDENCE.

WITH

REMARKS ON

MR. BIRKBECK'S "NOTES" AND "LETTERS."

By HENRY BRADSHAW FEARON.

SECOND EDITION.

LONDON:
PRINTED FOR LONGMAN, HURST, REES, ORME, AND BROWN,
PATERNOSTER-ROW.
1818.

ADVERTISEMENT

TO

THE SECOND EDITION.

THE early demand for a Second Edition of this work, affords decided evidence of the deep-felt interest which exists in the minds of the people of England upon the subject of Emigration to the United States.

With the success of my maiden effort I am much gratified, and hope most sincerely that the information contained in these "REPORTS" may be of benefit to my countrymen, and also assist in producing a correct and sound mode of thinking in relation to the country and people of America.

Some friends of general liberty have suggested that this work is calculated to injure the principles which they, in common with myself and my most intimate friends, revere: if this *is* its tendency, nothing can be more opposite to my design; but I feel confident that the publication of truth ought not, and indeed eventually cannot, be detrimental to the cause of political freedom and human happiness.

That the state of things in the American Republic should be so opposite to what the advocates of enlightened opinions in Great Britain imagine, is a fact which none can deplore with greater sincerity than myself; but that, in my opinion, this difference is not chargeable upon the political principles of their government, will be seen by a perusal of the review of the American character, which commences at page 350., and to which I beg to direct the attention of the reflective reader.

I have to solicit indulgence for the grammatical errors which exist in the first impression, and have also to state, that my avocations will not allow me to attend to their correction in the present edition, at least sufficiently early to meet the public demand for the work.

H. B. FEARON.

Adam Street, Adelphi,
Nov. 6th, 1818.

INTRODUCTORY REMARKS.

In submitting the following pages to the Public, it is my wish that the reader should be put fairly in possession of the circumstances under which they were written.

I was deputed by a circle of friends, whose persons and whose interests are most dear to me, to visit the *United States of America,* in order to furnish them with materials to regulate their decision on the subject of emigration. Into the motives and the views which led to this proposed measure on their part, it is not requisite that I should enter much in detail; they are, I fear, known and *felt* too generally to render description necessary.

Emigration had, at the time of my appointment, assumed a totally new character: it was no longer merely the poor, the idle, the profligate, or the wildly speculative, who were proposing to quit their native country; but men also of capital, of industry, of sober habits and regular pursuits; men of reflection, who apprehended approaching evils; men of upright and conscientious minds, to whose happiness civil and religious liberty were essential; and men of domestic feelings, who wished to provide for the future support and prosperity of their offspring.

Under such circumstances as these it was, that my friends directed their thoughts, in the way of enquiry merely, to the subject of emigration to America; having so done, they naturally set themselves seriously to investigate the state of the country and the character of the people; but, singular as it may appear, they were unable to obtain satisfactory information. Most of the books which they could procure contained statements which were evidently partial; some were written to exalt and some to vilify the situation of the country and its inhabitants, but none of them possessed that *kind* of information which was wanted by my friends; no lists of prices, of wages, rents, &c. *; no statements, or but imperfect ones, relative to individual trades or manufactures; little or nothing, in short, of that *homely* kind of intelligence which was wanted on such an occasion. It was, at length, resolved that some one should visit the country to make the necessary enquiries — the lot fell upon myself; but I owe it in justice both to the public

* It may be proper to observe that, in the following pages, the prices of live stock, &c. are often stated in what may appear singular amounts; this arises from turning American dollars into British currency.

and *to* myself to state, that circumstances, which, at the time, left me free from my usual pursuits, rather than any supposed peculiar fitness for the undertaking, guided their choice of me for the task; although it is among the first pleasures of my life to reflect that they relied, at least, upon my faithfulness and industry.

Recurring to the fact of publication, I pretend to few, if any, of the accomplishments which are deemed necessary for the regular traveller, writing professedly for the instruction or amusement of the public. The information, however, which I was deputed to collect, I sought for with all the diligence, and forwarded with all the accuracy, in my power. *It was my wish to put my friends as much as possible into my situation*—to inform them both of what I saw myself, and what I learned from others, where I thought *that* information might be relied upon. My enquiries were facilitated by various introductions, and aided by some personal friends who had previously emigrated to America.

I arrived in the city of New York August 6th, 1817, and finally quitted that place May 10th, 1818, after having made a tour, including both the Eastern and Western States of the American Union. Returned to England, I have, naturally enough, received applications for information relative to the country I had visited, from many persons disposed to settle there: some of these were parties of respectability and capital, not dissimilar in their views and objects from those which my friends had proposed to themselves. To these, therefore, the information I had collected might be supposed to be not unacceptable; many others, for various reasons, may wish to be possessed of these facts: such are the motives which have induced me to submit my "Reports" to the public. In forming their estimate of this production, I have therefore to request of my readers to bear constantly in mind the view with which I have written, and not expect to find the work *that which the author does not pretend it to be.* My object has not been to make a book; but circumstances having occurred to give me information which appears valuable because it may be useful, I wish to give it to the world,—and am content to do so in a plain, unvarnished manner.

The work may have many faults and numerous imperfections. Little accustomed as I am to write for the public eye, the critic will probably find in it much to censure—in style—in arrangement—and perhaps in materials; but the object I have had in view will, at least, be a pledge to the public of the *faithfulness* and *sincerity* of my statements. My intention in writing has certainly been neither to flatter nor deceive: my Reports were originally composed neither with a view to fame nor profit, — neither to exalt a country, to support a party, nor to promote a settlement. I have had every motive to speak what I thought the truth, and none to conceal or pervert it. The interests of my dearest friends depended most intimately upon the correctness of my statements. I wished to put them in possession of every thing I knew: the public will now decide whether what I have found to communicate be either useful or instructive.

TO

THE FRIENDS

OF

CIVIL AND RELIGIOUS LIBERTY,

THROUGHOUT GREAT BRITAIN AND IRELAND,

THESE PAGES

ARE RESPECTFULLY SUBMITTED,

BY

H. B. FEARON.

Plaistow, Essex,
October 2nd, 1818.

SKETCHES OF AMERICA.

Voyage in the Ship Washington from Isle of Wight.— Celebration of American Independence on board.— Debating Society.— Off Sandy Hook.— First Impressions of the People and of the City of New York.— Mrs. Bradish's Boarding-House.— Commodore Rogers.— Conversation at Dinner.— Suspicion of Corruption in the American Government Contracts.— Prices of Articles and Rent of Shops.

New York, August 9th, 1817.

MY DEAR FRIENDS,

I EMBRACE the first opportunity of communicating my safe arrival in this land of liberty, which I am enabled to do by the politeness of Sir James Yeo, who sails this day. We landed here on Wednesday the 6th instant. You are aware that the vessel in which I sailed is the Washington, Captain Foreman, which left London the 4th of June. I went on board at the Isle of Wight on the 14th, and we proceeded on our course the following day. The cabin was crowded, having nineteen passengers, amongst whom were Mr. or (according to American etiquette) The HONOURABLE John Quincey Adams, (late ambassador at the Court of St. James's, but now Secretary of State,) his lady and family: the gentlemen were chiefly Americans. You will be somewhat surprised to learn that Mr. George Washington Adams (eldest son of the Secretary) and myself were the only warm friends of political liberty; a subject which, of course, often came under discussion. All were its advocates in some limited or refined sense; but we stood alone in wishing its extension to England, to unfortunate Ireland, to France, to the European Continent generally, and to the brave South Americans. I delivered the letters of introduction, with which Alderman Wood and others had favoured me, to Mr. Adams; and wish to acknowledge the polite attentions which, in consequence, I received from him.

My passage-money was forty guineas, exclusive of wines, &c. A sea-life was to me more novel than pleasing. Sickness, the usual lot of fresh-water sailors, was my companion. It was extreme for eight days, and did not take its final leave for fifteen: indeed I had but little appetite the whole of the passage. The weather has been boisterous for the season; though I believe we were not in imminent danger, except upon one occasion, arising from neglect in not taking in sail. The wind blew a tremendous gale, which the ship, in consequence, was not so well prepared to withstand as she might and ought to have been. My fears were extreme:

there was but the turn of a hair between us and eternity. I prayed fervently to that Being, who is the God of the sea as well as of the land, and who has protected me throughout my life.

The 4th of July is a great American day, being the anniversary of their declaration of independence. It was kept on board with, I presume, its usual sanctity — by good eating and drinking. I felt warm in the cause, viewing that declaration as the common property of every friend of freedom. Several songs were sung. Two by the mate were the most remarkable: they were the evident production of *seventeen hundred and seventy-six;* their allusions being to those occurrences which peculiarly belonged to the first stages of the revolution. The toasts were also indifferent. I was not gratified with even an approach to the old English sentiment of " Civil and religious liberty all over the world."

In the steerage there were thirteen passengers. These paid twelve pounds each, and had to find themselves in every thing but water. Among them was a Mr. Davis, an ingenious, clever man. He organized a debating society, which was held in the steerage twice a week, " weather permitting." Young Mr. Adams and myself frequently attended their sombre discussions. Upon one occasion the question was, " Which is the best form of government, a democracy or a monarchy?" It was strongly contested on both sides, and at length determined in favour of the former by the casting vote of the chairman — who was seated in presidential state on a water-cask.

On the 5th of August, the sound of "Land O!" from the topmast, though communicated by the gruff voice of a hardy son of Neptune, sounded in my ears "most eloquent music." In the evening we stood out to sea, being too near shore. On the morning of the 6th I was called up at four o'clock. We were off the Jersey shore, which was crowded with small craft. We soon made Sandy Hook, the entrance into the bay, and thirty miles from the city of New York. The busy scene around me, the consciousness that I was about to be relieved from the worst of prisons, the serenity of the morning, and the extreme beauty of New York bay, conveyed impressions which mock description. Every object was to me an interesting one: first our pilot, his stature, his manners, his dress, were all, at this time, objects of my attention; though under other circumstances I should have viewed them with entire indifference. He brought us the newspaper of the morning. Many of the advertisements had to me the character of singularity. One announcing a play, terminated with, "Gentlemen are informed, that no smoking is allowed in the theatre." A newsman from the "Evening Post," and a custom-house officer, were our next visitors. Several sailing-boats passed with gentlemen, many of them wearing enormously large straw hats, turned up behind. At one o'clock we anchored close to the city. A boy procured us two hackney coaches, from a distance of about a quarter of a mile. I offered him an English shilling, having no other small coin in my possession. He would not take so little; "For as how I guess it is not of value. I have been *slick* in going to the stand right away." This was said with a tone of independence, which, although displeasing to my pride, was not so to my judgment. Mr. Adams satisfied the young republican by giving him half-a-dollar, (2s. 3d.) There was no sense of having received a favour in the boy's countenance or manner; a trait of character which, I have since learned, is by no means confined to the youth of America. A simple "I thank you, Sir," would not, however, derogate from a free man's dignity; but I must not be too fastidious. We should not expect every thing; and, after all, even cold independence is preferable to warm servility. Another question, and one of leading importance, suggested itself to me on this occurrence; namely, Is not labour here well paid? A great number of people were on the wharf looking at us and our vessel. Many of them were of the labouring class. They were not better clothed than men in a similar condition in England; but they were more erect in their posture, less care-worn in their countenances; the thought of "the morrow" did not seem to form a part of their ideas; and among them there were no beggars. Intermixed with these were several of the mercantile and genteeler classes. Large straw hats prevailed; trowsers were universal. The general costume of these persons was inferior to men in the same rank of life in England. Their whole appearance was loose, slovenly, careless, and not remarkable for cleanliness. The wholesale stores which front the river, have not the most attractive appearance. The carts are long and narrow, drawn by one horse; the hackney coaches are open at the sides, being suited to this warm climate — lighter and much superior to ours: the charge 25 per cent. higher than in London. The streets, through which we passed to Mrs. Bradish's boarding-house, in State-street, opposite the Battery, were narrow and dirty. The Battery is a most delightful walk, on the edge of the bay. The houses in State-street are of the first class. The one in which I am now writing is about the size of those in Bridge-street, Blackfriars. The rent is 2400 dollars (540l. sterling) per annum; taxes are about 80 dollars, (18l. sterling.) The general mode of living for those who do not keep house, is at hotels, taverns, or private boarding-houses. My present residence is at one of the latter. Here are two public apartments, one for a sitting, the other a dining room. At present, about forty sit down to table. The lady of the house presides; the other ladies, who are boarders, being placed on her left. The hours are — breakfast, eight o'clock; dinner, half past three; tea, seven; supper, ten. American breakfasts are celebrated for their profusion: presenting eggs, meat of various kinds, fish, and fowls. My London habits are not yet overcome; I cannot enjoy any addition to plain bread and butter. The hours of eating are attended to by all with precision: charge, two dollars per diem, exclusive of wine. The expense of living here is about 18 dollars per week. There are here at present, the celebrated Commodore Rogers, and several other naval officers; among whom are Decatur, Warrington, and Bidel, all of whom distinguished themselves in the late war: also Mr. Graham, the under-secretary of state, and Mr. Brackenbridge, author of a history of the late war. The two latter gentlemen are said to be upon the point of embarking in the sloop of war Ontario, on a mission to South America. That the object of their voyage may be to assist the patriots in shaking off the yoke of the infamous Ferdinand, is my heartfelt desire.

Last evening, while I was conversing with Commodore Rogers, a naval officer, attended by two black servants, ascended the steps: he proved to be Sir James Yeo. Commodore R—s, supposing me to be an American, was free in the expression of his feelings; which, in truth, were honourable to him, and not derogatory to Sir James, or the British navy generally. He referred to the disgraceful conduct of Admiral Cockburn at Havre de Grace, with a forgiving liberality which did him much credit. In his appearance he has more of the English than the American seaman, conveying an idea not dissimilar to the personifications of such characters by Bannister. He is an American by birth, but of Scotch parentage. His anecdotes of persons claiming relationship or acquaintance with him are numerous. One man met him in Baltimore, assured him that he had gone to school and eaten porridge and drunk whisky with him when a boy, at Aberdeen; another, a very old man, accosted him, in the Scotch dialect, in Broadway, New-York, and insisted upon it that he was his (Commodore R.'s) *father*. Commodore Rogers is now the president of the Board of Naval Commissioners at Washington; an establishment whose objects and powers are nearly similar to those of our Admiralty Board. His present business is, in conjunction with Commodore Decatur, to lay the keel of a seventy-four gun ship. His account of the climate of Washington is favourable. He states that he has there a family of seven children, and that for two years they have had no illness in the house.

Immediately upon landing, I treated myself with a glass of cider and some fruit: the charge was dearer than in London. As yet I cannot, of course, communicate any useful particulars. I have walked alone through the streets for the purpose of forming an independent judgment. Every object is new. I hardly dare trust myself in forming conclusions: one most cheering fact is indisputable, the absence of *irremediable* distress. The street population bears an aspect essentially different from that of London, or large English towns. One striking feature consists in the number of blacks, many of whom are finely dressed, the females very ludicrously so, showing a partiality to white muslin dresses, artificial flowers, and pink shoes. I saw but few well-dressed white ladies, but am informed that the greater part are at present at the springs of Balstan and Saratoga.* The dress of the men is rather deficient in point of neatness and gentility. Their appearance, in common with that of the ladies and children, is sallow, and what we should

* A place of fashionable summer resort, about 200 miles from this city. The route is by way of Albany, which is 160 miles up the Hudson river, and to which some of the finest steam-boats in the world go three times a week. The fare, including board, is seven dollars, and a tax of one dollar. The time usually occupied from New York to Albany is from eighteen and a half to twenty-two hours.

call unhealthy. Our friend D—— tells me that to have colour in the cheeks is an infallible criterion by which to be discovered as an Englishman. In a British town of any importance, you cannot walk along a leading street for half an hour without meeting with almost every variety of size, dress, and appearance among the inhabitants; whilst, on the contrary, here they seem all of one family; and though not quite a "drab-coloured creation," the feelings they excite are not many degrees removed from the uninteresting sensations generated by that expression. The young men are tall, thin, and solemn: their dress is universally trowsers, and very generally loose great coats. Old men, in our English idea of that phrase, appear very rare.

Churches are numerous and handsome: the interior of one which I have just visited in Broad-way is truly elegant, being fitted up with more taste, splendour, and, I presume, expense, than many in London. Several hotels are on an extensive scale: the City Hotel is as large as the London Tavern; the dining, and some of the private rooms, seem fitted up regardless of expense. The price of boarding at this establishment is, I understand, cheaper than where I reside. The shops (or stores, as they are called) have nothing in their exterior to recommend them: there is not even an attempt at tasteful display. The linen and woollen drapers (dry good stores, as they are denominated) leave quantities of their goods loose on boxes in the street, without any precaution against theft. This practice, though a proof of their carelessness, is also an evidence as to the *political* state of society worthy of attention. Masses of the population cannot be unemployed, or robbery would here be inevitable. A great number of excellent private dwellings are built of red painted brick, which gives them a peculiarly neat and clean appearance. In Broad-way and Wall-street trees are planted by the side of the pavement. The city-hall is a large and elegant building, in which the courts of law are held. In viewing this structure, I feel some objections which require farther observation either to remove or confirm. Most of the streets are dirty: in many of them sawyers are preparing wood for sale, and all are infested with pigs, — circumstances which indicate a lax police.

Upon the whole, a walk through New York will disappoint an Englishman: there is, on the surface of society, a carelessness, a laziness, an unsocial indifference, which freezes the blood and disgusts the judgment. An evening stroll along Broad-way, when the lamps are alight, will please more than one at noon-day. The shops then look rather better, though their proprietors, of course, remain the same: their cold indifference may, by themselves, be mistaken for independence, but no person of thought and observation will ever concede to them that they have selected a wise mode of exhibiting that dignified feeling. I disapprove most decidedly of the obsequious servility of many London shopkeepers, but I am not prepared to go the length of those in New York, who stand with their hats on, or sit or lie along their counters, smoking segars, and spitting in every direction, to a degree offensive to any man of decent feelings.

The prevalence of Dutch names tells me I am here a stranger; but this impression is often counteracted by viewing the immense quantities of British manufactured goods with which the shops are crowded, as also the number of English works which are advertised, and such placards as "Hone's Riot in London," "Prince's Russia Oil," "Reeves and Woodyer's Colours," and "Day and Martin's Blacking."

My abode here has, as yet, been so short, that you cannot expect solid information. Some things which I state may appear trifling, but I wish to communicate to you my first impressions, and to place you, as far as I am able, in my own situation: in that point of view you will regard the following circumstances.

I have been with Mr. Cook (a fellow-passenger of mine, and very pleasant young man, a resident of Kaskaski, in the Illinois territory) into three shops. The first was a chemist's: of him we enquired the state of trade. He replied that the only business which was good for any thing at this time in New York was shaving, meaning the buying and selling bank-notes. The rent which he paid for his small place astonished me. The next was a hatter's, at which Mr. C. was not suited. While waiting, a beggar came in, and was relieved with a Spanish silver piece called a sixpence: it was the sixteenth of a dollar. Beggars, I am informed, are very uncommon. The third shop was in the same business, at which Mr. C. bought a hat: it was of American manufacture, very narrow in the brim, according to the present fashion; the price was ten dollars (45s.); the quality nearly as good as those sold in London at from 24s. to 27s. The proprietor of this concern complained of the want of business. He stated that it had not been known so bad as during the last and present years; but that labouring men who were inclined to work could generally obtain employment either in the city or back country; and that among mechanics, masons and carpenters were very good trades. I asked him the reason of trade being bad. He replied that he did not know the reason; that they did not trouble themselves about reasons. To my remark, — business is also dull in London, he answered, " I guess *that* is the reason; for we take all our things from them in the old country." His rent I thought extravagantly high: he stated that it was one-fourth cheaper than last year; and that he expected it would be altered next May. This variation in rent flows from a mode of letting houses different to that practised in England. * You will not, of course, take information so loosely collected as the present as authentic. I do not myself, and therefore I am sure you will not do so.

Yesterday, at the dinner-table, my attention was strongly fixed by a conversation between Commodore Decatur and a gentleman, I presume a resident of this city: the following is nearly an accurate report. I would remark that Commodore Decatur is a member of the Navy Board, and, of course, concerned in the contracts issuing from that body.

Gent. " Well, Commodore, there were some good bargains made by *some* people during the war."

Com. D. " So I guess."

Gent. " M——, the contractor, did not lose any thing by *turning round:* his rations paid well."

Com. D. " A man ought to profit by what he sells."

Gent. " Yes; but democrats only had the chance."

Com. D. " Contracts are conducted with the most perfect fairness. Government deals with

* Houses are seldom let on long leases in the cities of America, the usual period being for one year, taking date from the 1st of May. Upon this day the removals are so numerous, that the streets have a very singular appearance.—Nov. 1818.

that man who can supply the country to the most advantage."

Gent. "If so, how is it that throughout the whole war, and up to the present moment, not a single federalist in any part of the Union has been a contractor?"

Com. D. "I guess they have not made application."

Gent. "That I know they have, and myself for one, and at a lower rate by — per cent. than M—— supplied them."

At this part of the conversation, a gentleman sitting on my left remarked that government were perfectly right in pursuing that line of policy; that they ought to favour those who supported them: this was partially assented to by Commodore Decatur. The gentleman before alluded to continued, with some feeling, to complain of jobs and peculation. These were terms which I had imagined unknown in the language of the United States: I had hoped that this *refined* order of things would never be imported from our great but oppressed country to this land, at the emancipation of which from tyranny and taxation every free mind throughout the world joined in exultation and triumph.

The inns and boarding-houses are crowded. At this time great numbers are here from the more southern states. Among other inducements, they come to avoid the present or apprehended existence of the yellow fever. The room in which I write is in the attic story, every other being occupied. In this small apartment are two beds. The heat of the weather is excessive, and the visits of the musquitoes not the most pleasing. I have not yet been enabled to sleep until three or four o'clock in the morning. Our furniture consists of two old chairs; the bedsteads are temporary; a mattress, cotton sheets and coverlid compose our bedding. There is no bell in the room—the attendance of servants is perfectly unattainable. This may arise from the full occupancy of the house, or it may be a general feature in the condition of the people: in either case it troubles me but little. If there be but a good government, a healthy and fertile country, and an enlightened people, I for one, and I am sure you will all join with me, shall be contented and happy, as little inconveniencies and personal privations must be set at nought, when put in competition with such important advantages. That the state of the country and people may realize the hopes I have entertained, is my constant and sincere prayer. With affectionate remembrances to you all,

I remain very sincerely your's,

HENRY FEARON.

I shall have a report, for it will be too long and too general to be called a letter, ready to go by the Amity, Capt. Stanton, which is to sail the 1st September.

FIRST REPORT.

Situation of New York. — Public Buildings. — Exaggerated Statements of America. — Particulars of, and Capital usually employed in, the Business of Carvers and Gilders, Timber-merchants, Distillers, Builders, Dyers, Boot and Shoe-makers, Tallow-chandlers, Taylors, Printers, Booksellers. — Present Prospect of Success for Emigrants. — Lawyers.—Doctors. — American Literature. — High Price of American-written Works. — American Editions of English Works. — Mechanics' Wages. — Schools. — Rents enormously high. — Country Houses to be sold. — State-Taxes. — Provisions; their Quality and Price. — Charge for Boarding per Week. — Price of Clothing. — Indian and French Goods. — Religious Sects and Character of the People of New York. — Military Service. — Proposal for a Settlement on the Banks of the Hudson.

New York, August 31st, 1817.

In a letter, dated the 9th instant, I apprised you of my safe arrival at, and my then impressions of, this place, as far as respects the inhabitants, and the appearance of the city: those impressions have been, in general, confirmed. Concerning the important object of my journey, you will be best capacitated to form your judgment from the following details. They have been collected with as much industry and discrimination, as my own capacity, and the circumstances in which I was placed, have enabled me to exercise.

The city of New York, when approached from the sea, presents an object truly beautiful. It is built at the extreme point of Manhaltan, or York Island, which is thirteen miles long, and from one to two miles wide. The city is on the south end, closely built from shore to shore, and extends in length about two miles and a quarter. The population is said to be 120,000. The East river separates it from Long Island, and the Hudson river from the State of Jersey. Ships of any burden, and to any extent, can come close up to the town, and lie there with perfect safety, in a natural harbour, formed by the above-named fine rivers, and a noble bay, completely protected by the surrounding lands: there are at present a great number of ships in harbour. New York is without competition the first commercial city in America. This will be seen by a slight view of Mr. Pitkin's "Statistical Account of the Commerce of the United States;" a work which no person ought to be without, who views the subject of America as an important topic. The port of New York being open at all seasons gives it a powerful advantage; the more so, as not only its northern but its two southern rivals, (Philadelphia and Baltimore,) are deprived of this convenience, so desirable in an extensive commerce.

The public buildings of a city of such recent birth as that of New York, must appear trifling to the native of an European city, accustomed to contemplate the collected works of successive ages; but you, my friends, in common with myself, look not at such establishments with the eye of the architect or the painter, but as plain men, desirous of knowing every thing concerning a country, around which some of our most endeared political opinions are entwined: and as we contemplate a possible removal to this new world, we feel interested in that land, which may not only affect our interest and happiness as individuals, but likewise those of many generations yet unborn.

The town-hall of this city is a noble building of white marble. The ground around it is planted and railed off. The interior appears well arranged. In the rooms of the mayor and corporation, are portraits of several governors of this State, and some distinguished officers. The State-rooms, and courts of justice, are on the first floor. In one of these, a gentleman pointed out to me the celebrated Mr. Emmett, well known in the history of Ireland. He is a plain man, of the middle size, in a small degree inclined to corpulency. His dress was not perhaps so respectable as that of a gentleman of his high legal estimation in England, but it accorded with the ideas and habits of the people of this country. His reputation at the bar is of the first order. I was grieved to find native Americans speak of him with great jealousy. It appears that, in *their eyes*, he has been guilty of two unpardonable crimes — two sins against the Holy Ghost: the first is in being, as they term it, *a foreigner!* the second and greatest of all, in being an *Irish rebel!* But to proceed with the city-hall; the staircase is circular, lighted by a cupola. The situation of this building is excellent in point of effect, and highly ornamental to the city. It would be much more so, had not the basement story, which is of red granite, the appearance of brick.

In the immediate neighbourhood of the hall is an extensive building, appropriated to the "New York Institution," the "Academy of Fine Arts," and the "American Museum." There are also a State-prison, hospital, and numerous splendid churches. I might fill many pages were I to follow in detail the deceptive example of some recent writers, whose views may perhaps be easily appreciated. One of these I have now before me, who names every house in which public business is transacted — "a public building." "There is," says this writer, "a custom-house, post-office, public forum, &c." The first is a private house, formerly a bookseller's, belonging to Messrs. Eastbourn and Kirk; the second is also a private house, of a very mean description, and indeed quite a disgrace to a commercial city of the magnitude of New York; the third is merely held in the winter months, in the ball-room of the city hotel. American habits, prosperity, and intelligence, are described upon the same model, and with, I regret to say, an equal degree of exaggeration. Such accounts would appear to answer no other ends than those of imposition; and the nation which really stood in need of these arts, would not deserve to rise and prosper: but as to the veil thus thrown over the real situation of this country by these writers, it is equally the interest of native and emigrant that it should be withdrawn. Every American, if he be a man of sense, would wish to see pourtrayed the real character and condition of his country, in order that he might not only perceive what was excellent, but also be enabled to discover what there was to amend and improve; while to the respectable emigrant and his family, the consequences must be lamentable, when he finds that he has been incited to a change of country by the exaggerated and base misrepresentations of romantic or interested individuals. When I survey this city, and remember that but two centuries since, the spot on which it stands was a wilderness, I cannot but be struck with its comparative extent and opulence. Like the country of which it forms a part, it is a striking evidence of the advantages of a cheap and popular government; but that country is not, as some would represent it, a paradise, any more than the city of New York is as yet a rival either in population, riches, or extent to that of London.

In answer to the various enquiries relative to their trades and professions, made by our several friends, I shall now proceed briefly to give the purport of all the information which I have hitherto collected either by my own observation or through the means of the introductions given me; and in doing this, I shall not confine myself to their form of question and answer, as the same fact will, in many instances, reply to several of their queries; and I should wish to give the information in as clear and compressed a manner as lies within my power.

Building appears brisk in the city. It is generally performed by contract. A person intending to have a house erected contracts with a professed builder; the builder, with a bricklayer; and he, with all others necessary to the completion of the design. In some cases, a builder is a sort of head workman, for the purpose of overseeing the others; receiving for his agency seven-pence per day from the wages of each man; the men being employed and paid by him. There are occasional instances in which there is no contract, every thing being paid for according to measure and value. In the city, houses of wood are not now allowed, but in the environs they are very general; and many of them handsome in appearance. They are commonly of two stories, and painted white, with green shutters. The expense of a frame (wood) house is materially affected by situation: on an average, they will cost to erect about the same as a brick house in England. The builder is sometimes his own timber-merchant. Indeed, all men here know a portion, and enter a little into every thing: — the necessary consequence of a comparatively new state of society.

The timber, or (as the term is here) lumber yards are not on that large and compact scale with which, in England, our friends C—— and M——— are familiar. Mahogany yards are generally separate concerns. Oak boards are this day 5l. 12s. 6d. per thousand feet. Shingles, (an article used instead of tiles or slates,) 1l. 2s. 6d. per thousand feet, to which is to be added a duty of 15 per cent. Honduras mahogany is five-pence halfpenny to seven-pence farthing the superficial foot; and St. Domingo, nine-pence three farthings to seventeen-pence halfpenny. Mahogany is used for cupboards, doors, and banisters, and for all kinds of cabinet work. Curl maple, a native and most beautiful wood, is also much approved. Veneer is in general demand, and is cut by machinery. Chests of drawers are chiefly made of St. Domingo mahogany, the inside being faced with boxwood: shaded veneer and curl maple are also used for this purpose. I would remark, that the cabinet work executed in this city is light and elegant, superior indeed, I am inclined to believe, to English workmanship. I have seen some with cut glass, instead of brass ornaments, which had a beautiful effect. The retail price of a three feet six inch chest of drawers, well finished and of good quality, is 3l. 16s. 6d.; of a three feet ten, with brass rollers, 5l. 8s. A table, three feet long, four and a half wide, 3l. 7s. 6d.; ditto with turned legs, 4l. 5s. 6d.; three and a half long, five and a half wide, (plain,) 3l. 12s.; ditto better finished, 4l. 10s.; ladies' work tables, (very plain,) 18s. Cabinet-makers' shops, of which there are several in Greenwich-street, contain a variety, but not a large stock. They are generally small concerns, apparently owned by journeymen, commenced on their own account. These shops are perfectly open, and there is seldom any person in attendance. In the centre, a board is suspended with the notice, "Ring the bell." I have conversed with several proprietors: they state their business to have been at one time good, but that there is now too much competition.

Chair-making here, and at the town of Newark, ten miles distant, is an extensive business. The retail price of wooden chairs is from 4s. 6d.

to 9s.; of curl maple with rush seat, 11s.; of ditto with cane seat, 13s. 6d. to 1l. 2s. 6d.; of ditto, most handsomely finished, 1l. 9s.; sofas, of the several descriptions enumerated above, are the price of six chairs. I have seen in parlours of genteel houses, a neat wooden chair, which has not appeared objectionable, and of which the price could not have exceeded 9s. Cabinet-makers, timber-merchants, and builders complain — they all say that their trades have been good, but that there is now a great increase in the numbers engaged, and that the times are so altered with the merchants that all classes feel the change very sensibly. These complaints I believe to be generally well-founded; but I do not conceive the depression to be equal to that felt in England. I would also make some deduction from their supposed amount of grievances. When did you ever know a body of men admit, or even feel, that they were doing as much trade, as in their own estimation they ought? or who did not think that there were too many in their particular branches? Every individual desires to be a monopolist, yet no wise legislator would ever exclude competition.

A good cabinet-maker, who should have no more than an hundred pounds after paying the expenses of his voyage, would obtain a comfortable livelihood; as would also an active speculating carpenter or mason, under the same circumstances. A greater amount of capital would, of course, be more advantageous.

A timber-merchant should have a capital of not less than a thousand pounds, as he ought to pay cash for his stock, with the exception of mahogany. The wages of a journeyman carpenter is 7s. 10½d. per day; of a mason, 8s. 5d. This difference arises, I believe, from the latter being an out-door business, which, in the winter months, from the extreme severity of the weather, is of necessity suspended. Cabinet-makers are paid by the piece. When in full employ, their earnings may amount to 50s. per week: a safe average is 36s. A man in either of the above trades, need not be apprehensive but that he should get a living.

Our friends A— and N—— are unfortunate in being "learned gentlemen." Lawyers are as common here as paupers are in England. Indeed for those friends I see no kind of opening. *Professional* men literally swarm in the United States. An anecdote is told of a gentleman walking in Broadway: a friend passing, he called "Doctor," and immediately sixteen persons turned round to answer to the name. This is even more characteristic of lawyers. At almost every private door, cellar, or boarding-house, a tin plate is displayed, bearing the inscription "Attorney at Law." Clerks are not in demand in this or any other occupation. There are here no very large concerns, and most men are capable of attending to their own business. A shopman or clerk, who would receive in London his board, and a salary of from 30l. to 100l. sterling per annum, would here experience great difficulty in gaining a situation; and if fortunate enough to obtain one, he would not receive more than from $3\frac{1}{2}$ to 7 dollars per week, exclusive of board and lodging. The causes which generate so great a number of "legal friends," lie beyond the sources of my penetration. Perhaps we may date the frequency of litigation to the intricacy of the profession, which is bottomed on English practice; while the cheapness of college instruction, and the general diffusion of moderate wealth among mechanics and tradesmen, enable them to gratify their vanity by giving their sons a learned education. This also opens the door to them for an appointment; and, by the way, the Americans are great place-hunters.

As it respects *distillation* — There are numerous distillers resident in the city and environs. During the late war this occupation was profitable, in consequence, I presume, of the difficulties attendant upon importation. There are none who carry on business upon an extensive scale. The capital employed is from one to twenty thousand pounds. The articles prepared are rum, gin, and whisky:

rum from molasses; gin from rye and Indian corn: malted grain is not used. Distillation is performed in stills made of wood, operated upon by steam: there is no particular mode required by law. There are two taxes paid; the first on the yearly capacity of the still, the second on the spirit, per gallon. The latter is a general government-tax, which is expected to be taken off the next session of congress. There are collectors, but no excisemen. The oath or affirmation of the proprietor is the mode prescribed by law of ascertaining the quantity distilled, which is certainly most consonant with civil liberty. Both wholesale and retail wine and spirit sellers are grocers: their establishments are called grocery stores. A great proportion of the retail are small chandlers' shops, and are often denominated grog-shops. They are usually at the corners of streets, and mostly owned by Irishmen. Their chief commodity is New England, or what is emphatically called "Yankee" rum. All spirits are commonly drunk mixed with cold water, without sugar. The price per glass, at the dirtiest grog-shops, is two-pence, where the liquor is of the most inferior description. At the more respectable, for a superior quality three-pence halfpenny. At what are called taverns and porter-houses, establishments similar to our second-rate public-houses, six-pence halfpenny. The size of the glass is half a gill. It is estimated that there are 1500 spirit-shops in this city; a fact opposed to my first impressions of American habits, which, on the point of sobriety, were favourable, judging from the absence of broils and of drunkards in the streets: but more attentive observation, aided by the information of old residents, enables me to state that the quantity of malt-liquor and spirits drunk by the inhabitants of New York, much exceeds the amount consumed by the same extent of English population. The beastly drunkard is a character unknown here; yet but too many are throughout the day under the influence of liquor, or what is not inappropriately termed "half and half!" a state too prevalent among the labouring classes and the negroes. Many date the source of this to the *extremes* of the climate. Another and a leading cause is, that numbers of the lower orders are European emigrants. They bring their habits with them. They are here better employed and better paid than they were in the country which gave them birth; and they partake too largely of the infirmities of our nature to be provident during the sunshine of prosperity.

Our friend C—— will not be displeased to learn that there are here several large carvers' and gilders' shops. Glass-mirrors and picture-frames are executed with taste and elegance;

but still the most superior are imported from England. Carved ornaments are general, though some composition-ornaments are used. Plate-glass is imported from France, Holland, and England, the latter bearing the highest price. Silvering looking-glasses is a separate trade: there is but one silverer in New York, and he is not constantly employed. Carvers and gilders are paid eight-pence three farthings per hour. The sale of prints and pictures is usually combined with this business. There are here two gold-beaters: one of them is a Mr. Jones from London. Leaf-gold is frequently imported; but they consider their own equal to foreign, and it bears the same price, 40s. 6d. per packet, containing 20 books. The duty on imported leaf-gold is fifteen per cent. A capital of from 800l. to 2000l. would be requisite for a moderately respectable concern. A journeyman gilder would not succeed; a carver may do so; but neither trades are (to use an Americanism) of the first *grade.*

To Mr. F—— I would remark, that boot and shoe-makers' shops are numerous, some of them extensive. The price of sole-leather is 11d. to 13½d.; of dressed upper ditto, 11s. 3d. to 15s. 9d.; to this is to be added a duty of 30 per cent. Wellington-boots at the best shops are charged 2l. 0s. 6d.; shoes, 13s. 6d. Spanish is much worn for upper leather. They are made neat and with taste: the workmanship appears to me quite equal to the best London. The American leather is very inferior in quality. Native workmen appear as good as English. The business is at present dull, which, I believe, is usual at this season of the year. A capital of from 500 to 1000 dollars is requisite in a moderate concern. A master shoe-maker will not be benefited by coming here; a journeyman may be so. C—, whom we knew in London, and who is first rate in his line, has been earning 2l. 5s. per week; but he is upon the point of going to Philadelphia, or perhaps to the Western country, as he cannot have a continuation of employment unless he work at an under price.

Mr. W. and his Son, who are dyers, would find some difficulty in stepping from the practice of their large concern in ———, to an American dye-house; which, from the non-existence of manufacturers in this country, must be essentially different from an English one. The articles usually done here, are old clothes and spoiled goods. A dyer's business in this city will best accord with an English scowerer, such as Sansom, in Fenchurch-street. The price for dyeing black woollen is 3s. per yard, $\frac{6}{4}$ wide; of brown ditto, 3s.; red, 2s. 6d.; yellow, 2s. 6d.; scarlet, 20s. a pound. There is no silk dyed in the skein, nor are there any silk-weavers in the United States. Fast blue is not done. Re-dyeing old silk is $6\frac{1}{4}$d. per yard. English alum is from 33s. 9d. to 36s. per cwt., to which is to be added a duty of 4s. 6d.; brazilletto, 140s. to 160s. per ton; cochineal, 24s. 9d. per pound, with a duty of $7\frac{1}{2}$ per cent.; logwood, 90s. to 112s. 6d. per ton. The business is of necessity limited. It is moderately good, and would not require a capital of more than from 200l. to 500l. A few journeymen are employed. They earn 2l. 5s. per week.

The trade of tallow-chandler is united by some with that of soap-boiler. Any other business may be connected with it, as the law raises no difficulty on the subject. The operation of melting must be removed a specified distance from the closely inhabited part of the city.

The pickle-trade is of no account, as families prepare their own.

The oil and colour-business might be combined with that of tallow-chandler, though perhaps without increased advantage. Oil is sold at grocery-stores, and by painters. The rent of a house to suit an oil-business, in a fourth-rate situation, (a better being unnecessary,) would be 135l. to 150l. per annum. A capital of from 800l. to 1200l. would suffice. For a journeyman or shopman it is a bad trade. They are paid 4s. 6d. to 5s. $7\frac{1}{2}$d. per diem. The chief work is done by apprentices. The Irish have got the greater part of this business; and they will, if possible, prevent an English journeyman from having employment. The wholesale prices of tallow are, foreign, 6½d. to 7½d., with a duty of ½d.; American, 7½d.: of soap, Castile, 8½d. to 9d.; turpentine, 5¾d., with a duty of 1½d. In the eastern States there is a superabundance of native tallow, but in the south it is scarce. Barilla is not used, American ashes being substituted; which are from 8¾d. to 10¾d. per bushel. A tallow-chandler in London who can save 50l. per annum, would not be benefited in his finances by a removal to this country.

Taylors are numerous: they are denominated, (in conformity with the accustomed vanity of the country,) "Merchant Taylors." Some keep rather large stocks of woollen piece-goods, all of which, I would remark, are of British manufacture. The price of a superfine coat is from 6l. 6s. to 8l. 2s. They are paid for making a common coat 18s.; a best ditto, 27s. If a journeyman find the trimmings, he receives for a best coat 45s. to 51s. For making trowsers, 9s. Apprentices can be had for the terms of three, seven, or ten years: seven is the usual period. A journeyman can have the work of an apprentice under him. If a man have not served his time, it is not of consequence in any business; *competency*, not legal servitude, being the standard for employment. A journeyman taylor I would rank but among the second-rate trades, so much being done by women and boys. A man that can cut out will be occasionally well paid: the women not being clever in this department, makes the employment of men necessary. There are ready-made clothes' shops, as in London, at which articles of a cheaper but inferior description are sold. Large quantities of clothing are imported from England, and many individuals have their regular London taylors. Black and coloured Canton crape, black stuff, white jean, white drill, and Nankin, are worn for trowsers; jean for coats; gingham for jackets in the house: all of which are made by women, at from 25 to 50 per cent. cheaper than if men were employed. A man will earn, when employed, from 36s. to 54s. per week. To carry on this trade as a master, and with a reasonable prospect of success, would require a capital of from 500l. to 2000l. The profits are large. Moderate credit is received; long credit is given. An additional taylor does not seem now wanted in New York, yet I should not be apprehensive of the success of a man of business who was possessed of the means above stated.

I have recently read a book which speaks highly of the literature of this country. From what source the writer derives evidence in support of his assertions I know not. A well-educated American, with whom I have had some agreeable conversation, candidly admitted their very lamentable deficiency in this particular; and in nothing, perhaps, is this more decidedly shown than in the scarcity of that greatest of literary curiosities — a native American standard work. The causes which produce this I shall endeavour to ascertain, when I become more conversant with this country and people. The fact is indisputable. Booksellers' shops here are extensive. Old works are scarce. Standard works are not so: by these I mean such as Shakspeare, Milton, Blair, and Johnson. Theological works (those only which are *orthodox*) are common, and I should suppose much in request. Hartley, Priestley, and the religious writings of Locke, are scarce; I may say unknown. English novels and poetry form the primary articles of a bookseller's business. They are quickly reprinted. An instance of dispatch in this line occurred a fortnight since at Philadelphia. "Manfred" was received, printed, and published all in one day. Walter Scott, Miss Owenson, Moore, Miss Edgeworth, Miss Porter, and Lord Byron, are favourites. The late Scotch novels have been very much read. The Edinburgh and Quarterly Reviews are reprinted by Messrs. Kirk and Mercien of this city. *English Tory writers* are neither unknown nor unpopular. Booksellers deal in stationary and various fancy articles.

Their stocks are large, but, what we should call in England, ill assorted. Mr. Eastbourne's is the only house which contains old English works. His general stock is valuable and extensive. I purchased from him gazetteers, and other American works, calculated to assist me in travelling. The price of all (which was the same as at any other house) surprised me: they were dearer than English books of a similar kind and size, and also very inferior in quality of paper, and general execution. Mr. Eastbourne politely invited me to his reading room — an establishment valuable to the city, and honourable to its proprietor. The great attraction of this department is a variety of native and English newspapers, and of English reviews and magazines. I spent a morning hour here with considerable satisfaction. American editions of many British writings are *lower* in price, but *not cheaper* than those issuing from the London press; the size as well as quality of paper being reduced. Folio is diminished to quarto, quarto to octavo, and octavo to duodecimo. The American edition, for instance, of "Lalla Rookh," which I have sent you, bears no comparison to that of Messrs. Longman and Co. Common stationary is of American manufacture; the superior, of British. Books pay upon importation 30 per cent.; printing types, 20; paper, 30; wafers, 30; playing cards, 30. Native binding is generally plain and common: many of the fine London pocket editions, bound, have been recently imported. A capital of from 1000l. to 10,000l. would be required in this business.— Query, Would it be judicious for our friend —— to transport his capital to this side of the Atlantic? His literary talents would indeed be a novelty in a New-York miscellany.

Printers are paid 2l. 5s. per week, but employment cannot be depended upon: a great portion of the work is done by boys. Stereotyping is practised: Messrs. —— are now engaged upon a work larger than any which has ever been stereotyped in England. An instance occurred in their office of the facility opened to learning a trade, in consequence of the non-existence of statutes to controul that which ought ever to be free. S——, a clever, active youth, who had been a shopman in London, came here in the Lorenzo: he had letters of introduction from his uncle, a highly respectable man in —— Lane, to several merchants in this city. The door of employment was however shut against him. Driven by necessity, he resorted to carrying the hod, and thus earned a few dollars; but the excessive heat of the weather overcame him, and, relinquishing his new occupation, he obtained a situation at the store of Mr. ——, in Broadway—was there eight months, transacting the most important part of their business—received 15s. 9d. per week, exclusive of board and lodging. Tired of this unprofitable occupation, he addressed a letter to the printers before referred to, requesting leave to attend in their office for the purpose of learning to be a compositor. Mr. ——, though a stranger, liberally consented, with the additional offer, that as soon as S—— was capacitated, he should have the full price of his labour. S—— has been there three months, was engaged in stereotyping a new edition of Sternhold and Hopkins, for the last month has received eight dollars per week, is now out of employment and upon the point of walking to Philadelphia, (distance 96 miles,) with the intention of working on the road.

The *Lancasterian system of education* is in practice here, but it has not spread so rapidly as in England; perhaps, because, among the lower orders, it was less wanted: there are 800 in the school of this city; the system at present is confined to free schools. One or two boarding seminaries exist here for ladies separately; but in general males and females, of all ages, are educated at the same establishment. The effect of this highly injudicious practice is not (at least judging from the surface of society) what I should have anticipated. American females are even more distant and reserved in their manners than English: the sexes seem ranked as distinct races of beings, between whom social converse is rarely to be held. Day-schools are numerous: some of them respectable, none large. A teacher, that is, an usher, at any of these establishments, is a situation not worth the attention of the poorest man. No species of correction is allowed: children, even at home, are perfectly independent; *subordination* being foreign to the comprehension of the youth, as well as the aged of this country. The emigrant proprietors of seminaries are Scotch and Irish: an instance has not occurred of a respectable English schoolmaster establishing himself here. Two English ladies have recently commenced a boarding-school for females only: they have been moderately successful. A capital of from one to five hundred pounds is essential: for a day-school none is required. The dead languages, music, surveying, drawing, dancing, and French are taught at the superior schools: the latter is rather generally understood, and in some measure necessary, French families being more frequently met with here than in England. At some of the academies plays are occasionally acted. The charges at several seminaries are, for arithmetic, reading, and writing, per annum, 40 dollars; for geography, philosophy, and the French language, 60; for Greek, Latin, and the mathematics, 80 dollars: these amounts are exclusive of board.

Rents form an important article for your consideration: I have therefore been very minute in my enquiries on this head. They depend much upon situation. In the skirts of the town a very small house, one story high, the front rooms of a moderate size, the back less, but suited for a bed, and with one room in the attic story, is from 12l. to 14l. per annum. This class of houses is similar to the least of those in Somers-Town, Commercial-Road, and the new lanes in Walworth. A mechanic who has a family can have two small rooms for 18l. a year. About half a mile out of the city is a small two-story house, in which Mr. —— has two rooms on the first floor, and two closet bed-rooms on the same, one room in the attic, and the use of the kitchen, for which he pays 24l. 10s. per annum: the landlord pays the taxes in both the above instances. I would remark, that many houses have closets between their rooms which serve for a bed, or sometimes are used as a pantry. It is also no uncommon occurrence for temporary beds to be laid out in dining-rooms and parlours: being, of course, removed sufficiently early in the morning to prevent inconvenience. At the distance of a mile from the city, a person of the name of Richards bought a small brick house, containing two kitchens in the basement, one front room, tolerable size, and one small back room on the ground floor, the same on the first floor, and three bed-rooms in the attic, for 300l. Garrets generally have no plaistered ceiling. A very small house, in a situation not convenient for business, containing in all six rooms, is worth from 75l. to 80l. a year; a similar house, in a better situation, 95l. to 105l.; a ditto in a good street for business, 130l. to 140l.; a ditto in first-rate retail situation, 160l. to 200l. per annum. You will remark, that this is the smallest class of houses. The house in which I am now writing is No. 53, Dey-street: it is neither good nor bad, in point of situation or gentility, being of a similar class to those in Hatton-garden, London: it contains a kitchen and servant's bed-room under ground; a dining-room, small parlour, and an intermediate closet on the ground floor; a drawing-room and large bed-room on the first floor, three bed-rooms on the second, three in the attic, and a small back yard; the rent is 202l. 10s. and the taxes 11l. 5s. Observe, these are the city and state, not United States taxes. A similar house to this, in a *first-rate* private-house situation, would be 300l. to 350l. per annum: were it appropriated to business, the rent would be higher. The concern at which S—— lived is in that part of Broadway which is first-rate for retail trade: the rent of the shop and cellar only is 292l. 10s.; the upper part of the house lets for 247l. 10s. A house and shop, equal in size and situation to those esteemed the best in Whitechapel, Fore-street, and the Surrey side of Black-friars, would be 320l. to 350l. per annum: a ditto, ditto to those in Oxford-street, Bishopsgate-Within, the best parts of Holborn and Gracechurch-street, would be 400l. to 600l. per annum. I am informed that Mr. Eastbourne, the very respectable bookseller before referred to, has bought his house, for which he gave 35,000 dollars: this house and situation I should esteem to be parallel with Mr. Waithman's, the corner of Bridge-street. Two moderate-sized houses in Wall-street, (the Lombard-street of New York,) were recently taken on lease by Mr. Gibson, for the purpose of an inn: he engaged to pay 1417l. 10s. per annum; the concern did not realize his expectations; he put up at public auction a nine years' lease, which it is said was knocked down to Mr. St. John for 2587l. 10s. per annum. Ground lots for building, even in the suburbs, are enormously dear.

To state the comparative expenditure for domestic wants, I find a difficult part of my communication. There are few families who keep an account of this essential portion of family economy; and still fewer who have any knowledge of *your* necessary expenses. The following list of prices may be of some assistance to you: beef is from 3½d. to 6d. per pound; mutton, 3½d. to 5½d.; veal, 5d. to 6½d.; ham and bacon, 7½d.

to 10$\frac{1}{2}$d.; dried beef, 8$\frac{1}{2}$d.; fowls, 1s. 9$\frac{1}{2}$d. to 2s. 9d. a pair; ducks, 2s. 3d. to 2s. 9d. a pair; geese, 2s. 3d. to 3s. 11d. each; turkeys, 3s. 4$\frac{1}{4}$d. to 5s. 7$\frac{1}{4}$d. each; pork, 6$\frac{1}{2}$d. to 8d. a pound; butter (fresh) 15d. to 20$\frac{1}{4}$d.; eggs, nine for 6$\frac{3}{4}$d.; cheese, old, 9$\frac{3}{4}$d., new, 6$\frac{1}{2}$d., English, 10d. to 16d.: I have seen but little of this article used; that which is of American manufacture is extremely bad: potatoes, 3s. 4$\frac{1}{2}$d. per bushel; cabbages, 2$\frac{1}{2}$d. each; turnips, 2s. 2$\frac{1}{2}$d. per bushel; peas, 6$\frac{3}{4}$d. to 10d. per peck; salt, 3s. 3d. per bushel; milk, 5$\frac{1}{2}$d. per quart; common fish, 2d. to 3$\frac{1}{2}$d. per pound; salmon, 1s. 1$\frac{1}{2}$d. to 3s. 4$\frac{1}{2}$d. per pound; brown soap, 6$\frac{3}{4}$d.; white ditto dressed, 8$\frac{1}{4}$d. per pound; candles, 8$\frac{1}{2}$d. per pound; mould ditto, 1s.; flour per barrel (weighing 196 pounds) is, of the best New York, 46s. 6d. to 49s. 10$\frac{1}{2}$d.; middling ditto, 36s. to 40s. 6d.; rye, 31s. 6d.; Philadelphia flour, 46s. 1$\frac{1}{2}$d. to 47s. 3d.; Indian ditto, 38s. 9d. to 41s. 6d.; hogshead of ditto, weighing 800 pounds, 148s. 6d. to 153s.; wheat, 7s. 10$\frac{1}{2}$d. to 9s. per bushel; rye, 6s. 4d. ditto; barley, 6s. 4d. ditto; oats, 1s. 10d.; hops, 19s. to 21s. 0$\frac{1}{2}$d. per pound; foreign feathers, 13$\frac{1}{4}$d. to 14d. a pound; American ditto, 3s. 1$\frac{1}{4}$d.; a loaf of bread weighing 17 oz., 3$\frac{1}{2}$d.; a ditto, 34 oz., 7d.; mustard, 3s. to 4s. a pound; table beer, 5s. 7$\frac{1}{2}$d. for 5 gallons; common ale, 5$\frac{1}{2}$d. per quart; best ditto, 7d., wine measure; a cask of 9 gallons of ditto, 24s. 9d.; apples, 10d. per peck; lobsters,

2½d. per pound; onions, (an article much used,) 3½d. a rope; cucumbers, 5 for 1s. 1½d.; common brown sugar, 7d. a pound; East India ditto, 10¾d.; lump ditto, 13½d.; best ditto, 16d.; raw coffee by the bag, 10¾d. a pound; souchong tea, 4s. 6d. to 5s. 7d. a pound; hyson, 5s. 7d. to 6s. 2d.; gunpowder, 10s. 1½d. The quality of provisions I think is, in general, very good: the beef is excellent, mutton rather inferior to ours; fowls are much larger but not better eating than the English. Candles are inferior to English; soap perhaps superior, at least less is required than of ours, for any given purpose.

Boarding.—Persons who are not house-keepers generally live at boarding-houses or hotels. A mechanic pays for his board and lodging 13s. 6d. to 18s. per week; the usual price is 15s. 9d.; for which he has three meals a-day, coffee, with fish or meat for breakfast; a hot dinner; and tea (called supper) in the evening; at which last the table is filled with cheese, biscuits (called Boston crackers), molasses, and slices of raw dried beef. Boarding at a moderately respectable house is 8 dollars a week, for what is termed "a transient man;" or, at the same house, 5 to 6 dollars per week for a three or six months' resident. Charges vary from 8 dollars to 14 dollars a week, according to situation, accommodation, and respectability. Very few allow four meals a day, as at that kept by Mrs. Bradish: indeed I am informed that

Mrs. B.'s is the best boarding-house in the United States.

Clothing and domestic utensils are chiefly of British manufacture: they are from 25 to 100 per cent. dearer than in England. India goods are much cheaper than with you: silk pocket-handkerchiefs not more than half the price. Canton crapes for ladies' dresses very moderate — in England they are prohibited: perhaps there are few articles to equal these for gentility, combined with economy and elegance. French silks, fancy articles, and ladies' gloves are also cheap.

Religion. — Upon this interesting topic I would repeat, what indeed you are already acquainted with, that *legally* there is the most unlimited liberty. There is no state religion, and no government prosecution of individuals for conscience-sake. Whether those halcyon days, which would, I think, attend a similar state of things in England, are in existence here, must be left for future observation. There are five Dutch Reformed churches; six Presbyterian; three Associated Reformed ditto; one Associated Presbyterian; one Reformed ditto; five Methodist; two ditto *for blacks;* one German Reformed; one Evangelical Lutheran; one Moravian; four Trinitarian Baptist; one Universalist; two Catholic; three Quaker; eight Episcopalian; one Jews' Synagogue, and to this I would add a small Meeting which is but little known, at which the priest is dispensed with, every member following what they call the apostolic plan of instructing each other, and "building one another up in their most holy faith." The Presbyterian and Episcopalian, or Church of England, sects take the precedence in numbers and in respectability. Their ministers receive from two to eight thousand dollars per annum. All churches are well filled: they appear the fashionable places for *display;* and the sermons and talents of the minister offer never-ending subjects of interest when social converse has been exhausted upon the bad conduct and inferior nature of *niggars* (negroes); the price of flour at Liverpool; the capture of the *Guerrière;* and the battle of New Orleans. The perfect equality of all sects seems to have deadened party-feeling: controversy is but little known. The great proportion of attendants at any particular church appear to select it either because they are acquainted with the preacher, or that it is frequented by fashionable company, or their great grandmother went there before the Revolution, or because (what will generally have a greater weight than all these reasons,) *their interest will be promoted by their so doing.*

Licences are not necessary, for either the preacher or place of meeting. According to the constitution of the State of New York, no minister of the gospel, or priest of any denomination, can ever hold any civil or military office or place within the State. In 1806, a law was passed, authorizing any religious denomination to appoint trustees, for the purpose of superintending the temporal concerns of their respective congregations. These trustees become by that act a body corporate, and capable of all legal transactions, on behalf of the congregation: they are allowed, on the part of the whole, to hold estates, which may produce 3000 dollars annually. The Episcopalians differ, I believe, in nothing from their *established* brethren in England, except that they do not form a part of the State: they have their bishops, &c. as in Great Britain. Ministers of all parties are generally ordained: they are exempt from military service. A case recently occurred in which a tradesman, who occasionally officiated, was declared exempt, though he had not been ordained. I feel little hopes of succeeding in conveying to you a faithful portraiture of this people in their religious character: they differ essentially from the English sectaries, in being more solemnly bigotted, more intolerant, and *more ignorant of the Scriptures.* Their freedom from habits of thinking seems to emanate from the cold indifference of their constitutional character; and *their attaching no importance to investigation.* There is also another feature in their religious national character, which will be considered by different men in opposite points of view. I do not discover those *distinctive marks* which are called forth in England by sectarianism. There is not the aristocracy of the establishment, the sourness of the presbyterian, or the sanctified melancholy of the methodist. A cold uniform bigotry seems to pervade all parties; equally inaccessible to argument, opposed to investigation, and, I fear, indifferent about truth: as it is, even the proud pharisaical quaker appears under a more chilling and more freezing atmosphere in this new world. Can it be possible, that the non-existence of religious oppression has lessened religious knowledge, and made men superstitiously dependent upon outward form *instead of internal purity?*

Military Service. — The laws upon this subject vary, I believe, in the several States. In that of New York, every male inhabitant can be called out, from the age of 18 to 45, on actual military duty. During a state of peace, there are seven musters annually: the fine for non-attendance is, each time, five dollars. Commanding officers have discretionary power to receive substitutes. An instance of their easiness to be pleased was related to me by Mr. ——, a tradesman of this city. He never attends the muster, but, to avoid the fine, sends some one of his men, who answers to his name; the same man is not invariably his deputy on parade: in this, Mr. ——

suits his own convenience; sometimes the collecting clerk, sometimes one of the brewers, at others a drayman: and to finish this military pantomime, a firelock is often dispensed with, for the more convenient warlike weapon—a cudgel.

Courts-martial have the power of mitigating the fine, on the assignment of a satisfactory cause of absence, and in cases of poverty. Upon legal exemptions I cannot convey certain information. During a period of three months in the late war, martial law existed, and no substitutes were received. Aliens were not called out. In the adjoining state (Jersey) they were compelled to serve. Instances occurred of residents, who had not taken up their citizenship, being banished to forty miles beyond tide-water.

You will probably expect some advice from me as to your emigration. At present I can hardly form an opinion; that is, such an one as would be deserving of respect. The preceding information has been collected from numerous sources, and with as much care and discrimination as I am capable of exercising. It may partly enable you to draw your own conclusions, which I shall greatly prefer to a dependence upon my judgment. Thus much I can safely say of this country, that every industrious man may obtain a living here; but that it is not that political Elysium, which a certain unprincipled author and bookseller has so floridly described, and which the imaginations of many have fondly anticipated.

In a few months I hope to be enabled to speak of America with more decision. That the Deity may bless me with a competent and discerning mind, and that all your steps may be directed aright, is my ardent and sincere prayer.

The Amity will sail in a few hours; I must therefore conclude. In my next report, which will be sent by Captain Foreman, of the Washington, I shall forward some particulars of the *interior* of this state.

The following letter has just come to hand.

" Sir,

" Understanding from Miss ———, " of Boston, who came with Mrs. Quincy " Adams, that you are looking out for a set- " tlement; I beg to offer one, which I think may " answer your purpose. It is at Fishkill-land- " ing, on the banks of the Hudson: sixteen frame " buildings, with a church, are already erected. " There is also a good lot of land. The whole " I am disposed to sell on moderate terms, and " with a liberal credit. For reference, I refer " you to the late president, at Quincy. The " distance is 60 miles from the city of New " York. Sloops and steam-boats pass every " day. I shall feel much pleasure in receiving

" a visit from you, previous to your return to
" Europe.

" J. P. De Wint.

" Fishkill-landing,
" State of New York."

*** The present report will be taken by Mr. Berthelé, of the house of Berthelé and Reeves, of Montreal; a gentleman who is going to pursue his medical studies in London, and who has politely consented to be the bearer of this. He sails in the Amity, for Liverpool, on the 4th September.

SECOND REPORT.

Courts of Law in New York.—Sloop of War Ontario.—Slavery; Anecdote of a black Barber.—Visit to Mr. Cobbett.—Soil and Agriculture of Long Island.—Prices of Stock, and of Land.—Man-Hatten, or York Island.—Country Houses on Sale; Prices.—Newark, in Jersey.—Fishkill.—Mr De Wint's Property.—American Servants.—Newburgh.—No National Monument to Washington.—American Emigration to Canada.—Cotton Manufactory.—Return to New York.—Academy of Fine Arts.—Mechanical Panorama.—Theatre.—Shamrock Society.—What Classes of Emigrants are likely to succeed, and what are not.

Newburgh, on the Banks of the Hudson.

In my last report, conveyed by the politeness of Mr. Berthelé, I gave particulars of various trades and professions. Their length prevented me from entering into those minor details, which perhaps may not be without their utility. My residence in this country has yet been but short; and whatever may have been my exertions and enquiries, I am not yet sufficiently familiarized with the habits and character of the people, to feel confident in my impressions. Minute traits and occurrences apparently trifling, frequently attract my notice; as I conceive it is by means of these, that we are frequently best enabled to form a correct estimate, either of an individual or an entire community.

The 9th of August was, I believe, the date on which I closed my first communication.

On the 10th, I attended at the city-hall, to witness an expected trial of our captain, on the charge of the second steward, for alleged ill usage: several passengers and sailors were in waiting to give evidence on both sides. I felt rejoiced to see even the latter; though, when on board, they had little of my respect: such is the attachment created by a long sea voyage. This trial was fifth on the list; the time spent in waiting I felt as no demand on my patience: my mind was occupied; the objects with which I was surrounded interested, because they were novel to me. The court is in size about one-fourth larger than the lord mayor's court in the Mansion-house. The presiding judge was a young man, about twenty-six; tall, thin, sallow, serious, and uninteresting: his dress was a long loose great-coat and trowsers. The counsel were of similar ages and appearance. The commencement of the first trial was delayed from the want of jurymen: twenty-four had been summoned; seven only were in attendance. The judge proposed that the first five should be taken from among the by-standers, who were from fifty to sixty in number. This proposition was opposed by the counsel for the plaintiff, who, among other arguments, urged the possibility that five so chosen might not all be citizens of the United States. This was overruled, and the trial proceeded. It was of a petty nature, not possessed of features useful to communicate: the decision seemed to me just. The technical language used, was borrowed from English practice; the general effect different, especially in the perfect equality of judge, counsel, jury, tipstaff, and auditors. Our case was called: it was not tried, in consequence of, I believe, the well-paid *management* of counsel. I am informed, on good authority, that great corruption exists in those minor courts. The judge is said to have *a good understanding* with the constable: *he receives too, a larger sum in cases of conviction than in those of acquittal.* It is indisputable that the constables are remarkably anxious for jobs; and that the judge strongly *participates* in their feelings. An important legal officer here, has been long known to practise the most disgraceful imposition; but his political views are in agreement with those of the State government, and therefore he retains his situation. My impressions of the court just referred to were, that it presented a character of more simplicity, (if the term be allowable in any case where lawyers are concerned,) but of less dignity, than those with which we are familiar. The justice awarded in each is perhaps about upon an equality: at least I see no fair reason to give the preference to this side of the Atlantic.

When at my boarding-house I am not unoccupied in observing the characters and conduct of fellow-residents. The manners of Americans differ widely from those of Englishmen: they are more easy, but less polite. A desire to please does not seem to form a feature of the national character. Their easiness of address seems not the result of reflection, or the polish of good society; but appears to proceed from the general diffusion of moderate wealth, and the national civil institutions. Every man feels not merely independent in his political, but also in his personal condition. The individual acts and thinks as an individual; and society seems to have diminished charms for men, who imagine that they have sufficient resources within themselves.

The following day, Major Biddle, of the United States' army, had the politeness to take me in the garrison boat on board the ship of war *Ontario*, which his brother commanded. She is waiting to take out commissioners to South America. This vessel is remarkably fine of her class: she carries twenty thirty-two pounders and two twelves. Captain Biddle, distinguished for his bravery in the late war, was in a hammock on deck, being indisposed with a slight fever, as were several of his officers and crew: his reception of me was most liberal and gentlemanly.

I was much pleased with one of the Lieutenants. Having adverted to their naval victories, he very modestly replied, "I make no claim "to superiority over the British. Men cannot "be braver than they are: but they were too "confident of success, and that feeling has "defeated men in many things besides battles. "Besides which, Sir, their long unrivalled suc- "cesses caused them to be lax in their dis- "cipline, while, on the contrary, we are remark- "ably strict in ours: our discipline is a model "in that particular, and nothing can be done "without it at sea."

The existence of *slavery* in the United States has, I know, long been to you all a subject both of regret and astonishment. New York is called a "free state:" that it may be so *theoretically*, or when compared with its southern neighbours, I am not prepared to dispute; but if, in England, we saw in the Times newspaper such advertisements as the following, we should conclude that freedom from slavery existed only in words. The first is from the New York Daily Advertiser. I have not made a memorandum of the paper from which I extracted the second; but no American will deny their originality; and, what is worse, I fear there are few who would acknowledge their iniquity:

"TO BE SOLD,

"A Servant woman acquainted with both city and "country business, about 30 years of age, and sold "because she wishes to change her place. Enquire at "this office, or at 91 Cherry-street."

"FOR SALE OR HIRE,

"A likely young Man Servant, sober, honest and "well behaved. He would suit very well for a house "servant or gentleman's waiter, being accustomed to "both. Enquire at this office."

The number of blacks in this city is very great: they have instituted a "Wilberforce Society;" and look upon the Englishman whose name they have taken as the great saviour of their race. At Mrs. Bradish's boarding-house I saw but one white servant, and I should suppose there were of her own, and of her boarders', at least sixteen blacks. A negro child, about six years of age, often waited upon us at tea: the strength and dexterity of the little thing frequently excited my attention and sympathy. Female blacks often obstructed my passage up and down stairs. They lie about, clinging to the boards as though that had been the spot on which they had vegetated: several belonged to families from the south, and were, as a matter of course, *held in unconditional slavery*. The men, whether regular servants of the house or not, equally attended upon all at table. There was one waiter on an average to four gentlemen; yet such was the want of system observed, that few could obtain what they desired. Soon after landing I called at a hair-dresser's in Broadway, nearly opposite the city-hall: the man in the shop was a negro. He had nearly finished with me, when a black man, very respectably dressed, came into the shop and sat down. The barber enquired if he wanted the proprietor or his *boss*, as he termed him, who was also a black: the answer was in the negative; but that he wished to have his hair cut. My man turned upon his heel, and with the greatest contempt, muttered in a tone of proud importance, "We do not "cut coloured men here, Sir." The poor fellow walked out without replying, exhibiting in his countenance confusion, humiliation, and mortification. I immediately requested, that if the refusal was on account of my being present, he might be called back. The hair-dresser was astonished: "You cannot be in earnest, Sir," he said. I assured him that I was so, and that I was much concerned in witnessing the refusal from no other cause than that his skin was of a darker tinge than my own. He stopped the motion of his scissars; and after a pause of some seconds, in which his eyes were fixed upon my face, he said, "Why, I guess as how, Sir, what "you say is mighty elegant, and you're an ele-"gant man; but I guess you are not of these "parts." — "I am from England," said I, "where we have neither so cheap nor so en- "lightened a government as yours, but we "have no slaves." — "Ay, I guessed you were "not raised here; you salt-water people are "mighty grand to coloured people; you are "not so proud, and I guess you have more "to be proud of; now I reckon you do not "know that my boss would not have a single "ugly or clever gentleman come to his store, "if he cut coloured men; now my boss, I "guess, ordered me to turn out every coloured "man from the store right away, and if I did "not, he would send me off slick; for the slim- "mest gentleman in York would not come to "his store if coloured men were let in; but you "know all that Sir, I guess, without my telling "you; you are an elegant gentleman too, Sir." I assured him that I was ignorant of the fact which he stated; but which, from the earnest- ness of his manner, I concluded must be true. "And you come all the way right away from "England. Well! I would not have supposed, "I guess, that you come from there from your "tongue; you have no hardness like, I guess, in "your speaking; you talk almost as well as we "do, and that is what I never see, I guess, in "a gentleman so lately from England. I guess "your talk is within a grade as good as ours. "You are a mighty elegant gentleman, and if "you will tell me where you keep, I will bring "some of my coloured friends to visit you. "Well, you must be a smart man to come from "England, and talk English as well as we do "that were raised in this country." At the dinner-table I commenced a relation of this occurrence to three American gentlemen, one of whom was a doctor, the others were in the law: they were men of education and of liberal opinions. When I arrived at the point of the black being turned out, they exclaimed, "Ay "right, perfectly right, I would never go to a "barber's where a coloured man was cut!" Observe, these gentlemen were not from the south; they are residents of New York, and I believe were born there. I was upon the point of expressing my opinion, but withheld it, thinking it wise to look at every thing as it stood, and form a deliberate judgment when every feature was finally before me. They were amused with the barber's conceit about the English language, which I understand is by no means a singular view of the subject.

The exclusion of blacks from the places of public worship where whites attend, I stated at the commencement. In perfect conformity with this spirit is the fact, that the most degraded white will not walk or eat with a negro; so that, although New York is a free state, it is such only on parchment: the black Americans are in it *practically* and politically slaves; the laws of the mind being, after all, infinitely more strong and more effective than those of the statute book; and it is these *mental* legislative enactments, operating in too many cases besides this of the poor negroes, which excite but little respect for the American character.

August 21st. (You see I am not very regular in my chronology, wishing rather to throw my ideas on the same subject as nearly as I can together.) On this day I went to Long Island, for the purpose of visiting Mr. Cobbett, at Hyde-Park Farm, which is 18 miles distant from the city. I had no previous personal knowledge of Mr. C. nor had I letters of introduction to him; but believing that he could give information and advice concerning America, and also feeling a strong desire to see a character so celebrated, I resolved to forego the usual pre-requisite in calling upon a stranger. The conveyance from the city to Brooklyn, on Long Island, is by a steam ferry-boat: the East River, at this point, is about one-third wider than the Thames at Greenwich: horses and carriages are driven into the boat, those who ride seldom dismounting. In order that I might be in time for the stage, I did not go to my lodgings for dinner, supposing that as Brooklyn was a place of considerable population, I should find no difficulty in obtaining an article so necessary for a traveller. I found there several places of public entertainment, the signs and outward appearance of which bespoke a similarity to English taverns. The first into which I went had one large public room, without a table, or, I believe, a chair, with a bar railed off like a prison. The inhabitant of this department was not dissimilar to many of his countrymen: tall, thin, yellow, cold, suspicious, and silent. At this place I did not venture to make known my wants. I passed several others before I presumed to make a second attempt: when I did so, it was at a "Tavern and Hotel;" the bar was like the one before described, but there was the convenience of a private room, the floor of which was covered with a neat and economical species of carpet, of domestic manufacture. I made known my wants to the landlady; saying, that I was not at all particular, and should be glad of any thing she had in the house: she walked on to her bar, answering, without looking at me, "I guess we "have got no feed for strangers; we do not "practise those things at this house, I guess." The stage was ready: the driver informed me that he would take me to Wiggins' Inn, a distance of about four miles from Mr. Cobbett's. The vehicle was a kind of light farmer's waggon, with three seats, carrying two persons each: there was no covering, and, of course, a want of protection from the sun and dust, both of which, on this occasion, were very unpleasant: my thermometer in the shade was 88°, in the sun 120°.

Long Island is called the garden of America. We passed some pleasing scenery, and several remarkably fine fields of Indian corn: this article can hardly be excelled in beauty of appearance. The residence of the celebrated Mr. Rufus King is on the road side: it is a frame house, painted white, with green shutters, and would class in England as a fourth-rate country seat. A gentleman informed me, that, were Mr. King travelling, he would not hesitate at riding in our waggon. Mr. K. is what is called a Federalist; but this trait of real dignity of character is not the peculiar feature of a party: it appertains to all public men in America; at once exhibiting an evidence of their good sense, and the wise institutions of this government.

The murder of American prisoners at Dartmoor was the subject of a conversation between myself and an American medical fellow-passenger, arising from Mr. King's son having been one of the commissioners appointed by the United States to investigate that most unfortunate and disgraceful transaction. The Doctor was unwilling to censure, in this instance, the conduct of the British. He stated, that there was a great deal to be said on both sides; and that, for himself, he had suspended his judgment. Lord Castlereagh and the English cabinet were, in this gentleman's estimation, "great men, who acted with good intentions "for the welfare of their country." Taxation was partially discussed; he labouring to convince me that, in proportion to their means, they (the Americans) were more heavily taxed than the people of England.

Upon arriving at Mr. Cobbett's gate, my feelings, in walking along the path which led to the residence of this celebrated man, are difficult to describe. The idea of a person self-banished, leading an isolated life in a foreign land — a path rarely trod, fences in ruins, the gate broken, a house mouldering to decay, added to much awkwardness of feeling on my part, calling upon an entire stranger, produced in my mind feelings of thoughtfulness and melancholy. I would fain almost have returned without entering the wooden mansion, imagining that its possessor would exclaim, "What in-"truding fellow is here coming to break in upon "my pursuits?" But these difficulties ceased almost with their existence. A female servant (an Englishwoman) informed me that her master was from home, attending at the county court. Her language was natural enough for a person in her situation: she pressed me to walk in, "being "quite certain that I was her countryman; and "she was so delighted to see an Englishman, in-"stead of these nasty guessing Yankies." Following my guide through the kitchen, (the floor of which, she asserted, was imbedded with two feet of dirt when Mr. Cobbett came there — it had been previously in the occupation of Americans,) I was conducted to a front parlour, which contained but a single chair and several trunks of sea-clothes.

A French gentleman, whom I found in the house, residing with Mr. Cobbett, interested me much by his character and conversation. He had been in the suite of Napoleon, and came over with Santini. His account of the Emperor's treatment corresponds with the published narratives. Of his late master he speaks in the most affectionate manner. He jumped about, whistled, and sang with a thoughtless gaiety, peculiarly French. At half past eight in the evening Mr. Cobbett had not returned. My design was to walk back to Wiggins' Inn. This idea I abandoned on the recommendation of an English servant, who, as it proved, knew little of the country. He conducted me to the road side, directing me to proceed in a direction opposite to that which led to Wiggins', stating, that in about one hundred yards' distance I should see a tavern. My walk extended for many hundred yards, but no human habitation appeared. The night fortunately was fine — the moon's brilliancy — the surrounding scenery — the serious turn of my mind, and the belief that, for that night, wandering without repose in a strange land was to be my lot, produced feelings which would have furnished my poetic friend D—— with a good subject for further "night thoughts." The coolness of the air was also a most pleasing treat after the oppressive heat which I had experienced during the day. I proceeded at a slow and thoughtful pace, willing to foster a faint hope that I might yet arrive at a tavern. A house appeared, but it was a private one, and all were gone to bed. I became very uneasy, having in my pocket a large remittance from Washington. At length, to my great joy, I saw a light at a considerable distance: it proved to come from a hut by the road side. Upon my approach to the door, a dog jumped out: when he was partially silenced, I enquired for a public house; none was near. This habitation belongs to an old woman, who once kept what is here called a tavern. After the repetition of my request, she answered, by desiring to know, "What do *you* want with a "public-house? What is your name? Where were "you raised? Where are *you* going? You are "from York (New York) I guess? You want a "bed I guess? now I guess if you be not a *hard* "*character*, I will let you have *elegant* lodgings "I guess?" I accepted the offer with a combination of fear and gladness. The old lady still sells liquors. Her present stock is contained in three dirty bottles, carefully preserved in a corner cupboard. At the moment of my entrance, she was supplying a black pedlar with a glass of New England, or what is here denominated "Yankee" rum. The old lady's witch-like appearance, and the cast of character of her guest, were strong drawbacks upon my desire for repose. This pair seemed living portraits of Dirk Hatterick and Meg Merrilies: they looked really terrific. I seated myself, and was busied in physiognomical research, when the man, holding a candle in my face, exclaimed "*She* wants to look at you." When I had passed my examination, the old woman withdrew to prepare a bed; her guest continued drinking, giving me a great many winks and nods, and saying "how wealthy the old baggage was." I was heartily glad to find that this sable hero was not to be an occupant of the same house with myself. As the old lady conducted me to an apartment, she apologized for the passage to it being through a room, in which were an entire family strewed over the floor. The wretchedness and poverty of my chamber must remain undescribed. Yet I never in my life lay down with more sincere gratitude to the Deity.

Before seven o'clock on the following morning I regained Mr. Cobbett's. His servant conducted me into a room in which he was writing, with his coat off. The first question was, "Are you an American, Sir?" then, "What were my objects in the United States? "Was I acquainted with the friends of liberty "in London? How long had I left?" &c. He was immediately familiar. I was pleasingly disappointed with the general tone of his manners. His sons, particularly the second, are genteel young men. Of their talents I had no opportunity to form a judgment. Mr. C. thinks meanly of the American people, but spoke highly of the economy of their government. He does not advise persons in respectable circumstances to emigrate, even in the present state of England. In his opinion, a family who can but barely live upon their property, will more consult their happiness by not removing to the United States. He almost laughs at Mr. Birkbeck's settling in the Western country. This being the first time I had seen this well-known character, I viewed him with no ordinary degree of interest. A print by Bartollotzi, executed in 1801, conveys a correct outline of his person. His eyes are small, and pleasingly good-natured. To the French gentleman he was attentive; with his sons familiar; to his servants easy; but to all, in his tone and manner resolute and determined. He feels no hesitation in praising himself, and evidently believes that he is eventually destined to be the

Atlas of the British nation. His faculty of relating anecdotes is amusing.— Instances when we meet.

My impressions of Mr. Cobbett are, that those who know him would like him, if they can be content to submit unconditionally to his dictation. "Obey me, and I will treat you kindly; "if you do not, I will trample on you," seemed visible in every word and feature. He appears to feel, in its fullest force, the sentiment,

> "I have no brother, am like no brother,
> "I am myself alone."

The little Frenchman was whistling, jumping, and singing, with all the gaiety of a delighted boy upon a gala day. In reply to my questions concerning the treatment of Napoleon, he was rapid, energetic, and nearly unintelligible. "Gover-neur, bad man, rascal man, "insult empe-reur: empe-reur not like gover-"neur, not speak to him, — Balcomb, Oh! Oh! "Oh! bad man, bad man — rats, run, run, run."

Mr. Cobbett complained of the difficulty of obtaining labourers, at a price by which the agriculturist could realize a profit: so much so, that he conceives that a farmer in America cannot support himself unless he has sons, who, with himself, will labour with their own hands. He had contracted with a man to do his mowing: the terms were, an equal division of the produce, Mr. C. took me round his grounds. The contractor complained that even half the hay, for merely his labour, was a hard bargain. With pleasing sensations I departed from Mr. Cobbett's residence; and most willingly express my obligation to him for a reception generous and liberal.

Long Island, a part of the State of New York, is chiefly occupied by farmers: their populous capital affords a ready market for produce. This island in length is 120, and in breadth 12 miles. It is divided into counties, two of which retain the names of royalty, after the disappearance of the reality; the first being called King's, the second Queen's County—such inveterate tyrants are ancient establishments. The west end has a good soil, and is in a state of moderate cultivation; the east has a considerable portion of sandy plains. The introduction of gypsum, and other improvements in their mode of agriculture, have much increased the annual produce. I am informed that within the last 14 years farms have risen in value 25 per cent. Land is worth from 3l. 7s. 6d. to 33l. 15s. per acre. A choice of farms may now be purchased in this island at from 15l. 15s. to 22l. 10s. per acre, including necessary buildings. Farmers do not live extravagantly: few of them have money in reserve. The high price of labour, indifference of the soil, and general want of capital, must cause a long continuance of this state of things. The agriculturist, who alone can, in this island, entertain rational hopes of profit, must have sons that will work, and be himself among the foremost by labouring with his own hands. There being no tax upon horses, their labour is preferred, and mules and asses are seldom if ever used. The breed of horses is good, but not large: one fit for a waggon is worth 22l. 10s.; a saddle or drawing horse, 35l.; gig horse, 33l. 15s. to 56l. 5s.; carriage ditto, 90l. to 120l.; fine riding ditto, 90l. to 120l. Cows are worth—lean, 9l.; fat, 11l. 5s. to 13l. 10s. Pigs are sold, per pound, alive; the present price is 7d.; sheep, 9s. They are very small: an entire carcase is not much larger than a Leicestershire leg of mutton. A sheep, when fattened for market, is 13s. 6d. A good farm cart is worth 7l. to 9l.; a ditto waggon, 22l. to 23l.; a farmer's man-servant, 24l. to 30l. per year; a ditto woman, 12l. to 16l. Early wheat is cut in the middle of July. The wheat and rye harvest is completed by the end of August; buck-wheat, in October; Indian corn, ditto; oats, middle of August; grass, from 1st to the end of July. The seed for winter, rye and wheat, is sown from end of August to end of September. The following advertisement, extracted from the New York Evening Post, may convey more specific ideas of the value of farms than the preceding statement. Previous to this notice of public sale, I applied, with a view to our friend L——, to know the lowest ready money price. Mrs. Ledyard, their owner, informed me that the first would be 100 dollars, and the second 70 dollars, per acre.

" FOR SALE AT AUCTION,

" At the T. C. H. on the 1st day of March next, the " farm belonging to the estate of the late Dr. Isaac " Ledyard, situated one mile south of the village of " Newtown, Long Island. The Williamsburgh turn- " pike runs through the farm, on one side of which is " a new excellent stone wall, half a mile in length. The " farm contains about 150 acres, 15 of which are a fine " wood lot, with two apple orchards, one old, the other " just beginning to bear well, and a suitable proportion " of good salt meadow. The mansion house is large " and convenient, four rooms on each floor, with a good " kitchen and cellars; attached is a large barn, crib, " hen house, smoke house, well, and a new cistern, &c. " The court-yard and garden contain a variety of fruit " trees and shrubbery, a large asparagus bed, rasp- " berries, and currants.

" Also — A farm adjoining the above, containing " about sixty acres; attached to which is an equal pro- " portion of salt meadow, and a lot of young wood, " situated within less than a mile of the farm, containing " ten acres, with a farm house, barn, well, garden, &c."

Wishing to see York Island, Mr. Dashwood, a fellow-boarder, had the politeness to accompany me, in a single horse chaise. We proceeded a few miles beyond Hearlem Bridge, where we visited a farmer with whom Mr. D. was acquainted. Apple trees were in profusion on the road side. There is no obstacle, and seems, indeed, no objection raised to any person's taking fruit. The scenery, during this ride, particularly on the margin of the East River, is pleasing and diversified. Country seats are rather numerous: one half of them, at least, are to be sold or let.

My excellent friend S—— could make a pleasing selection on York Island. I enquired the price of several places: they vary, of course, as being affected by causes similar to those which serve to lessen or to increase the value of houses in England. A residence, two stories high, sufficiently large for a family of ten or twelve persons, with a garden, and from two to fifteen acres of land, is from eight thousand to twenty thousand dollars (1800l. to 4500l. sterling); a variation occasioned by difference in the situation, or in the style of building.

The following description I extract from a letter, sent me by the solicitor of a person to whom I applied. The house referred to is four and a half miles from the city, and in the immediate neighbourhood of a good road:—

"The house and other buildings are substan-
"tially and neatly built.

"The cellar to the house is perfectly dry,
"being partly blown out of the rock.

"The house is filled in with brick, furrowed

" off, lathened and plaistered, so as to be as tight
" and comfortable as a brick house.

" The two wells on the place are both blown " through a rock; the one near the house for " twenty or thirty feet, and both contain ex- " cellent water for family use, particularly the " one near the house.

" Particular pains have been taken with the " garden, it being a fine level garden spot, and " filled up on one side, with mould carted into " it, to the height of eight or ten feet.

" There are a great number and variety of " fruit trees of the most improved and best " kinds.

" The situation is elevated and healthy, and " commands one of the finest prospects on the " island.

" The terms are 10,000 dollars, which can be " made payable, a small part in cash, and the re- " sidue in such payments as may be convenient."

B—— (a coach-maker), who sailed in the Ann to Boston, and M—— (a chair and fancy japanner), who came in the Criterion, have got work at Newark, a town in Jersey, ten miles from the city of New York. I have been with them several times, and through their means am possessed of some information relating to mechanics and manufacturers. I made several visits to Jersey: it is situated opposite New York, on the southern banks of the Hudson.

An excellent steam ferry-boat connects these States as completely as could be effected by a bridge. In the valleys are black oak, ash, palms, and poplars; in some parts there is considerable variety of the red and white oak; the hickory grows in those situations which are overflowed. The soil is not esteemed prolific.

NEWARK contains a population of about eight thousand persons, including slaves. It is a manufacturing town of some importance: carriages and chairs are made on a very extensive scale, chiefly for the southern markets. I saw a very beautiful model of a carriage at Campfield's factory, which was ordered for a Spanish patriot-chief. This town is delightfully situated, and contains a great number of excellent houses.

Wishing to see Mr. De Wint's property, at Fiskhill, (see the postscript of my first report,) I took a passage in the steam-boat "Chancellor Livingstone;" fare 3½ dollars, distance 60 miles, time of departure five o'clock in the evening, of arrival half past one the following morning. This vessel is, perhaps, equalled by none in the world: she may be denominated, without the charge of exaggeration, a floating palace; her length is 175 feet, and breadth 50, and she is propelled by a steam-engine of 80 horse power; there are beds for 160, and accommodation for 40 more by settees. The ladies have a distinct cabin: they seem cut off from all association or conversation with the gentlemen. On deck there are numerous conveniences, such as baggage rooms, smoking rooms, &c.; on the descent to the cabins are placed cards of tradesmen and hotels in the chief cities, and also religious tracts, which are chiefly reprints of English evangelical effusions—affording another instance of the slavish dependence of America upon British writers. The interior of this vessel is extremely splendid. The late period of the day at which we embarked, allowed me but a limited opportunity of viewing the bold and grand scenery of this majestic river. Near the banks is erected a monument to that great ornament of the federal party, Hamilton: he was in the administration, and some say the director, of Washington. Those who knew him best, state that he was a man far above the ordinary standard of public characters: endowed, indeed, with such talents as but few mortals are destined to possess; he was deprived of life by the celebrated Mr. Aaron Burr, thus adding another and a splendid victim to the barbarous practice of duelling—which, by the way, is very general and almost uniformly fatal in this country. A slight provocation produces a challenge, and if the parties consider themselves of what is called "equal standing," that is, of families and in worldly circumstances of equal respectability, they rarely decline the combat; and the Americans being generally good shots, and as remarkable for their cool deliberation as, too frequently, for deadly malignity, it is seldom that both parties escape with life.

In the churchyard of New York there is a monument to Alexander Hamilton; there is also one to Captain Lawrence, of the Chesapeake: that the latter may be deserving of this distinguished honour I wish not to dispute, but surely Washington is, to say the least, entitled to as much respect as a rash naval officer; yet, singular to relate, to Washington, the father and saviour of his country, there is no national monument! unless, indeed, you will call by that name an existence in the hearts and affections of the remaining few who are deserving of his unexampled exertions, and equally unparalleled devotion to the sound interests of his country. But if Washington has no national monument in America, he has one in England that never can decay but with the annihilation of the British character; he lives in their generous and liberal minds as a model to the general and the politician of the present and every succeeding age.

Relative to Hamilton, I extract the following from a New York publication, written by one, an Englishman by birth, but an American by adoption: — "General Hamilton was born in "one of the English West-India islands; he

" came to the American colonies *when a lad;* " entered into the revolutionary war with zeal; " became early in the war one of the aids of " General Washington; gallantly commanded " a regiment at the capture of Cornwallis; " fought through the revolution; was a member " of the convention from which our national " constitution originated; was the first secretary " of the treasury, or chancellor of the exche- " quer, under the national government; he " formed the department, and brought order " out of chaos; he was, perhaps, the ablest " writer, and most eloquent man in America. " Even Hamilton, one of the most ingenuous " and disinterested of mankind, was called and " considered and treated as a *foreigner.* His " early distinctions are to be ascribed to the " circumstances of the times, to a poverty of " talents. The late President Adams says, in " his recent publications, that *Hamilton being* " A FOREIGNER, it could not be supposed that " he could have American feelings, or be well " informed on American affairs!!!" But to return to my detail, the boat in which I had embarked for Fishkill was well filled with passengers. The general occupation was card-playing; one or two had a book in their hands: those whose beds were in the births fitted up for that purpose were passengers going the entire route (to Albany), and who had taken the precaution to have their names early entered in a book kept by the captain for that purpose. Mr. Tompkins, the Vice-president of the United States, was among the number going to Albany, the seat of the New York State government: he was seated among the other passengers, without assuming consequence, or receiving any particular attention. In person he is of the middle size, in complexion dark, with a countenance at that time thoughtful to an extreme; he is taller than Mr. Waithman, but in other respects the latter gentleman will convey an idea of his cast of character: his solemnity may not have been habitual, for I am told by those who knew him, that he carries jocularity and lively good-nature to an extreme.

Newburg, the town where I stopped, is 60 miles from New York; I obtained a bed after one or two unsuccessful applications at the hotels which keep open regularly for steam-boat passengers. The following morning I crossed the Hudson to Fishkill-landing. The gentleman to whose house I was going was a fellow-passenger in the ferry-boat, though at that time unknown to me. The property for sale consisted of one hundred acres of land, and fourteen small frame (not log) houses; the price for the whole is 25,000 dollars (5625l.): there is on this lot a neat frame church, which may be purchased for 2500 dollars (562l. 10s.); it is not fitted up, except a few common seats, and a pulpit of rather primitive simplicity. A credit of four years will be given, charging the interest: the present cash price is not lower.

Mr. De Wint's residence is within half a mile: I had the pleasure of dining with him in company with several ladies and gentlemen of a very superior class. The following day Judge Vanpelt, a neighbouring gentleman and farmer, had the politeness to take me to his house. My reception at both, as well as the style of living, the substantial elegance of the furniture, and the mental talents of the company, was *essentially English.* I felt, indeed, for the first time, that I was once more in your little island. That *peculiarly* British word *comfort* was well understood in these hospitable mansions. Another thing, too, was here an evident favourite, though, I lament to say, scarcely known on this side the Atlantic — *cleanliness:* the servants also were in their dress neat, and in their manners attentive, forming a striking contrast to what I have too often seen on other occasions.

Servants, let me here observe, are called "helps:" if you call them servants they leave you without notice. Englishmen often incur their displeasure by negligence in continuing to use this prohibited word. The difference, however, would appear merely verbal; for indeed I should misrepresent the impressions

I have received on the subject, if I stated that the Americans *really* shewed more feeling, or were more considerate in their conduct towards this class of society than the English: every one who knows them will, I think, pronounce the direct contrary to be the case. A friend of mine, the other day, met with a rebuff at his hotel, which taught him the necessity of altering — not his ideas indeed, but his words. Addressing the female "help" he said, "Be kind "enough to tell your mistress that I should be "glad to see her." — "My *mistress*, Sir! I tell "you I have no mistress, nor master either. "I will not tell her, Sir, I guess; if you want "Mrs. M——— you may go to her yourself, "I guess. I have no mistress, Sir. In this "country there is no mistresses nor masters; "I guess I am a woman citizen." — The term "boss," as I have before observed, is substituted for that of master: but these, I would remark, are not the only instances in this country of the alteration of *names*, while *things* remain the same: indeed some very absurd, and even indelicate changes have been made which cannot well be communicated on paper.

Servants are usually engaged by the week: enquiry as to character is not practised: blacks and whites are seldom kept in the same house; they are chiefly blacks, and, though held in the most degraded estimation, appear to do almost what they please. The condition of their kitchens is what in England would be considered very objectionable: there seem usually several black friends of the servants in this apartment. Their children I observed frequently sprawling about the floor like kittens or puppies.

Judge Vanpelt is a large farmer: his sheep, I think, he stated at 500, — a large flock for this country. His land appeared rather barren. — Mr. De Wint informs me that their winters are dry and severe: they commence about the 5th of December, and end by the middle of March. At this time the ice begins to break in the Hudson. The thermometer is from 56 to 70, from the 1st of April to the middle of May; in July and August it is 78 to 90; in March and April the weather is subject to sudden changes: the cold sometimes intense, with much rain and easterly winds. June is a delightful month, as are also part of September, and the whole of October. The summer heats and winter colds are usually extreme. The advance in the value of land, in this part of the State, has made many of the old settlers men of large property. The general style of living consists of a plentiful supply of the necessaries of life, with but few of what in England we should call its comforts. I visited the mountain adjoining Fishkill-landing — a walk to the summit was fatiguing, but the prospect amply repaid the labour. The town from which I am now writing (Newburgh), appeared situated in a most delightful and fertile valley, with many fine roads connecting it with several parts of this immense continent. Newburgh has a population of 3000, many of whom are of Dutch descent. There are many new and excellent buildings: the genuine log house I have not yet seen. Paper currency seems to be the only circulating medium: it is of every amount, and with a reputation infinitely varied; being regulated according to the distance, and the reputation of the bank. I see no man in absolute want, nor any who appear particularly anxious about their future prospects. These are, perhaps, the natural signs of an improving country, and one whose resources, so far from being exhausted, are yet not even called wholly into action. A Lieutenant in the United States' army, who has just arrived from his station on the lakes, and is now sitting opposite to me, states that the number of Americans who emigrate from the western part of this State to Canada, is very considerable. I asked, with surprise, what could be their inducement. His reply was, that "the King gives them great "encouragement, with land for nothing; — no "taxes, and a present of the implements of "husbandry." This is, indeed, "great en-"couragement!" and such as we old friends of His Majesty would be happy to see imitated in our native land.

Upon returning from my mountain excursion, I visited Vanskank's cotton manufactory. It is advantageously situated on a fine fall of water, which empties itself into the Hudson. The proprietor conducted me over every part of this establishment. It was erected in 1814, has withstood the brunt of British competition, and is said to be profitable. There are sixteen hundred spindles in operation. Children perform the same kind of labour that they do with us: they receive 3s. 4½d. per week; women, 11s. 3d.; men, 31s. 6d. Every part of the machinery is manufactured on the premises. There is also a general shop or store on the ground floor, at which the work people are supplied with any thing they may want, in payment of their wages. The chief articles made are ginghams, plain chambrays, calicoes, and bed ticks; the latter at a price to exclude English cotton tick. Linens are still imported. The fabric of all the articles is coarser and stronger than ours: the *finishing* department is very defective; but this will be amply compensated by the wear. This concern is modelled upon British establishments. Hearing in New York that native manufactories were ruined, I felt astonished in witnessing the prosperous appearance of Mr. Vanskank's; which may be accounted for perhaps by the able way in which it is conducted, and the excellence of the machinery. Their connection is chiefly with the southern merchants. The question as to the success of domestic manufactories, is one in which I cannot but feel personally a particular interest. My present design is to proceed to the New England States, for further information upon this and other subjects.

Returned to New York, I visited the several public exhibitions. The first in order was the "Museum," the collection of which is small — in excellent condition, and displayed with much taste. The charge is 1s. $1\frac{1}{2}$d.

"The Academy of Fine Arts," as it is called, is exhibited in the same building. The collection is small; and, upon the whole, very indifferent, with the exception of two or three rustic pieces. Among the casts, there are a Venus, an Apollo, and a fighting gladiator. — Admission, 1s. $1\frac{1}{2}$d. The printed particulars of this exhibition are pompously denominated, "A catalogue of "paintings, statues, busts, drawings, models, "and engravings, exhibited by the American "Academy of Fine Arts. Sept. 1. 1817. — "*Auditque vocatus Apollo.* — The third Exhi-"bition. *N. B.* The catalogue of pictures is "entirely new. — Printed for the Academy." Then follows a list of directors and officers for the year 1817; containing a president, vice-president, eleven directors, a treasurer, a secretary, a librarian, and sixteen academicians!!

Mr. Van Derlyn, an artist of considerable merit, has a small exhibition, in which is a well-executed copy of Lefebre's Napoleon. — Charge, 2s. 3d.

There is a mechanical Panorama, exhibiting much ingenious mechanism. The wax-work exhibition is tolerably good: the dresses are splendid. The figure of the Goddess of Liberty feeding the American eagle is beautiful and interesting.

The *Theatre* is about the size of the "Royal Circus," and as well fitted up as the second-rate London theatres. The prices are, Boxes, 4s. 6d. Pit, 3s. 4½d. Gallery, 2s. 3d. I went to the pit, concluding that, with an allowance for the difference of country, it would resemble the same department in an English establishment; but found it consisted of none in dress, manners, appearance, or habits above the order of our Irish bricklayers; — a strong fact this to prove the good payment of labour. Here were men that, if in London, could hardly buy a pint of porter — and should they ever think of seeing a play, must take up their abode among the gods in the upper gallery: yet, in America, they can pay three-quarters of a dollar — free from care, and without feeling, on the following morning, that they must compensate, by deprivation or extraordinary labour, for their extravagance. Many wore their hats, and several stood up during the performance: there did not seem to be any power which could prevent either practice. The boxes were respectably filled: the female part of the audience made considerable display. Between the acts gentlemen withdrew: indeed at this period the house, in every part, was deserted, except by the ladies. The cause of this practice is to indulge in the fatal habit of rum-drinking. A part of the gallery is allotted for negroes, they not being admitted into any other part of the house. Women never go to the pit. The entertainments were, "Laugh when you can," and the "Broken Sword:" both performed very respectably. The dresses, scenery, and decorations were superior to what I had expected to find them.

Agreeably to your wishes I waited upon the gentlemen of the "Shamrock Society," who lately published a pamphlet, entitled, "Hints to Emigrants." This association is composed chiefly of Irishmen. Among the gentlemen present was the distinguished Dr. M'Neven. Their place of meeting is at the Globe public house, in William-street, where their business is conducted with much regularity. The society bears a high character for benevolence, and is no doubt of material service to their distressed countrymen. One of their members had just prevented an imposition which is commonly practised in this city, and which, in common with all my fellow-passengers, I had submitted to — the payment of two dollars to the port doctor. Their room is decorated with flags commemorative of American victories. Their hatred of the English ministry is implacable; but they do not seem to distinguish between our government and people. It would prove, I think, impossible to make a native of Ireland, who had never been in England, believe that you have among you men who feel for their wrongs, and sympathise with their sufferings. These gentlemen being engaged in a variety of town occupations, their acquaintance with America has hardly extended beyond the city of New York; and, as far as I can form a judgment, their capability of giving such information as can be relied upon is very limited; much more so, indeed, than their pamphlet might have caused us to expect. Mr. Alexander Pike, their secretary, is a young lawyer: from him I received much attention, though but little faith can be placed in his answers to our queries: not that he designs to deceive, but he affects to give intelligence concerning rents of houses, profits of trade, and domestic expenditure, upon each of which I generally found his statements about 50 per cent. too low; — the fact is, he is not informed upon these subjects.

To-morrow (the 8th) I shall depart from Boston. My old captain has offered to be the bearer of this. I shall write again as soon as I have leisure and materials. Even yet I must withhold my advice as to emigration — — — — — — — — — — — — — — — —

The capitalist may manage to obtain 7 per cent. with good security. The lawyer and the doctor will not succeed. An *orthodox* minister would do so. By the way, the worn-out, exposed impostor Frey, who said he was converted from Judaism to Christianity, has been attracting large audiences in New York. The proficient in the fine arts will find little encouragement. The literary man must starve. The tutors' posts are preoccupied. The shop-keeper may do as well, but not better than in London—unless he be a man of superior talent and large capital: for such requisites, I think, there is a fine opening. The farmer (Mr. Cobbett says) must labour hard, and be but scantily remunerated. The clerk and shopman will get but little more than their board and lodging. Mechanics, whose trades are of the *first necessity*, will do well: those not such, or who understand *only* the cotton, linen, woollen, glass, earthenware, silk and stocking manufactures, cannot obtain employment. The labouring man will do well; particularly if he have a wife and children, who are capable of contributing, not merely to the consuming, but to the earning also of the common stock.

THIRD REPORT.

Leave New York for Boston.—East River, Hell Gate.—American Dislike to Emigrants.—Steam-Boats, Connecticut and Fulton.—First Landing on Continent of America.—Stages.—Roads.—Taverns.—Military.—Condition of People.—Mrs. Fisher's.—Public Roads, and Ideas of their endangering Liberty.—No Slaves in New England.—Face of the Country of Connecticut, and Rhode Island.—Arrival at Providence.—Rents.—Prices of Provisions.—Of Labour.—Trades.—Cotton Manufactories at Pawtucket.—Price of Lands.—Size of Farms.—Entrance into Boston.—Character of the Bostonians.—The Atheneum.—Cambridge College.—Religious Sects.—State of Society.—People of New England aristocratical.—Climate.—Health.—Morals.—State House.—Scenery.—Bunker's Hill.—Visit to the late President Adams.—Servants, superior to those of New York.—European Politics in New England.—Leave Boston for Albany.—Pittsfield.—Military.—Hudson.—Face of Country.—Condition and Character of Americans.—Albany.—Population.—Rents.—Prices of Provisions.—Of Labour.—Feelings concerning America.

Albany, the River Hudson, &c. Sept. 1817.

On the 8th of September I left New York for Boston, in the steam-boat "Connecticut," Captain Bunker; fare to New London, seven dollars, including board; distance, about 140 miles; time, $21\frac{1}{2}$ hours. The various characters on board a steam-boat, for ten minutes before starting, afforded a fruitful source of observation. I supposed we should have been much crowded, but found that at the ring of the bell, three-fourths went on shore. The banks of the East River are pleasing: by Americans and some *interested* European flatterers, they are bepraised most extravagantly. On the York Island side, there is fine hill and dale scenery: among which are scattered several country seats, belonging to the city merchants. The view of Long Island is not so interesting. We passed the navy yard, in which is the far-famed steam-frigate. Eight miles from New York is the difficult passage called Hell Gate. At the moment of passing this strait, a bell rang for breakfast; the ticket for the partaking of which is a receipt given by the captain for the passage-money. My appetite and my curiosity had a strong struggle; the latter, however, prevailed. There are here numerous whirlpools, which at a state of the tide lower than when I passed, produced a loud roaring noise. The whirlpools are said by Mr. Morse to be occasioned by the narrowness and crookedness of the passage, and a bed of rocks, which extend quite across it. A skilful pilot may conduct a ship of any burden with safety through this strait, at high water with the tide, or at low water with a fair wind. There is a tradition among the

Indians, that at some distant period their ancestors could step from rock to rock, and cross this arm of the sea on foot.

The *sound* now opened upon our view, with a light-house, at eighteen miles' distance. A Dutch ship sailed by, full of passengers. This sight did not meet with the approbation of my American friends. One of them, who was a farmer, was the first to express his opinion: "There (said he) is some more of them 'ere salt-" water fellows I guess; curse them I say; I guess" if I had my will there should never be a salt-" water man employed in the States." This was warmly assented to by those who stood near him. He continued, "What a *jag* (a load) there is of" them 'ere salt-water fish lately come into the" States. I guess they are starving in the old" countries, and when they come here they soon" get *kedge* (brisk, or in good health and spirits)," I wish every vessel that brings such freight" might go to the bottom!" Other objects now attracted the old man's attention. His train of illiberal ideas, which I hope are not national, gave way to general observations upon business. He wanted a plaisterer at his farm; here his antipathies were lost in a sense of his interest. "I guess I should like one of them" 'ere, if he was a plaisterer; I would not mind" his salt-water lingo a *cent*, so that he could" plaister."

After a passage of twelve hours, we arrived off New Haven, a city in Connecticut, distance from New York by water, almost ninety miles. This small city is said to have a population of about five thousand, and has the reputation of ranking among the first towns in respect to beauty in the United States. I have since understood that Colonel Humphreys resides here: he is largely engaged in Merino sheep, and the woollen trade. I regret very much that I do not take up my residence for a few days, feeling, as I do, the subject of manufactures to be very important, not only to myself, but to all our friends in Yorkshire.

The greater part of our passengers went on shore. The following day was to be a grand one at the college; it was what is here called "commencement day." The college is said to be a very excellent one. Those who, like myself, were bound for New London, were removed to the steam-boat "Fulton." "The Connecticut" has an engine (en-gīne, is the American pronunciation) of forty horse power: two cabins for gentlemen, one for ladies, a very extensive kitchen and other conveniencies. It is fitted up with minute attention to accommodation, and with much elegance: the chief fault consists in its having too many erections on deck. In a conversation with Captain Bunker he expressed his decided opinion that steam-vessels, as now constructed, could safely navigate the ocean; this passage from New York to New Haven was often, he said, very boisterous; and upon one occasion a gale blew so violently that he accomplished the route in the extraordinary short period of six hours. The "Fulton," in most respects a similar boat, has, however, some variations in her construction. The engines of both are on Bolton and Watt's principle. She was built for the Emperor Alexander, and contracted for to be in Russia at a specified time. Captain Hall, the conqueror of our "Guerrière," was to have had the command: had he successfully navigated her across the Atlantic, he would have added another unfading laurel to his own brow, and that of his country. We landed in New London before day-light: our passage was so rough that I was once more approaching towards the sick list.

At New London I took a place in the coach for Providence. American stages are a species of vehicle with which I know none in England that will compare: they carry twelve passengers — none outside. The coachman, or "driver," (and who is not unfrequently a military officer,) sits inside with the company. In length they are nearly double that of English stages. Few go on springs. The sides are open — the roof being supported by six small posts. The baggage is carried behind, and inside. The seats are pieces of plain board. There are leathers which can be let down from the top, which are useful as a protection against wet, but of little service in cold weather. Few of them have doors; the places of entrance and exit being by the horses. They form, upon the whole, both in construction and management, a very unpleasant mode of conveyance. The charges are nearly equal to English *inside* fares.

We breakfasted at the town of Norwich (a city, I believe, it is denominated); distance from New London fourteen miles, and at the head of the navigation of the Thames: three-mast ships can come up to the town. It was in this river that Commodore Decatur was blockaded during the last war: and so approachable are the Connecticut men represented on the side which promotes their pecuniary interest, that they are said to have had the baseness to betray their country by giving information to the English admiral whenever their shipping attempted putting out to sea. The mode of doing this is said to have been by throwing up blue lights; a circumstance which has given rise to the party appellation of "blue-light men,"—a term of reproach used by the democrats against the federalists.

Our dinner was at the well-known Mrs. Fisher's, at Scituate. She is certainly a most original character; but I must, for the present, pass over a description of this oddity of oddities.

The supply for our whole party consisted of beef, a ham, two fowls, potatoes, cabbage, and apple pie. They grumbled at the scantiness of the supply: for myself, no epicure ever enjoyed his dinner more, and chiefly because every thing was cleanly. At the back of Mrs. Fisher's house there is a fine orchard, from which any person may take as much fruit as they please, free from charge, and without the act being considered a liberty. Mrs. F. makes from forty to a hundred barrels of cider per annum: this year apples are so abundant that it scarcely pays for the trouble. Farms are here worth from thirty to forty dollars per acre. An old man was sitting in the room; I supposed that he was a day labourer; I addressed him with a remark that their roads were bad: "Yes," said he, "roads, I guess, are unpopular in this State: we think, I guess, that they are invasions of our liberties: we were mightily *roiled* (vexed) when they were first cut, and we always spoiled them in the night!"

At six o'clock in the evening we entered Providence, the capital of Rhode Island. We had been thirteen hours travelling fifty miles. Of the general appearance of the country I wished to *force* myself to think well; but I must tell the truth, and therefore honestly say, that, as it respects my bird's-eye view of its soil and cultivation, I am rather disappointed—but we must suspend our judgment. The western States are said to be very superior. Where I now am is that part of America which has been colonized almost since the days of Columbus; and, of course, is too well occupied to offer present encouragement to English emigrants.

In Connecticut and Rhode Island there are numerous dairies. Cheese is sold, for exportation, at from ten to twelve cents a pound. Farms contain from ten to two hundred acres. All houses within sight from the road are farm-houses. The genuine country seat has not yet made its appearance in the four States which I have seen. The condition of the people in Connecticut and Rhode Island is an absence of the extreme either of wealth or of poverty. The land is very stony, and the price of produce not commensurate to that of labour. The absence of negroes from these last-mentioned States gives me much pleasure: certainly not on account of a prejudice against our darker-tinged fellow-creatures, or from a belief that they are of an inferior order in creation; but from a hatred of oppression, whether exercised in a monarchy or a republic, more especially, indeed, in the latter, which, professing to be built on the basis of freedom, *ought* to respect the rights and protect the liberties of all. In the States of New York and Jersey the treatment of Americans of colour, by their white countrymen, is illiberal and barbarous.

A few of the aborigines still reside here. Their ill-shapen miserable huts exhibit but a small remove towards civilization.

With regard to the agriculture. — Stones are cleared from the surface of the land by large holes being dug, into which they are rolled. Fields of Indian corn, which struck me with so much beauty in Long Island, are here a comparatively melancholy sight. The stalks are not half the height, are at a greater distance from each other, and look as though they were springing from a bed of broken rock.

On entering Providence, the capital of Rhode Island, I was much pleased with its beauty. In its appearance, it combined the attractions of Southampton and Doncaster. There are manufactories in the neighbourhood. On that account I took up my abode at Chapotan's Inn until the 11th.

All places of public social worship are, in the State of New York, called churches — not, as with our dissenters, chapels. In these States, the old English distinction of "church," and "meeting house," continues. Here is an excellent market-house, a *workhouse*, four or five public schools, an university with a tolerable library, a public library, and an hospital. Several of the churches are very handsome: they, as well as many orivate houses, are built of wood, painted white, with green Venetian shutters, presenting a neat elegance very superior to our smoky brick buildings. I have not seen a town in Europe or America, which bore the appearance of general prosperity equal to Providence. Ship and house-builders were fully occupied, as indeed were all classes of mechanics. The residents are native Americans. Foreign emigrants seem never to think of New England. Rent and provisions are much lower than at New York.

At Pawtucket, four miles from Providence, are 13 cotton manufactories; six of which are on a large scale. They are not the property of individuals, but of companies. I visited three of these. They had excellent machinery; not more than one half of which was in operation. The articles manufactured are the same as described at Fishkill. Children from six to ten years of age, of both sexes, are paid 6s. 9d. per week; ditto, 11 to 16, 10s. per week; women, 12s.; men, 27s. to 31s. 6d. Very few of the latter are employed. Several of the manufactories of this place are situated on a fine fall of water, 50 feet in length, and passing through several chasms in a rock which extends across the river. The scenic effect of the fall is most materially injured by the situation of Pawtucket bridge.

To a labouring man who accompanied me through the manufactories, I gave half a dollar. I remarked that he addressed men of similar appearance to himself by the titles of "major," "captain," and "colonel." The population of this village is very trifling, yet it has "TWO BANKS!" The persons employed at all the manufactories combined, are not equal in number to those at *one* of a moderate size in Lancashire. A considerable portion of weaving is done by women, who have or live in farm-houses. They receive 3½d. per yard for ¾ wide stout dark gingham; an article which is sold at 13½d. wholesale, and 15d. retail. These female weavers do not in general follow the occupation regularly; it is done during their leisure hours, and at the dull times of the year. Some, who have no other means of support except service, (which is unpopular in America,) lodge with farmers, and give half the produce of their labour for their board and lodging.

The Pawtucket manufacturers have shops or stores in Providence. On their doors a board is affixed, "Weaving given out." During a conversation with a proprietor of one of these establishments, a woman came in, who, from her independent (though not impudent) air, I supposed must be a customer. His address to her, "I'll attend to you directly," confirmed my opinion. She replied, "I want work, Boss, I guess, for Harriet Angel." He immediately called to his assistant, "Where is that work for "Miss Angel."—What would a starving Manchester *weaveress* say to this? and how would Sir Robert Peel feel if addressed in the true language of honest independence?

The road from Providence to Boston is much better than that from New London to the latter place. The appearance of the country also improves; but there is nothing in either as to mere appearance which would be inviting to an inhabitant of our beautiful and cultivated island. From New London to Providence (50 miles), the number of cows which I saw were 16; horses, 6; pigs, 10. From Providence to Boston (44 miles), 38 cows, 10 horses, 25 pigs, and 18 sheep. I met several waggons, all of which were drawn by two oxen and one horse. When, travelling in the stage, we passed boys or girls, they bowed or curtsied. Some of them brought apples to sell, the amount of payment being left to our liberality. We did not meet many persons on the road, and no pedestrians, except a black man and woman. There were no beggars—none that seemed distressed—all either were at work, or going to or from their labour; and in all my enquiries of farmers, inn-keepers, store-keepers, manufacturers, their servants, and others, I understand that employment is not difficult of obtainment by industrious and honest men.

I separated from an English fellow-traveller at Providence;—he proceeded in the stage. During our journey he directed nearly all his discourse to me, so much so that it was supposed we were old friends. I was by no means proud of this impression, as my fellow-countryman was so full of the importance and superiority of England, that any thing American did not, in his eyes, seem worthy of notice. A man passed us on horseback without bowing or speaking; *my friend* exclaimed, "There, you see they "have neither manners nor common sense in this "country; if we were in England, you know, "and a man passed the stage, he would bow and "say, How do you do?" To this gentleman the old story was strictly applicable of two Englishmen and an American travelling in a stage from Boston. They indulged their patriotism by abusing every thing American. The butter was not so good as the English—nor the beef—nor the mutton—nor the peaches—nor the laws, nor the people—nor the climate—nor the country. Their fellow-traveller was displeased, but he remained silent. At length there came on a tremendous storm of thunder and lightning. He then burst forth, boiling with rage—"There, "d—— you, I guess that that thunder and lightning is as good as any you have in England."

As far as I have proceeded I have not seen much good land. It may do for grazing, but upon the whole, it is stony and sterile:—and what would seem remarkable is, that in these old settled States, a large portion remains uncultivated. Travelling in this country conveys none of those delights which are connected with an English country excursion: here, when your eye carries you in imagination to the distant eminence, you feel no relief in the fancied contemplation of your elevated position's presenting a view of fine seats, and extended cultivation. On the contrary, you first feel that you could hardly arrive at the summit through the density of a gloomy forest; and even if you could, that your eye would be fatigued with forests and the parched monotony of unproductive nature.

Arable land in the immediate neighbourhood of Boston, is worth from 50 to 100 dollars per acre (11l. 2s. 6d. to 22l. 5s.), farm-house and buildings included. The same quantity of land at from 8 to 30 miles from Boston, brings from 20 to 30 dollars; — meadow and pasturage, from 10 to 30 dollars; orchard ditto, 50 to 100 dollars per acre. Wood land, *near* towns, is, of course, more valuable than any other, its worth also increasing yearly. Moderate-sized farms usually contain all the different kinds of land, in, of course, varied proportions. Plaister of Paris is used for manure; — it does not succeed, I believe, in those lands within the influence of the sea air. There are some rich farmers in the New England States, but generally it is not an occupation by which more than a living can be obtained.

Gentlemen-farmers do not make more than from two to three per cent. of their capital. The more wealthy farmers, from 20 to 40 miles from Boston, own large pastures, at the distance of from 30 to 60 miles from their residence; and in the mountainous parts of New Hampshire and Vermont, cattle and sheep are fattened for the Boston market.

My entrance into Boston was not favoured by the weather. From its irregularity, and other circumstances, this town in appearance has more of an English character than New York. The names are English, and the inhabitants are not so uniformly sallow. In proceeding along the street with my baggage, to Jones's boarding-house in Pearl-street, a gentleman accosted me—"Where are you from? When did you arrive? "Any thing new in York? What is your name? "Any thing special?"

Boston has a population of 40,000, yet it is not a city: this arises from an apprehension in the inhabitants, that the powers vested in corporations would be injurious to their liberties. This town is the head-quarters of federalism in politics and unitarianism in religion. It contains many rich men. The Bostonians are also the most enlightened and the most hospitable that I have yet met with: they, in common with all New Englanders, have the character of being greater sharpers, and more generally dishonourable, than the natives of the other sections of the Union: for myself, I should be inclined to think otherwise; and if I *must* affix such a reputation, I should be disposed to remove it further south.

The *Atheneum* public library, under the management of Mr. Shaw, is a valuable establishment. It contains 18,000 volumes, four thousand of which are the property of the present secretary of state. In this establishment I observed American editions of the following works: Rees's Cyclopædia, Edinburgh ditto, Calmet's Dictionary and Fragments, Unitarian Version of the New Testament, the Writings of Mosheim, Jeremy Taylor, Bishop Lowth, M'Knight, Newcomb, Paley, Murphy's Tacitus, two or three editions of Shakspeare, Edinburgh Review, Quarterly ditto, and the Christian Observer. English magazines and newspapers are filed regularly: among the latter were the Examiner, Courier, and Morning Post: the former are miscellaneous, and collected apparently without regard to party. Mr. Shaw obligingly offered me access to this library:—he is a singular character:—his whole soul is engrossed by his pursuits; at the same time he knows every body, and every body knows him. I have walked with him in the streets:—our progress was slow indeed:—every few yards we were accosted, "Ah, Mr. Shaw, I have got something for the

" Atheneum—a Russian copper."—" Well, Mr.
" Shaw, I have thought of you—such a snake!"
—" How do you do, Mr. Shaw? I have got a
" prize—such a prize!"

Mr. S. " What, something for the Atheneum,
" I guess?"

" Yes, a stuff'd rat, in fine preservation; my
" brother brought it from Pernambuco."

At Cambridge, four miles from Boston, is situated a college, upon a large and liberal scale. Mr. Washington Adams, who is a student, took me to view it: it contains 250 apartments for officers and students. There is a philosophical apparatus, a hall for public recitations, a dining hall, and a valuable library, which contains a few, and almost the only standard works in the United States. Admission into the college requires a previous knowledge of mathematics, Latin, and Greek. All students have equal rights—each class has peculiar instructors—they meet twice a day. There are quarterly and annual public examinations. This college is regarded by the orthodox party as heretical in religious subjects—it being observed as somewhat remarkable, that most of the theological students leave Cambridge disaffected towards the doctrine of the Trinity. The staunch advocates of this system taking the alarm, they have established an academy for the education of young men, " *who must be compelled to* "*learn and to defend the doctrine of their* "*fathers,*" as the most effectual means to oppose the "Cambridge heresies." A legislative act has not yet been obtained to incorporate this establishment as a college. From my brief observation of these two prominent parties, I should be induced to consider the Trinitarians to be much behind their English orthodox brethren in theological knowledge, liberality, and sincerity; and the Unitarians (or more properly, the Anti-Trinitarians, for few have gone the whole length of Dr. Priestley) to be at the best too worldly-minded;—the open avowal of their opinions being a point upon which they appear to maintain general reserve.

The state of society in Boston is better than in New York, though the leaven, not of democracy, but of aristocracy, seems to be very prevalent: many of the richer families live in great style, and in houses little inferior to those of Russel-Square. *Distinctions* exist to an extent rather ludicrous under a free and popular government: there are the first class, second class, third class, and the "old families." Titles, too, are diffusely distributed.

Foreigners are not often met with in New England;—neither are Jews, or Quakers. There once existed a law in Massachusetts, which awarded the punishment of death to the high crime of being a Quaker! It is hardly necessary to observe, that this barbarous statute, enacted by a people who themselves had fled from religious persecution, is not at present in existence. It is not now, therefore, civil disabilities which exclude the Society of Friends from this "land "of steady habits," but a cause is said to exist for their absence, perfectly adequate to the effect — *the New Englanders are as keen as themselves.* The same fact applies, perhaps, to the descendants of Abraham.

Boston is not a thriving, that is, not an increasing town: it wants a fertile back country, and it is too far removed from the western States to be engaged in the supply of that new and vast emporium, — except, indeed, with inhabitants, a commodity which, I am informed, they send in numbers greater than from any other quarter.

The winds here are violent; as are also rains, but not nearly so frequent as in England. A clear sky is, I believe, the general characteristic of America: the evenings are certainly most delightful.

The *police* of Boston must be very far superior to that of New York; at least, if *effects* may be taken as the criterion. The state of *morals* I cannot speak upon; but medical gentlemen inform me, that their town is not an exception to others with regard to purity:

one fact is, however, apparent, that, unlike some other towns, gross vice is not obtruded upon the public gaze.

On an eminence in the Mall (a fine public walk), is built the State House, in which the legislature hold their meetings. The view from the top of this building is surpassed by nothing which I have seen: the bay with its forty islands — the shipping — the town — the hill and dale scenery for a distance of thirty miles, present an assemblage of objects which are beautifully picturesque. A great increase of interest is communicated by the knowledge of the fact, that Boston is the birth-place of the immortal Franklin, and that here broke forth the first dawnings of the ever-memorable revolution. The heights of Dorchester and Bunker's Hill are immediately under the eye of the spectator.

On the 20th of September I walked to *Bunker's Hill:* it is about two miles from the centre of Boston. The young gentleman who accompanied me is a native of the town, and yet did not know the road to this spot — sacred to patriotism and to liberty. The hill is one of moderate height. The monument placed here in commemoration of the victory is of brick and wood, without an inscription; — except what is supplied by the boyish tricks of visitors, who disfigure it with their names. "J. Fessenden, "1817," is cut in every direction; so anxious are obscure blockheads for posthumous fame. At the bottom of this hill are now lying two most unexpected and far-famed American monuments of national glory — the frigates Guerrière and Java, named after two taken from the British. What would a Franklin, a Patrick Henry, or a Washington have felt, could they have foreseen these things? In the afternoon of this day, young Mr. Adams came from Quincy to conduct me to his grandfather's (the late President) at that place. We sailed out of the harbour by way of Hingham: this route increases the distance 13 miles. The inner and outer harbours are both handsome: they are more extended, but have not that compact and varied beauty which so peculiarly belongs to those of New York. We passed Forts Warren and Independence, near which the inhabitants, in 1814, were stationed in shoals of boats, viewing the contest between the Chesapeake and Shannon. So confident were they of the success of their countrymen, that dinners were absolutely prepared in Boston for both the victors and the vanquished: — but in this they were sorely disappointed by the event.

The ex-president is a handsome old gentleman of eighty-four; — his lady is seventy-six: — she has the reputation of superior talents, and great literary acquirements. I was not perfectly a stranger here, as a few days previous to this I had received the honour of an hospitable reception at their mansion. Upon the present occasion the minister (the day being Sunday) was of the dinner party. As the table of a "*late king*" may be amusing, take the following particulars: — first course, a pudding made of Indian corn, molasses, and butter; — second, veal, bacon, neck of mutton, potatoes, cabbages, carrots, and Indian beans; Madeira wine, of which each drank two glasses. We sat down to dinner at one o'clock: at two, nearly all went a second time to church. For tea, we had pound-cake, wheat bread and butter, and bread made of Indian corn and rye (similar to our brown home-made). Tea was brought from the kitchen, and handed round by a neat, white servant-girl. The topics of conversation were various — England, America, religion, politics, literature, science, Dr. Priestley, Miss Edgeworth, Mrs. Siddons, Mr. Kean, France, Shakspeare, Moore, Lord Byron, Cobbett, American revolution, the traitor General Arnold. Concerning the popularity, among the mass of the people, of this latter personage, Mr. Adams related a characteristic occurrence. Washington, Arnold, and himself were viewing a spot of ground for the purpose of erecting a fortification. A man, with great anxiety depicted upon his countenance, enquired of Mr. A., "Which is General Arnold? the "brave Arnold? the victorious Arnold?" His curiosity being gratified, he exclaimed with an oath, "I guess, if I should not glory even in "going to hell, provided General Arnold led "me on."

The establishment of this political patriarch consists of a house two stories high, containing, I believe, eight rooms; of two men and three maid servants; three horses, and a plain carriage. How great is the contrast between this individual — a man of knowledge and information — without pomp, parade, or vitious and expensive establishments, as compared with the costly trappings, the depraved characters, and the profligate expenditure of ——— House, and ———————! What a lesson *in this* does America teach! There are now in the United States no less than three Cincinnati!

The charge at my boarding-house for eight days, being part of the time I spent at Boston, was 3l. 1s. 8d. I should remark, that neither beer nor cider was served at dinner, — brandy and rum were so; and the charge, in this instance, was upon the *presumption* that I availed myself of them accordingly.

Education is rightly valued in this State as one of the most important features of legislation. There are public schools, and amongst them some at which the learned languages are taught. The expenses of instruction at private academies professing to give a classical education are about 100 dollars per annum ; 50 at a best English school ; 32 for a middling ditto ; board from two to three dollars per week extra ; female education about $12\frac{1}{2}$ per cent. cheaper. The Lancasterian system is not in operation. Masters of free classical schools are exempt from military duty and *taxes :* the same exemptions are enjoyed by ministers of every denomination. *Clerical* gentlemen have here an astonishing hold upon the minds of men : the degree of reverential awe for the sanctity of their office, and the attention paid to the *external forms* of religion, approach almost to idolatry ; — these feelings are, perhaps, never encouraged without becoming the substitute of *real religion,* and expelling the active and mental principles of Christianity. A man who values his good name in Boston, hardly dare be seen out of church at the appointed hours ; — this would be viewed as a heinous crime by men who would consider the same individual's cheating his creditors as of small import. They seem, in these respects, not unlike the peculiarly religious among the Jews of old, who showed their sanctity by a solemn countenance and a broad garment, who would not eat with unwashen hands, and who regarded it as profane to pluck ears of corn on a Sabbath-day ; — but the founder of Christianity, in those days drew aside the veil of hypocrisy ; declaring, that it was fornication, false witness, and evil thoughts which defiled a man — and that neglecting these outward observances did not defile a man. His use of the language of Isaiah would, I fear, be but too applicable to the religious bodies of this place: "They draw nigh unto me with their mouths, "and honour me with their lips, but their "hearts are far from me."

The number of churches is as follows: viz. twelve Congregationalists (nine of which are said to be Anti-Trinitarian); two Episcopalian; three Baptist; one ditto for blacks; one Quaker; one Universalist; one Roman Catholic; two Methodist; one travelling preacher ditto. There being here no peculiar state religion, men are allowed the liberty of choosing to which of the sects existing here they shall belong. *To the support of one of these, however, they are compelled to contribute:* and should they neither attend to the worship, nor believe in the doctrines of any of them, the payment must equally be made — and it then goes to the funds of the Congregationalist body. This enactment would appear rather at war with enlightened legislation, and scarcely reconcileable with that extreme jealousy of their liberties, which would appear to have dictated an opposition to their town being incorporated as a city. — Americans, and especially New Englanders, ought to have known that religion, in all its details, is an affair between

God and the individual only, and that any attempt at human interference, is a violation of the rights of conscience, and ranks foremost among the basest of tyrannies.

Politics. — You may expect some report as to the *political* principles of the inhabitants of this place; — the following document will speak for itself, and show, more fully than I can pourtray them, what are the prevailing views and opinions on the subject of European politics. It consists of the

" *Appendix*" to " *A discourse delivered in*
" *Boston, at the solemn festival in commemora-*
" *tion of the goodness of God, in delivering the*
" *Christian world from military despotism, by*
" *William Henry Channing, minister of the*
" *church in Federal-street, Boston.*"

" After receiving intelligence of the late asto-
" nishing revolutions in Europe, ascertaining
" beyond all doubt the entire subversion of that
" atrocious military despotism, which had so
" long desolated the Christian and civilized
" world, a number of the citizens of this
" metropolis and the commonwealth at large,
" assembled on the 8th inst. at the house of
" His Honour William Phillips, to consult upon
" the propriety of noticing these events in a
" manner suited to their character and import-
" ance, and to the sentiments which they were

" calculated to inspire. Deeply impressed with
" the magnitude and the beneficial and lasting
" influence of this revolution, upon the best and
" dearest interests of society, they had no hesi-
" tation in recommending to their fellow-citizens
" the observance of a solemn religious festival
" in commemoration of the goodness of God,
" in humbling unprincipled ambition, in crush-
" ing wicked and unjust power, in delivering
" the world from cruel and disgraceful bondage,
" in restoring to mankind the enjoyment of their
" just rights *under the protection of legitimate*
" *government*, and in giving to nations the cheer-
" ing prospect of permanent tranquillity. For
" that purpose a large and respectable committee
" was chosen to make the necessary arrange-
" ments.

" Concluding prayer and benediction—Rev.
" Dr. Lathrop.

" The musical performances, vocal and in-
" strumental, were executed by a very full choir
" and band, in a style of enthusiasm, taste and
" excellence, seldom equalled in this metropolis.
" The celebration was attended by *the governor,*
" *council, and both branches of the legislature.*

" After the religious services of the day were
" closed, the Honourable Mr. Gore, chairman
" of the committee of arrangements, introduced

" the following resolutions, by remarking on the " happy state of Europe prior to the French " revolution, the depraved and deplorable con- " dition to which that event reduced the civilized " world, the just apprehensions of wretchedness " and barbarism from the continued despotism " of Bonaparte, and the consequent joy that " must arise from his destruction and the " establishment of *order and public freedom in* " *Europe.*

" RESOLUTIONS.

" A large number of citizens of the State of " Massachusetts convened at Boston for the pur- " pose of expressing, in a solemn manner, their " thanks to Almighty God, for his late gracious " and wonderful interposition, in delivering " Europe from that most fearful despotism, " under which a great portion of the nations " were actually suffering, and which the rest " had just reason to apprehend: and for the " further purpose of manifesting their sympathy " and participation in the general joy of one " hundred millions of the Christian world, and " their delight at the prospect of a speedy and " durable tranquillity to suffering and distracted " nations, the following Resolutions, having " been duly matured, were introduced.

" *Resolved,* That the citizens of Massachusetts

"here assembled, contemplate with unfeigned
"joy the emancipation of the French people
"from the usurped power of a ferocious military
"adventurer; and they rejoice in the prospect
"that thirty-five millions of their fellow men,
"have *a reasonable expectation of being blest*
"*with temperate liberty, adapted to their state*
"*of society and habits, and a constitution and*
"*administration of government, apparently con-*
"*formed to their wishes.* They congratulate
"the venerable head of the *house of Bourbon*
"on his restoration from exile, to the throne
"of his ancestors, *to which he is called by the*
"*entreaties of his people*, and from which he
"has been excluded by a series of crimes, at
"which humanity shudders. They remember
"the language of their revolutionary sages and
"patriots, glowing with affection and respect
"toward the late unhappy and injured possessor
"of the throne of the Bourbons; nor can they
"forget that the good understanding between
"this country and France was never interrupted
"so long as that family were in power, but that
"injuries and insults, such as no nation ever
"before submitted to, have been heaped upon
"it by all their successors, from the transient
"despot of a day, to the more permanent tyrant,
"clothed with imperial authority. It is not
"more from a conviction that the *interest* of
"the United States will be promoted by the

" late auspicious events, than from their regard " to the happiness of other nations, that they " congratulate the Sovereign and People of " France, on the voluntary renewal of their " ancient ties.

" *Resolved*, That the people of Massachusetts " recollect the generous sympathy of the Dutch " towards the American people during the dark- " est period of their revolutionary struggle; and " rejoice most fervently in *the glorious emanci-* " *pation* of the United Netherlands. They bless " God, that whilst this people appeared to human " eyes for ever blotted out of the list of nations, " He was at that moment preparing its restor- " ation to independence, and, it may be hoped, " to glory and power. *They rejoice with the* " *patriotic Hollanders at the return of the illus-* " *trious house of Orange to their first magistracy,* " *and do not wonder at their enthusiastic joy* " *upon the occasion, when they remember that* " *this ancient family have been always the gallant* " *and zealous defenders of the rights and liberties* " *of the Dutch people.*

" *Resolved*, That the liberation of Germany, " Italy, and Switzerland, and especially of " Prussia, with whom this country is connected " by treaty, are also causes of the most exalted " pleasure to this assembly.

" *Resolved*, That they have always witnessed " with deep emotion, and watched with con-

" stant anxiety, the struggle of the Spanish and " Portuguese nations for their independence: " and it therefore gives sincere delight to find " this independence fully confirmed, and nothing " but the unhappy situation in which this coun-" try is placed in relation to *one* of the allies, " prevents their expressing a just sense of the " *virtues* and talents of that chief, to whom, " under God, whole nations are so greatly " indebted.

" Resolved, *That this assembly view with* " *mingled emotions of admiration and gratitude,* " *the unexampled magnanimity of the great head* " *of the Confederacy for the deliverance of* " *Christendom. The name of* ALEXANDER THE " DELIVERER, *will be always dear to every lover* " *of national freedom, while the moderation, dis-* " *interestedness, foresight, and determination of* " *all the Confederates, to sacrifice every thing to* " *the future repose of Europe, will cause their* " *names to be venerated, and the epoch to be for* " *ever memorable. It is with the greater joy they* " *perceive this liberality and true wisdom in the* " *allied councils, as it affords a well-grounded hope* " *of a restoration of peace to this country, on* " *terms compatible with its interest and its honor.*

" It is because the recent events in Europe " have a direct tendency to render liberty secure, " *to check anarchical propensities,* to restrain am-" bition, foster morals and religion, and to pro-

"tect property and the arts, and finally, to give "solid peace to the Christian world, that this "assembly hail them as blessings, that they bow "in humble gratitude before the Almighty, "from whose goodness they all proceed: and "it is from a desire it may be known that, *with* "*many thousands of their countrymen,* they "partake in the joy of all civilized nations, "that these feelings and sentiments are now "proclaimed.

"*These resolutions, having been severally con*"*sidered, were cordially approved and unani*"*mously adopted by the assembly.*

"*In the evening fire-works were exhibited, and* "*by a resolve of the Legislature the State-house* "*was illuminated, as were some private houses,* "*in a manner to complete the sober and dignified* "*enjoyment of the vast multitudes who united* "*in the celebration.*"

This is, I think, a curious document. *The gentlemen, whose names it contains, are the leading men in Boston;* and it may be taken as speaking the general sentiments of the inhabitants, not only of Boston, but of New England generally, and even of some persons in New York, upon a subject clearly illustrative of *their* views, at once, of European and general politics.

24th September, 1817, I left Boston for Albany, in the stage: the distance is 180 miles;

the fare, 2l. 14s.; charge for all meals on the road, 2s. 3d. each; for bed, 2s. 3d.: nothing given to waiters or coachmen. The stage called at my lodgings at two o'clock in the morning. There was, upon my entrance into it, but one passenger; he was an American, and, of course, soon obtained from me the information that I was going to Albany. We were driven about the town for an hour, taking up others; so that, before our starting, we were well filled with passengers and their luggage. The man before referred to was going but ten miles; yet he must know from every person how far they were travelling, and whether or not they were "*natifees*" of Boston. An old man, partially deaf, was the last object of his attack. His seat being central, the first question put to him was, "Where are you going, middle on'?" This being answered satisfactorily, the following dialogue ensued: —

Q. Do you keep at Boston? — *A.* No.

Q. Where do you keep? — *A.* Fairfield.

Q. Have you been a lengthy time in Boston, eh, say? — *A.* Seven days.

Q. Where did you sleep last night? — *A.* —— street.

Q. What number? — *A.* Seven.

Q. That is Thomas Adonis ——'s house? — *A.* No; it is my son's.

Q. What, have *you* a son? — *A.* Yes; and daughters.

Q. What is your name? — *A.* William Henry ——, I guess.

Q. Is your wife alive? — *A.* No, she is dead, I guess.

Q. Did she die slick right away? — *A.* No; not by any manner of means.

Q. How long have you been married? — *A.* Thirty years, I guess.

Q. What age were you when you were married? — *A.* I guess mighty near thirty-three.

Q. If you were young again I guess you would marry earlier? — *A.* No; I guess thirty-three is a mighty grand age for marrying.

Q. How old is your daughter? — *A.* Twenty-five.

Q. I guess she would like a husband? — *A.* No; she is mighty careless about that.

Q. She is not awful (ugly), I guess? — *A.* No, I guess she is not.

Q. Is she sick? — *A.* Yes.

Q. What is her sickness? — *A.* Consumption.

Q. I had an item (a supposition) of that. You have got a doctor, I guess? — *A.* Guess I have.

Q. Is your son a trader? — *A.* Yes.

Q. Is he his own boss? — *A.* Yes.

Q. Are his spirits kedge (brisk)? *A.* Yes; I expect they were yesterday.

Q. How did he get in business? — *A.* I planted him there. I was his sponsor for a thousand *dallars.* I guess he paid me within time; and he is now progressing slick. He bought his store at a good lay (a good bargain).

The young man's arrival at his destination put a stop to this course of question and answer; and the inquisitive catechiser invited his elderly friend, when he should come that way, "*to go by* his house and dine with him."

Northampton, 97 miles from Boston. We arrived at this town at ten o'clock at night.

We started hence at two o'clock the following morning. The road leads over the Green Mountain, and is both tedious and difficult. There seemed scarcely a spot upon the mountains capable of cultivation. In one place there were ten frame buildings, among which a skeleton church was not the least prominent.

At *Pittsfield*, 140 miles from Boston, we stopped for an hour and a half. This town is singularly situated, in a beautiful and fertile valley, on the banks of the Hausatonic River. There are here two inns, five stores, 100 houses, a congregationalist church, and a military barracks. We arrived on a military field day: soldiers were exercising in the street: they were dressed in their common clothing;—to distinguish officers from men was difficult: some were armed with sticks, some with umbrellas, some with muskets; all were talking, and each seemed to do as he pleased. At the church door, where a man was retailing cider, the sons of Mars were actively engaged in making purchases; their officers joining in this department of *military* service.

One of our passengers was a labouring man: he conversed with ease and with good sense. I particularly remarked his correct pronunciation, and concluded that this class of society were much superior to the lower orders in England. He afterwards proved to be a Londoner, and had recently emigrated to this country, in the ship Perseus; — an instance this how cautious travellers ought to be in drawing general conclusions from particular facts.

The country from Boston to Albany did not equal my expectations. The soil appears sterile, and there still remains immense tracts uncultivated. The towns look new and handsome. A barren rock over which we travelled is named Lebanon; — this, I observe, accords with a point of national character, which shows itself in a love of striking, of ancient, and of hard names. Counties or towns are denominated Athens, Homer, Virgil, Horace, Cincinnati. Men — Cicero, Brutus, Solomon. Women — Penelope, Adeline, Desdemona.

Upon the condition of the people I have little more to say than to repeat my former remarks. There seems no absolute want: all have the essential necessaries of life; few its luxuries. Their habits and manners are similar to those I have observed in their countrymen generally:

all seem to have a great deal of leisure, and few or none to occupy it for the purposes of mental improvement. The grossly coarse and vulgar man is as rare as the solidly intelligent and liberal. Ignorance, I suspect, exists a great deal more in *fact* than in *appearance.* Men seldom converse upon any subject except those connected with their immediate pecuniary interest;—few appear to have any regard for the general extension of liberty to the whole human family.

In order to gain an idea of the agriculture and population of the country, it occurred to me to take an account, as far as I could, of the live stock, &c. which I saw from the road. This may appear trifling—perhaps almost ridiculous; but by comparing it with what you would yourself see, under similar circumstances, on an English road, you may gain some useful ideas on the subject. During the route of 180 miles, then, which I have just traversed, I counted twenty-five cows, ten horses, six small farmers' waggons, three men travelling on foot, four on horseback, two families in waggons removing to the western country, one on foot pursuing the same course. There were no beggars;—none who appeared much distressed. The cows and horses are smaller than ours; but they are compact in shape, and well fed. After having passed through Westboro, Worcester,

Northampton, and Pittsfield, (all towns of considerable importance, and containing many excellent buildings,) I arrived late in the evening at

Albany, the capital of the State of *New York*. It is distant from the city of New York about 160 miles, and lies at the head of the sloop navigation of the Hudson River. Should the canal to Lake Erie be completed, this must become a first-rate town: it is, even at present, a place of extensive business. The building in which the State-legislature meet is called "The Capitol;" — it is situated on an elevation at the termination of the main street, and certainly presents a fine appearance. — I have only time to give you the following unarranged information concerning Albany.

The *population* is about 12,000. Shopkeepers, of whom I have conversed with several, complain most bitterly of the state of trade. A large body of mechanics recently left here for want of employment; — the wages given to those who remain are the same as at New York: their board is three dollars per week. I pay at my inn one and a half dollar per day. Rent of a house and shop in a good situation, is from five to seven hundred dollars per annum, and the taxes about twenty dollars. There are many small wood houses, which are from fifty to one hundred and fifty dollars per annum, according to size and situation. Beef, mutton, and veal, are 5d. to 6½d.

per pound ; fowls, 8d. to 9½d. each ; ducks, 13d. to 16d.; geese, 2s. 3d.; butter, 14d. a pound; potatoes, 20d. a bushel; flour, 45s. a barrel; fish, 4d. to 7d. a pound; rum and gin, 4s. 6d. per gallon ; brandy and hollands, 9s. 6d.

I must still withhold my advice upon the general subject of emigration. I am not yet possessed of evidence from which I can form that matured judgment, which should either give you encouragement, or the contrary. My feelings are certainly those of disappointment; but *feeling* is a bad guide, and therefore its suggestions must remain, at present, confined to my own bosom. Perhaps one cause of these unfavourable impressions is, that my ideas of this country, in common with your own, were higher than an experience of mankind, or a deliberate view of all the circumstances of this people, would have justified. Thus much, however, I can say, that, although I see no decidedly prominent inducement to emigration, yet the poor industrious man, who has got a family, and the mechanic who is not earning more than a guinea a week, would find their pecuniary affairs improved by becoming citizens of this republic. To the capitalist, I can as yet give no satisfactory information. With anxious hopes that I shall receive letters when I arrive at Philadelphia, I must for the present take my leave, intending to forward a further report by the very first opportunity.

FOURTH REPORT.

Citizen Genet. — Scenery of Hudson River. — Return to New York. — View it more favourably. — Enormous and dangerous Powers vested in the Governor. — Leave New York for Philadelphia. — Trenton. — General Moreau. — River Delaware. — Joseph Bonaparte. — Appearance of Country from New York to Trenton. — Arrival in Philadelphia. — Fine Appearance of that City. — Want of domestic Comfort and Cleanliness. — Preparations for a General Election. — Full Particulars of that Occurrence. — Copies of Electioneering Hand Bills. — Reflections upon Political Liberty in America. — Visit to Mayor's Court. — Law Proceedings. — Visit to the Prison. — Its excellent Management. — The Pennsylvanian Hospital. — Public Buildings and Institutions. — Fine Arts. — Peale's Museum. — Markets. — Prices of Provisions; of Labour. — Rents. — Religious Sects. — Fanaticism of some. — Estimation of Negroes. — Military Service. — Climate. — Diseases. — High Charges of Medical Gentlemen. — Poor Laws. — Police. — State of Morals; of Manners. — Character of Philadelphian Ladies. — What Classes of Emigrants would be likely to succeed. — America rising in my Estimation. — Taxes.

Philadelphia, Oct. 12. 1817.

THE well-known citizen *Genet* boarded at the inn at *Albany*, in which I took up my abode. When ambassador from the republic of France to the republic of America, he was peculiarly prominent, as having under his influence a large party, who were actively in opposition to the administration of General Washington: he was in consequence recalled. At present he is an almost unnoticed individual; though his politeness in this "land without manners," will cause him to be remarked, at least during his seat at the dinner-table.

When I arrived at the inn, I was extremely cold. All the fires were surrounded by gentlemen smoking segars, and lolling back on chairs, with their feet fixed against the chimney-piece. An idea of making room for a shivering stranger, seemed not to enter into their minds. I left *Albany* in the steam-boat Richmond, and proceeded to the city of *Hudson*. I hasten on in my detail to the city of *New York*, the interior of the State not having furnished me with any features peculiarly different from those already communicated; but I must not quit the noble Hudson without first contributing my share of praise, in acknowledgment of the delight I experienced in viewing the varied scenery of this magnificent river. Upon leaving Albany, the views which presented themselves were mild and pleasing; as we approached the Catskill Mountains, the scene assumed the true character of bold and fearless grandeur.

The city of *New York*, upon a second visit, improved in my estimation: such is the effect of comparison! The season having advanced, many had returned from "the springs," as Balston and Savatoga are denominated. This produced a most striking improvement in the effect of the public promenade, particularly with respect to the females: many of them were handsome, and had the appearance of health, while nearly all of them were even splendidly attired.

My former acquaintances were eager to know my opinion of Boston, and to discover how it stood in a "stranger's judgment," as compared with their own idolized city. I endeavoured to be impartial in drawing the parallel; but no *qualification* of praise, as to their own place of residence, would satisfy them. Every sentence terminated with an appeal to some peculiar beauty or excellence which they possessed and the other town wanted; as, "Remember Broad-"way, Mr. Fearon!" or "You know, Sir, the "battery, Sir!—the battery, Sir! and Broad-"way, Mr. Fearon—and the battery; there "can be nothing like these in the world." The Bostonians on their part are equally bigotted in favour of their town; and indeed I find, almost universally, that sectional prejudices are as strong amongst themselves, as those which exist generally against England; for there seems to be no *reasoning* in the likes and dislikes of this people.

Upon *politics* I have little to communicate. —I am told that the situations which are in the gift of the Council of Appointment (and they comprise almost every civil office in the

State) are bought and sold as commonly as the poor oppressed men of colour are in the neighbouring States; or, to bring the matter nearer home, as frequently as seats in our House of Commons.

2d October. Left New York for Philadelphia, in the steam-boat "Olive Branch."

In the evening I arrived at *Trenton*, which is the capital of New Jersey. General Moreau's stables are still standing in this neighbourhood: his dwelling-house was consumed by fire. King Joseph *was* negotiating for a house here, in anticipation of his brother Lucien's arrival: the price was to have been 30,000 dollars. At six o'clock in the morning we recommenced our journey for Philadelphia. Joseph Bonaparte's house is situated on the Jersey banks of the river Delaware: in appearance it is equal to a moderate English country seat. He is said to have bought it for 10,000 dollars, and to have laid out 20,000 more in having it completed in a splendid style. At present he is from home, having gone to view Niagara Falls. His associates are French gentlemen, but he is easy of access, and appears to participate in the interests of the country; — owns a steam-boat, and would be popular, if it were only on account of his riches. When he arrived in New York from Europe, an anecdote is currently related of the American porter who was removing his baggage from the vessel. It was heavy. King Joseph was standing on the wharf; —the honest republican called to him, "Come, Boney, lend "a hand."

At ten o'clock we arrived at Market-street Wharf, PHILADELPHIA. Before I enter upon a description of this truly fine city, it may be well to occupy a few lines with what remarks I have made on the country through which I have passed. The banks of the Rariton are low, but contain some fine salt meadows. The country from New Brunswick to Trenton is well cultivated, but the soil appears indifferent: the roads are extremely bad. Easiness of circumstances, or rather an absence of poverty, appears to characterise the condition of the inhabitants: the negroes are sorely oppressed. There are many good houses in the towns. Six steam-boats passed us on the Delaware: the scenery of this river possesses no character in common with that of the Hudson: there is a total absence of the bold and the grand: yet it possesses much that may be termed beautiful, with a calm serenity which is very pleasing.

When our boat arrived we were inundated with porters, the greater part of whom were blacks, the rest were Irish: they had tin plates on their hats or breasts, upon which were written their names and residences. I, for the first time, allowed my trunk to go out of my sight.

In England, among strange porters, I should have been more particular, but here such things are done without hesitation. I should not suppose that this proceeded from any peculiar feelings of national honour, or a general spirit of integrity: the real cause lies, I rather think, in the simple fact, that any man may obtain work, and when it is completed, will be liberally paid. The inducements to dishonesty are thus lessened at their true source.

My first impressions of this city were decidedly favourable: it gave me ideas of a *substantial* cast. In the possession of a character essentially different from New York — it has not so much business, not so much gaiety, not so much life; but there is in Philadelphia a freedom from mere display, a relief from gaudy trappings, an evidence of solidity, of which its more commercial rival is nearly destitute. The streets are clean, well and regularly built. First-rate private houses are numerous, as are also public buildings; but their architecture is not of the highest order. The foot-paths are impeded by an injudicious mode of constructing cellars, by which they project into the street; and also by a very slovenly practice of the store-keepers, which is common in America, namely, placing quantities of loose goods outside of their doors.

The quality of some of the water of Philadelphia may be estimated from the experiment of Mr. Hunter, who, upon analysing 220 gallons from a pump in Second-street, found it to contain the following ingredients: 12 oz. chalk, 32 oz. salt-petre, 17 oz. magnesia, 24 oz. common sea-salt.

The Delaware, of which the Indian name is Poutaxat, upon the banks of which this city is built, rises in the State of New York. At this city it is 1360 yards wide, and is navigable for vessels of any burden. It is frozen in the winter months; a circumstance which materially affects the commercial interests of Philadelphia, and gives a great advantage to New York, as the latter port is rarely closed.

The present population of Philadelphia is estimated at 120,000, many of whom live in houses which would adorn any city in the world. Rents are about 25 per cent. lower than in New York: this, I should apprehend, does not proceed either from a comparative want of prosperity, from cheaper materials, or lower-priced labour; but from a more general equality of desirable situations, combined with the existence of more real, though perhaps less apparent capital. It may be also that rents are influenced by the calculating habits of the society of friends, who reside here in great numbers.

After a residence of three days at the hotel, I removed to a private boarding-house, in one of the bed-rooms of which I am now writing. The dining-room of this establishment is genteel; but the other apartments, and more particularly the kitchen, are of a kind not much to excite admiration. I perceived here what—unpleasant as may be the discovery, I think I have observed elsewhere, and — worse still, what I fear pervades this new world, an affectation of splendour, or what may be called *style*, in those things which are intended to meet the public eye; with a lamentable want even of cleanliness in such matters as are removed *from* that ordeal. To this may be added, an appearance of uncomfortable extravagance, and an ignorance of that kind of order and neatness which constitute, in the sight of those who have once enjoyed it, the principal charm of domestic life. I should rejoice to find myself in an error in this judgment; but all I have seen myself, and all I have collected from the observation of others most competent to form a correct opinion, tend to its confirmation.

Last evening I drank tea at a genteel private house.—The furniture was splendid, the table profusely supplied, being loaded with fish, dried beef and sausages; the bread and butter was roughly cut in huge hunks piled zig-zag. The children's faces were dirty, their hair uncombed, their dispositions evidently untaught, and all the members of the family, from the boy of six years of age, up to the owner (I was going to say master) of the house, appeared *independent* of each other. I have seen the same characteristics in other families—in some indeed decidedly the contrary; but these latter would seem to be the exceptions, and the former the general rule.

Funerals are uniformly attended by large walking processions. In the newspapers I have frequently observed advertisements stating the deaths, and inviting all friends to attend the burial. The dead are seldom kept more than two days. At the time appointed, intimate friends enter the house, others assemble outside, and fall into the procession when the body is brought out. Sorrow does not seem depicted in the countenances of any, but few wear mourning, and many smoke segars; none appear chargeable with the hypocrisy described by the poet of "mocking sorrow with a heart not sad."

The present is a most busy time at this place, to-morrow being the day of election for the governor of the State of Pennsylvania. I have been fortunate in having letters of introduction to the leading man of one of the great political parties which divide this State; inasmuch as by that means I have witnessed all the novel machinery which is now in such active operation.

The governor has the gift of from forty to fifty offices, amongst which are those of recorder, alderman, and indeed every minor as well as important civil occupation. Auctioneers also receive their authority to sell from the governor; and their number being small, the profession becomes a most valuable monopoly. By means of this statement you will see the value and importance of the office of governor, and will not be surprised that its obtainment should be the object of a severe contest.

16th Oct. The election being now closed, I can sit down and review it calmly as a whole. It has been to me a highly interesting scene. The political parties at present range I believe as follows:

1st. The violent democrats, denominated "Patent Democrats."

2d. The moderate democrats, called by the several names of "Independent Republicans," "Democrats of the Revolution," and "Old "Schoolmen."

3d. Federalists, denominated also "Tories," "Hartford Conventionalists," and "Blue Light "Men,"

4th. No party men, called "Quids."

The present candidates for the office of governor are each of them of the democratic party. General Hiester is of the moderate faction, and is also supported against his opponent by the federalists and quids. Mr. Finlay has the powerful aid of the unyielding democrats; and, though he is in a minority in the proportion of one to three within the city of Philadelphia, little doubt is entertained of his election's having been carried by a large majority through the State at large. All that are citizens, whether native or naturalized, of the age of 21 years and upwards, and who have paid their taxes, have the right of voting. It is not necessary that a man should be a householder in order to pay taxes, there being here a direct or poll tax of 9s. per annum, which alone, when paid by men possessed of the previous qualification of citizenship, establishes the right to vote. The general election is preceded by an election in the different wards of officers called Inspectors, whose business it is to receive the ballot ticket of voters: parties try their strength in this first step. I witnessed the mode of voting: the persons choosing inspectors attend at a stated place in their own ward, and deliver in their ballot through a window. The number assembled at any one time did not exceed twenty. There was no noise, no confusion, in fact, not even conversation. I was astonished to witness the anxiety felt by leading men, that *their* party should be elected *inspectors*. The eventual choice at the general election seemed, in fact, in their estimation, actually to rest upon the having "Inspectors" of their own party. I remarked to them that it could be of no consequence of what party these gentlemen were, as they were protected from partial or corrupt conduct by the mode of voting being by ballot. One of them informed me afterwards, that the fact of the inspectors being on one side or the other had been calculated to make a difference of upwards of 200 votes in a particular section! — arising from the reception of improper, and the rejection of good votes. The means by which an inspector can effect this, though the mode is by ballot, is said to be remarkably exact. That there may be some truth in this statement, would seem probable from a scene which I witnessed in the evening. I called upon the gentleman before alluded to. His room was completely crammed with the *managers* of the forth-coming election; and here, instead of finding that the general anxiety was at all connected with the advancement of correct political principles, I heard the following conversation: —

"I'll bet you fifty (dollars) on Hiester in Chesnut ward."

"What majority will you give him?"

"One-fourth."

"Give old Sour Kraut (Hiester) a hundred and thirty, and I'll take you."

"Done."

"What will you give Finlay in Lower Delaware ward?"

"One hundred."

"And what to Hiester?"

" Three hundred."

" Give Bill three and a half, and I'll take you for five hundred."

" No: I'll give him three and half for a pair of boots."

" 'Guess I'll take you for a pair and a hat. — What for Dock ward?"

" I won't bet on Dock: they're all a set of d——d Tories."

" Will you give Joe four hundred in South Mulberry?"

" I won't take Joe, I guess, in that ward?"

" What will you give Billy in South Mulberry?"

" A couple of hundred."

" Done for five hundred."

All. " What majority upon the whole election, Friend ——, will you advise us to give?"

Fr. " You must be cautious in your majorities. We do not know how Beaver and Dauphin (the counties of Dauphin and Beaver) may turn out.—Mind! save yourselves.—If you find Billy (Finlay) going down, take up Sour Kraut (Hiester)."

I should have explained, that elections are managed, and even governed, by a something (a species of meeting) which, I confess, I do not yet perfectly understand: it is called a " *Caucus.*" Candidates do not personally appear. Those who wish to be chosen obtain, as a preliminary step, what is termed " The Appointment." This is said to secure them the support of the whole of that party from which "the appointment" emanates. An announcement, called "The Ticket," issues from this Caucus a few days before the election; in this case there were three of these "tickets," severally headed, *Federal, Republican,* and *Democratic.* The federalists sent to an acquaintance of mine their "ticket," enclosed in the following circular letter; though I would remark, that *canvassing,* in the English meaning of that word, is not allowed: —

"Fellow Citizen,

"The exercise of the elective franchise is at "all times a privilege of the highest value: — "on the present occasion every federalist has "an opportunity to aid in dispelling preju-"dices — in lessening the malignity of party "spirit — *in restoring the right of free election,* "*and of resisting those dangerous abuses in* "*government, introduced by office holders, which,* "*if not promptly and steadily checked, threaten* "*to become inveterate and irremediable.* Let "every man be vigilant, active, and firm, on "this day, and success will crown our efforts.

"The inspectors have resolved to open the "poll precisely at 9 o'clock.

"*October* 14, 1817."

The democratic party adopt the same mode. I enclose you two of their circulars. These documents, as well as others which will follow, are, perhaps, better calculated than any other plan which I could adopt, to put you in possession of the state of parties, their mode of conduct and feelings towards each other, and also the general political condition of the whole people.

(CIRCULAR.)

" SIR,

" We enclose you the *Democratic* Ticket, " which is recommended by the delegates and " conferrees fairly chosen, after *public notice.* " We request you to VOTE IT and give it *all* the " SUPPORT to which you may deem it entitled. " We consider THIS election as involving the " most important consequences. Federalism, " conscious of its own feebleness and inability " to wrestle with the STRENGTH of democracy, " has made a *union* with a FEW disappointed " men; hoping through them to turn over, " not only this city and district, but the State " and Union to Federal misrule.

" Be careful to *bring with you* your *receipt* " *for* COUNTY *tax.* If a *naturalized* citizen, be " sure to *bring* your CERTIFICATE of naturalization, as it will, in all probability, be required. " These cautions are deemed more than ever " necessary, from the shameful conduct and

"persecuting spirit manifested by the Federal
"Judges, at the late ward election. Be on the
"ground early. It is of an importance, that
"*every* citizen votes, because it may be that a
"vote would carry a candidate.

"*Philadelphia, October* 6, 1815."

DEMOCRATIC ADDRESS.

"Citizens, Democrats, Americans! *This is*
"*the Day of the General Election!* If you value
"your own rights, your own happiness, your
"political characters, your liberties, or your Re-
"publican institutions, every man to the poll,
"and vote the *Democratic Ticket;* it is headed
"with the name of the patriot WILLIAM FIND-
"LAY.—*Citizens!* the times are momentous!
"the seceders from the Democratic ranks have
"joined with our old and inveterate political
"enemies to *put down Democracy.* It is an
"*unholy league* between *apostates* and political
"traitors on the one part, and on the other the
"anglo-federalists, the monarchists, the aristo-
"crats, the Hartford conventionalists, the blue-
"light men, the embargo-breakers, the Henry-
"ites, the men who in time of Peace cried out
"for *War! War!* but who in time of war,
"called themselves the *Peace party.* — Huzza
"for WILLIAM FINDLAY, and no bribery. — A
"long pull, a strong pull, and a pull altogether."

FEDERAL ADDRESS.

" WILLIAM FINDLAY —

" 1. A selfish politician, who never served his
" country, and always on the look-out for office.
" 2. An apostate federalist and time-server.
" 3. A constant office-hunter. 4. A treasury
" broker and public defaulter, who exchanged
" and *used public money for his own benefit.*
" 5. One who holds morality in contempt, and
" maintains and practises the maxim, that the
" end justifies the means. 6. One who has re-
" sorted to the basest falsehoods to support him-
" self. 7. *One who intrigued and bargained*
" *for the office*, and openly electioneered for
" himself. 8. A state inquisitor, who would
" gag, if not immolate every man, not of his
" own sect. 9. A man who has blended the
" public money with his own, and is yet to ac-
" count for misdemeanor in office. 10. A bar-
" barian, who holds that ' the study of the law
" disqualifies a man from being a judge.' "

" *Take notice* who are the friends of WIL-
" LIAM FINDLAY, — 1. Traitors and apostates.
" 2. Inveterate aristocrats. 3. Office-holders and
" office-hunters. 4. Cormorants for the loaves
" and fishes, and friends only to themselves.
" 5. Fugitives from British gaols and justice.
Take care !!! — WILLIAM FINDLAY's election

"will be sure, 1. If the Republicans stay at "home. 2. If they are negligent or timid on "the election ground. 3. *If election, like trea-* "*sury frauds, are not detected and prevented.*

"*Take advice,* — 1. Look well to your tickets. "2. Look well to your boxes. 3. Look well "to your tallies. 4. Look well to your returns; "and, 5. Look well to those who vote, that they "are qualified."

The following morning I was early on the election ground. The place appointed to receive votes * for the city (exclusive of Southwark and the northern liberties), was in the State-house — the same building in which that immortal document was passed — THE DECLARATION OF INDEPENDENCE! There were two inspectors for each ward of the city placed at separate windows. The electors delivered in their votes from the street. The ground was what is here called *manned;* that is, persons in the interest of the parties have written on their hat or breast, "Federal Ticket," or "De-"mocratic Ticket," soliciting citizens as they approach the poll "to vote their ticket;" for which purpose they are prepared to furnish them with the printed balloting list of their party. The neighbouring public-houses were, of course,

* The city and state are divided into election districts. The whole terminates in one day.

occupied by the electioneerers. I resolved to devote to this as much of my time as possible, in obtaining an insight into the character and mind of this people, and to observe them acting in their political capacity. They were all betting upon the election; but I lament to say, that few, if any, appeared to care one straw about principle. Old General Barker (whom I had heard the previous evening make a most able speech in favour of Mr. Findlay, at a public meeting of the democrats) was travelling about to the several depôts of leading characters. I could hardly credit my sight that he was the same person whom I had heard the previous evening. His chief employment during the day seemed drinking rum and gin, with any and every body. I made some remarks to him concerning his speech: he pleasantly answered, "My good "fellow, I did as well as I could, I guess: they "made me open the ball." This old general was the companion in arms of Washington: he has been both sheriff and mayor: he has the character of possessing a good heart, and very improvident generosity.

The election terminated throughout the State in *one day*. The excitement of party and pecuniary feeling, by the universality of gambling upon the occasion, was very great; yet there was no confusion, no disturbance. Let it be borne in mind, that here was the right of voting to the utmost extent, and exercised by a people, concerning whom it is high praise to say, that they are not superior in intellect, in information, in honest zeal, and in temperate ideas of liberty, to the English nation; yet there is much to lament here. The original documents given in the preceding pages are too full upon this point: they, indeed, are far from complimentary to our nature; but at the same time we should recollect, that in the political, as in the moral and natural worlds, we must endure evils, in order to insure a preponderance of good. The extent of my approbation, then, upon this occasion, is a conviction of the compatibility of popular election with peace and good order; and, if possessed by the English people, I should presume, it would not be attended with so many abuses.

REDEMPTIONERS.

A practice which has been often referred to in connection with this country, naturally excited my attention. It is that of individuals emigrating from Europe without money, and paying for their passage by binding themselves to the captain, who receives the produce of their labour for a certain number of years.

Seeing the following advertisement in the newspapers, put in by the captain and owners of the vessel referred to, I visited the ship, in company with a boot-maker of this city:

" THE PASSENGERS

" On board the brig Bubona, from Amsterdam, and
" who are willing to engage themselves for a limited
" time, to defray the expences of their passage, consist
" of persons of the following occupations, besides women
" and children, viz. 13 farmers, 2 bakers, 2 butchers,
" 8 weavers, 3 taylors, 1 gardener, 3 masons, 1 mill-
" sawyer, 1 white-smith, 2 shoe-makers, 3 cabinet-
" makers, 1 coal-burner, 1 barber, 1 carpenter, 1 stock-
" ing-weaver, 1 cooper, 1 wheelwright, 1 brewer,
" 1 locksmith. — Apply on board of the Bubona, op-
" posite Callowhill-street, in the river Delaware, or to
" W. Odlin and Co. No. 38, South Wharves.

Oct. 2.

As we ascended the side of this hulk, a most revolting scene of want and misery presented itself. The eye involuntarily turned for some relief from the horrible picture of human suffering, which this living sepulchre afforded. Mr. ——— enquired if there were any shoemakers on board. The captain advanced: his appearance bespoke his office; he is an American, tall, determined, and with an eye that flashes with Algerine cruelty. He called in the Dutch language for shoe-makers, and never can I forget the scene which followed. The poor fellows came running up with unspeakable delight, no doubt anticipating a relief from their loathsome dungeon. Their clothes, if rags deserve that denomination, actually perfumed the air. Some were without shirts, others had this article of dress, but of a quality as coarse as the worst packing cloth. I enquired of several if they could speak English. They smiled, and gabbled, "No Engly, no Engly, — one Engly "talk ship." The deck was filthy. The cooking, washing, and necessary departments were close together. Such is the mercenary barbarity of the Americans who are engaged in this trade, that they crammed into one of those vessels 500 passengers, 80 of whom died on the passage. The price for women is about 70 dollars, men 80 dollars, boys 60 dollars. When they saw at our departure that we had not purchased, their countenances fell to that standard of stupid gloom which seemed to place them a link below rational beings. From my heart I execrated the *European cause* of their removal, which is thus daily compelling men to quit the land of their fathers, to become voluntary exiles in a foreign clime: — yet Americans can think and write such sentiments as the following: "We rejoice with the patriotic Hollanders at "the return of the illustrious house of Orange "to their first magistracy, and do not wonder "at *their enthusiastic joy* upon the occasion, "when they remember that this ancient family "have been always the gallant and zealous "defenders of *the rights and liberties of the* "*Dutch people.*"

An interesting occurrence is said to have taken

place the other day, in connection with the German Redemptioners (as by a strange misnomer the Dutch are denominated). A gentleman of this city wanted an old couple to take care of his house;—a man, his wife, and daughter were offered to him for sale;—he purchased them.—They proved to be his father, his mother, and sister!!!

I must now conduct you back to the city. The mayor's court is for the trial of petty offences. It is four times as large, and ten times more convenient for the public than our lord mayor's court. When I visited it, the mayor and two judges were upon the bench. The first case was for assault and battery. The plaintiff had a stall in a particular field, on the fourth of July, (the great national day, being the anniversary of the declaration of independence;) the defendant claimed a right to the spot of ground, not that it was his property, but because he had occupied it the preceding year. The plaintiff, to rid himself of troublesome interference, had, at the time, given the defendant five dollars. This sum satisfied the latter for the moment, but afterwards conceiving that he could induce or compel him to pay more, he took with him three men, and they had assaulted and ill-used the plaintiff.

Mayor. "How long have you been in "prison?"

Defend. " Two months."

Mayor. " Have you not been brought to " trial before?"

Defend. " No,"

Mayor. " In consideration of your having " been that period of time in confinement, we " discharge you."

Second case. Thomas Rapoon, brought up at the suit of his wife, for ill usage: the charge was fully proved.

Mayor. " What do you wish to have done to " your husband?"

Mrs. R. " Nothing, Sir, I discharge him, " Sir, I guess; but only I cannot live with him, " he beats me regularly before mass."

Mayor. " I will consider the case."

Third. William Jackson, for ill-treating his wife. The charge proved, but no decision given during my stay.

Fourth. V. Fitzgerald for stealing two tumblers. He spoke in rather a low tone of voice. The court stated to him, " Unless you speak " louder, we cannot attend to your case." — " There," (said the clerk, whose voice was singularly weak,) " raise your voice as high as " mine." A decision was not given in this case.

Fifth. A man of colour for stealing a saw.

Mayor. " Yellow boy! what have you to " say against this charge, are you guilty or not " guilty?"

Prisoner. " Not guilty, gentimman, I was " going long street groggy, man groggy too ; " (laughing in the court,) me go long so bad " groggy, lay down, put saw by side, man steal " saw from me, me not steal saw from no " man."

Mayor. " I guess, you have not been long " in this country, yellow boy ?"

Prisoner. " No: quite long enough," (Laughing in the court.)

Mayor. " Where do you come from ?"

Prisoner. " Jamaica ; you let me out, me back " Jamaica pretty quick." (Universal laughing.)

Mayor. " How long have you been in " prison ?"

Prisoner. " Seven weeks."

Mayor. " In consideration of your having " had that period of punishment before trial, we " sentence you to pay the fine of one cent only, " and to be further confined for one calendar " month."

MUSEUM, PAINTINGS, &c.

A brief account of some of the exhibitions of this city may not be uninteresting; and may serve, too, incidentally to communicate some ideas as to the manners and pursuits of the people.

PEALE'S MUSEUM contains an extensive collection of the curiosities usual in such establishments, divided into three departments. The

Mammoth skeleton complete, is a most tremendous object. I remarked that there were several quart bottles filled with ashes of the paper called " Continental money." This was the circulating medium of the Revolution, and by the means of which they carried on that glorious struggle. The nation have not redeemed their notes, nor I presume will they ever. I boarded at the house of a widow lady at New York, whose whole family had been utterly ruined by holding these notes. I remarked Talleyrand's oath of allegiance to the United States in his own hand-writing! a cake of portable soup, which was sent from England in 1775, for the use of the British army! Penn's curtains; and a scrap of poetry called " The Cow Chase," in the hand-writing of the gallant and interesting André, written a few hours before his execution. The portraits in this establishment are very numerous, including those of Americans of great, down to those of very limited celebrity. I also remarked the likenesses of Paine, Arthur O'Conner, and Dr. Priestley. The style of their execution is but little creditable to the talents of the artist (Mr. Peale), and would seem to be below the standard of his ability, if we judge at least from the specimen which he has given in a fine portrait of Napoleon, after David; where, by the way, he has committed the error of substituting an American horse, marked by the very long shaggy hair near the hoofs, by which they are distinguished.

The painting of the *Anaconda*, which was exhibited in Spring Gardens, is now here, at the house of Mr. Earl. It is certainly a first-rate production. I remarked in the same room a table of the Connecticut marble, which is so beautiful that it has become, I am told, an article of export to France.

Mr. Sully's collection of paintings is small, but select. They are chiefly of his own execution. "Madame Ricamier returned from the bath" is by a French artist. This is a beautifully executed and delicate picture. The "Country Wedding" by Sully is interesting, and in the style of our best domestic pieces. The idea of the "American village politicians" is taken from Wilkie, with much variation in particulars and general effect, the national characters having hardly one part of contact. "The Capture of Major André" is particularly interesting: I shall long have before my eyes the lively figure of this accomplished gentleman. Mr. Sully is a portrait painter: his charges are for a full-length 500 dollars; half, 200; head and hands, 150; bust, 100.

The Academy of Fine Arts is a highly respectable institution, which, without the pretence and puff of its sister establishment in New York, possesses a most decided superiority. There are numerous excellent paintings, and a hall of statuary, in which are some fine specimens of Venus, the Gladiator, Apollo, &c.

There is here exhibited what I believe is the first attempt at panoramic painting in America — a view of the city of Newhaven. Its merits are of a very negative kind. The charge for each of these exhibitions is a quarter of a dollar, (1s. 1½d.)

PENITENTIARY, MARKETS, &c.

The *Penitentiary* system for the rational punishment and reform of criminals, being a subject with which you are familiar, I shall not trouble you with the details of the humane and enlightened management of the gaol in this city. I visited it on Saturday last. The keeper accompanied me into every apartment, giving, as we proceeded, the most full explanations. The scene was novel, and I had almost said delightful; but a recollection that I was viewing the consequences of vicious pursuits, checks the expression, and draws a tear for the weakness of humanity; — yet I could not but be pleased, and highly so, on drawing a comparison between what I saw here, and what I have witnessed in the London prisons. Here, instead of the prisoners passing their time in idleness, or in low debauchery and gaming, all was sobriety, life, and activity. A complete manufacturing town was in fact collected within the narrow precincts of these otherwise gloomy walls. The open court was occupied by stone-cutters, chiefly negroes. It would appear, on first seeing this department only, that these were either more vicious, or more hardly dealt with in the courts of law, than their white countrymen. But the true reason of their numbers in the yard is, that few of them being mechanics, they are set to labour upon those things for which they are fitted, and which they can undertake with little previous instruction. The rooms in which the mechanic arts are carried on, have a very great proportion of whites, so that crime would by no means seem to be monopolized by our darker brethren. The produce of the labour of prisoners nearly supports the whole of this extensive establishment. Some have earned a sufficiency by their own work to enable them to commence business on the expiration of their term of confinement. Those who conduct themselves with industry and propriety, receive a remission of part of their sentence. Several have become honest and useful members of society. When the gaoler spoke to the prisoners, they addressed him with confidence, but with proper respect. He is a plain intelligent man, liberally, though not profusely paid for his services. To have offered him money for his trouble, would, I am sure, have been considered an insult. What a contrast does such a man afford to our prison-keepers, the majority of whom are perhaps greater criminals than those over whom they tyrannize. Surely, the example of Pennsylvania will not be lost upon our country. Here is the best of all evidence, DEMONSTRATIVE PROOF, that brutal treatment, hangings, and gibbeting, are neither the most economical nor the most efficacious, as they are certainly neither the most humane, nor the most enlightened modes of punishing crime or reforming society; and if we wish to preserve the character of a feeling and enlightened people, we must reform that foul disgrace to England, and to the age in which we live — our CRIMINAL CODE. One fact, in connection with the prison, I have omitted to mention; and as it is a characteristic trait of national character, it ought to be recorded — white criminals will not eat with the negroes, the latter therefore have a separate table!!!

From this receptacle of moral evil, I walked to one of physical pain and suffering, the PENNSYLVANIA HOSPITAL, an institution in every way a national honour. The medical reputation of the gentlemen connected with this establishment would be highly estimated in the first European cities.

The *markets* are large and well supplied; — the chief is in Market-street. The time of sale is from day-light to 2 o'clock from the 1st of April to the 1st of September, and from day-light to 3 o'clock the remainder of the year. No butchers are allowed to kill in the city, nor are live cattle to be driven to the city markets.

PRICES.

The prices of fish vary from 2d. to 6¾d. per pound; beef, which is of excellent quality, 4d. to 5¼d.; mutton, 3¼d. to 4½d.; veal, 5¼d.; pork, 5¼d. to 7d.; bacon, 7d. to 8d.; butter, 17d. to 20d.; cheese, 9½d.; English ditto, 16d.; onions, 13d. per peck; potatoes, 3s. 4½d. a bushel; cabbages, 2½d. each; fowls, 12½d. to 2s. 3d. each; ducks, 20d. to 2s. 3d.; geese, 3s. 4½d. to 4s. 6d.; turkeys, 5s. 6d.; these four last articles are one half larger than those you have in England, but I am inclined to think their flesh is inferior in quality; strong beer, 20d. per gallon; apples, 3s. 4½d. per bushel; flour, 10 dollars per barrel of 196 pounds; dipt candles are 10d. per pound; moulds, 12½d.; moist sugar, 6¾d. to 9d.; lump ditto, 1s. to 1s. 5d.; tea, 4s. 6d. to 9s.; soap, 6¾d. to 10d.; chocolate, 13½d. to 20d.; raw coffee, 10d. to 13½d.; Liverpool salt, 3s. 4½d. per bushel; loaf of bread, weighing 2 pounds 2 ounces, 5¼d.; Indian corn, per bushel, 4s. 6d.; buck-wheat flour, 4s. 6d. Mechanics pay 13s. 6d. to 15s. 9d. per week for board and lodging: many board with their employers: all eat, work, and sleep in companies.

Moderately respectable boarding is from 20s. 3d. to 27s.; genteel ditto, 31s. 6d. to 54s. Charge at the best inns, 9s. per day, exclusive of beer and liquors.

WAGES.

Labourers are paid 4s. 6d. to 5s. 7½d. a day; female servants, 4s. 6d. to 9s. per week, with their board; cooks, 6s. 9d. to 9s.; men-servants, 54s. to 67s. 6d. per month; carpenters earn 36s. to 47s. 3d. per week, time of work from sun-rise to sun-set; cabinet-makers, 36s. to 45s., working generally by the piece; bricklayers, 31s. 6d. to 45s.; tinmen, 27s. to 54s.; shoemakers, 31s. 6d. to 40s. 6d. — they work more hours than in London; saddlers, 31s. 6d. to 45s. — this business at present is not good; coachmakers, 36s. to 45s. — at present bad here, but tolerably good at Newark in Jersey; taylors, 36s. to 45s. — a variable business, sometimes good employment, often not, it is largely in the hands of women; printers, compositors and pressmen, 36s. to 45s. — employment tolerably good, but not certain; apprentices perform a large portion of the work.

Individuals may get employment in any of the above trades, but there is no actual want of mechanics. Many leave here for the southern States and the western country. Men of this class of society may decidedly make themselves extremely comfortable in this place. Those who are here, speaking generally, receive higher wages, are more independent of their masters, live better, have less anxiety for the morrow, drink more, and are less intelligent than men following the like occupations in England.

PRICES OF WEARING APPAREL, &c.

Shoes are 13s. 6d. to 15s. 9d. a pair; Wellington boots, 38s. 3d. to 45s.; Hessian ditto, 42s. 9d. to 45s.; jockey ditto, 67s. 6d.; ladies' shoes, 4s. 6d. to 5s. $7\frac{1}{2}$d.—the leather is not good; upon a fair average, two pair of English will last as long as three pair of American; the best beaver hats are 40s. 6d.; superfine cloth coats, 8l. 1s. 6d.; surtout ditto, 11l. 5s.; pantaloons and trowsers, 45s. to 54s.; waistcoats, 27s. Clothes made of inferior materials, are from 25 to 50 per cent. lower. India and French silks, China crapes for ladies' dresses, and India handkerchiefs, are one half cheaper than in England. Other articles of wearing apparel, and almost every thing used in domestic economy, are of British manufacture. They pay an import duty of 25 per cent., and when retailed, are from 25 to 100 per cent. dearer than in London.

RELIGIOUS SECTS.

Having heard that American methodists were distinguished for an extreme degree of fanatical violence in their religious exercises. I visited the African church, (all houses of religious assembly being denominated churches,) in which were none but blacks; and in the evening, "Ebenezer Church," in which were only whites. As the latter possessed all the characteristics of the former, with considerable additions of its own, to that only is it necessary that I should call your attention. I went at 8 o'clock in the evening. The door was locked; but the windows being open, I placed myself at one of them, and saw that the church within was crowded almost to suffocation. The preacher indulged in long pauses, and occasional loud elevations of voice, which were always answered by the audience with deep groans. When the prayer which followed the sermon had ended, the minister descended from the pulpit, the doors were thrown open, and a considerable number of the audience departed. Understanding however that something was yet to follow, with considerable difficulty I obtained admission. The minister had departed, the doors were again closed, but about four hundred persons remained. One (apparently) of the leading members gave out a hymn, then a brother was called upon to pray: he roared and ranted like a maniac; the male part of the audience groaned, the female shrieked; a man sitting next to me shouted; a youth standing before me continued for half an hour bawling, "Oh Jesus! come down, come down, "Jesus! my dear Jesus, I see you! bless me, "Jesus! Oh! oh! oh! Come down, Jesus!" A small space farther on, a girl about 11 years of age was in convulsions: an old woman, who I concluded was her mother, stood on the seat, holding her up in her arms, that her ecstasies might be visible to the whole assembly. In another place there was a convocation of holy sisters, sending forth most awful yells. A brother now stood forward, stating, that "although "numbers had gone, he trusted the Lord would "that night work some signal favours among his "dear lambs." Two sisters advanced towards him, refusing to be comforted, "for the Lord was with them:" another brother prayed—and another. "Brother Macfaddin" was now called upon, and he addressed them with a voice which might almost rival a peal of thunder, the whole congregation occasionally joining responsive to his notes. The madness now became threefold increased, and such a scene presented itself as I could never have pictured to my imagination, and as I trust, for the honour of true religion and of human nature, I shall never see again. Had the inhabitants of Bedlam been let loose, they could not have exceeded it. From forty to fifty were praying aloud and extemporaneously at the same moment of time: some were kicking, many jumping, all clapping their hands and crying out in chorus, "Glory! glory! glory! Jesus "Christ is a very good friend! Jesus Christ is "a very good friend! Oh God! oh Jesus! "come down! Glory! glory! glory! thank you, "Jesus! thank you, God! Oh, glory! glory! "glory!!!" Mere exhaustion of bodily strength produced a cessation of madness for a few minutes. A hymn was given out and sung; praying then recommenced; the scene of madness was again acted, with, if possible, increased efforts on the part of the performers. One of the brothers prayed *to be kept from enthusiasm!* A girl of six years of age became the next object of attention. A reverend brother proclaimed that she "had just received a visit from the "Lord, and was in awful convulsions—so hard "was the working of the spirit!" This scene continued for some time; but the audience gradually lessened, so that by ten o'clock the field of active operations was considerably contracted. The women, however, forming a compact column at the most distant corner of the church, continued their shriekings with but little abatement. Feeling disposed to get a nearer sight of the beings who sent forth such terrifying yells, I endeavoured to approach them, but was stopped by several of the brethren, who would not allow of a near approach towards the holy sisterhood. The novelty of this exhibition had, at first sight, rendered it a subject of amusement and interest; but all such feelings soon gave way to an emotion of melancholy horror, when I considered the gloomy picture it represented of human nature, and called to mind that these maniacal fanatics were blaspheming the holy name of Christianity. Notwithstanding my warm love of liberty, I felt that, were I an absolute lawgiver, I would certainly punish and restrain men who thus degraded their nature, who set so wicked an example of religious blasphemy, and so foully libelled the name and character of revelation.

I have since understood that one of the female converts upon this occasion had been turned away from her situation the previous evening for stealing five dollars.

A gentleman informed me that he was at "Ebenezer" a few days since, when the preacher stopped in the midst of his discourse, and directed those among his audience who were for King Jesus to stand up. Numbers of men and women immediately rose, shouting "I am "for Jesus," "I am for Jesus," "I am for "King Jesus." "Oh, that I could press him to "my bosom!" "There he comes." "I am for "King Jesus." I am informed that these exhibitions are neither singular in occurrence nor partial in extent, and feel at a loss to account for such fanatical enthusiasm in this country: it is by no means an essential part of the creed of either Wesley or Whitefield; and, in Great Britain, few bodies of men conduct their meetings with more order than the methodists. In Wales, I understand, and perhaps in some country parts of England, there may be occasional exhibitions of the same kind; but they are of rare occurrence, and comparatively moderate in their excesses. In Ireland I have also witnessed occasional violence; but never any thing at all equal to that exhibited at "Ebenezer." In the latter country, too, we make some allowance for national character: they are all fire—all feeling; but with Americans, whatever may be their excellences or their defects, they are certainly not chargeable with possessing a superabundance of warm blood: they are, on the contrary, most remarkable for complete and general coldness of character and disposition. That, therefore, *they* should be enthusiastic, even in matters of religion, would appear a matter of difficult solution. In the individuals, it would seem to burst forth upon prepared occasions, and to exist in common with—perhaps actually to spring from, a cold-blooded callousness of disposition. The general theory which attributes *warmth* of feeling to the fanatic is perhaps, after all, a false one. Who so bigoted, so exclusive, so illiberal towards others, so wholly devoid of every generous sentiment? The extreme fanaticism of these maniacal saints may perhaps therefore actually spring from the absence of *real* enthusiasm, combined, of course, with gross and excessive ignorance.

The sects of this city, and the number of their places of assembly, are as follow: 1 Swedish Lutheran, 3 Quakers, 1 Free ditto, or Whig Quakers, called also Fighting Quakers, 4 Episcopalian, 4 Baptist, 5 Presbyterian, 4 Roman Catholic, 6 German Lutheran, 1 Moravian, 1 Covenanters, 3 Methodists, 1 Universalist, 1 Unitarian, 1 Independent, 1 Jews, 2 Black Methodist, and 1 Black Episcopalian.

Religious controversy appears unknown. Every man is expected to choose one of these churches; and when that is done, he must abide by it as solemnly and as regularly as he does his segar, his rum, and his business. *Whatever degree of religious intelligence exists, is confined to the clergy;* who, perhaps, have lost no advantage by the abolition of a state-religion.

ESTIMATION OF NEGROES.

The three "African churches," as they are called, are for all those native Americans who are black, or have any shade of colour darker than white. These persons, though many of them are possessed of the rights of citizenship, are not admitted into the churches which are visited by whites. There exists a penal law, deeply written in the *minds* of the whole white population, which subjects their coloured fellow-citizens to unconditional contumely and never-ceasing insult. No respectability, however unquestionable,—no property, however large,—no character, however unblemished,—will gain a man, whose body is (in American estimation) *cursed* with even a twentieth portion of the blood of his African ancestry, admission into society!!! They are considered as mere Pariahs—as outcasts and vagrants upon the face of the earth! I make no reflection upon these things, but leave the facts for your consideration.

CLIMATE, DISEASES, &c.

Of the climate of this city I can say but little from personal observation. The weather, at present, is at once healthy and delightful; the thermometer ranges from 56° to 70°; the sky is perfectly serene, and each day is as fine and clear as the preceding, forming a pleasing contrast to the humidity and frequent changes of our island. The heats of summer, I am told, are excessive, while the colds of winter are equally in the extreme. Spring, in the European understanding of that delightful season, there is none at all. If the appearance of the inhabitants be taken as a criterion, and if that appearance be not produced or aggravated by other causes, (such as excess or unhealthy practices of many kinds,) I should say that this climate is not so congenial to the well-being of the human constitution as that of England. A Philadelphian (particularly a female) is as old at 27, as a Londoner at 40. Neither sex possesses the English standard of health — a rosy cheek. The young females indeed are genteel; but their colour is produced by art, but for which disgusting practice, many of them might pass for beautiful. You will be surprised to hear, that in the practice of *rougeing*, the junior branches of *the society of Friends* are not at all deficient! Englishmen are said to improve in appearance for the first 12 months of their residence, but after that time the face becomes sallow and flabby.

In estimating the character of the climate, as shown by the health of the inhabitants, it may be well to take into account, on the part of the females, the effect of close stoves and want of exercise; on the part of the males, the excessive use of rum and tobacco; and, with regard to both sexes, the early period of life at which the mass of the population enter into the marriage state. There are, at any rate, it has been observed, two things but rarely seen here — "good teeth" and "green old age."

The leading class of diseases are inflammatory. The yellow fever to any great or important extent has not existed here for the last

11 years : a few cases occur each year, both here and in the more northern cities. The average of deaths per day, during the present year, has been eight; which, with a city population of 120,000, is not more in proportion than those of London and Paris. *Superior* medical aid is not cheaper than in London.

PROVISIONS FOR THE POOR, POLICE, &c.

The poor-laws are administered by sixteen citizens, who are chosen annually *by the corporation*, to superintend the provision for the poor. They are empowered, with the approbation of four aldermen and two justices, to levy an assessment not exceeding, at any one time, 100 cents (4s. 6d.) on 100 dollars (22l. 10s.), or one per cent.; nor more than three dollars per head, on every free man not otherwise rated. The average annual number of paupers supported in alms-houses of this city is 1600; the expence of keeping them 70,000 dollars a year; the produce of the poor-tax for the city and county of Philadelphia 100,000 dollars.

The police is strict, at least in some departments. There are fourteen constables and two high constables, whose business it is to perambulate the streets, which they do with a mace in their hands, and to examine all suspicious looking persons. If such refuse to give a satisfactory account of themselves, they are taken before the mayor. There are thirty-six watchmen who cry the hour (to imitate which, subjects the offender to immediate imprisonment), and six others who visit their boxes to see that they perform their duty. The whole are under the direction of a "captain," who attends to receive vagrants, rioters, and thieves. Watchmen are paid fourteen dollars (63s.) per month, fourteen-pence extra for every lamp under their care, and are supplied with a great coat: they are fined for neglect of duty. The cost for lighting and watching Philadelphia is 25,000 dollars per annum. I had intended saying something concerning the heads of the police, but shall reserve my remarks for the next communication. Circumstances have recently occurred, which, if true in all particulars, would prove the magistracy here to be as corrupt as that of London in the days of Fielding.

MORALS, MANNERS, &c.

Of the state of public morals, I find considerable difficulty in forming my judgment. The habits of the people are marked by caution and secresy. Although the eyes and ears of a stranger are not insulted in the openness of noon-day with evidence of hardened profligacy, I have, nevertheless, reason to believe in its existence to a very great extent; though perhaps there is no Philadelphia parent would say to me what a respectable inhabitant of New York did — "There is not a father in this city but "who is sorry that he has got a son."

To classify the population of this city, I should only have to repeat what I have communicated concerning other parts of the Union. There is, of course, here no rank of society correspondent to the peerage, or the "*haut-ton*," in England; but there are many who keep carriages, have truly elegant houses, and superb furniture. These are called of the "first class;" and although they have not the pomp or the titles, they have the pride of an aristocracy. The small and middling tradesmen do not make much exertion, live easily, save no money, and appear to care nothing about either the present or future. If they find business getting bad, they do, what is called, "sell out," and pack up for the "back country." The labourer and mechanic are independent, not in purse, but in condition. Neither they nor their masters conceive that any obligation is conferred by employing them. They live well, and may always have a dollar in their pockets. Men are here independent of each other: this will show itself even in half an hour's walk through the streets of Philadelphia.

The dress of the gentlemen is copied from the fashions of England; that of the ladies from France, — who very modestly believe, and indeed have no hesitation in declaring, that they combine the excellences of the French and the English character, without possessing the defects of either. For myself, I can trace no resemblance to the former, unless it consist in kid gloves and artificial flowers; nor to the latter, except in a fondness for Lady Morgan's writings, and an admiration of Lord Wellington's achievements. Could American ladies be content to despise instead of copying the vanity of their country-men, and take a few practical lessons from the English female in the management of domestic concerns, and the cultivation of their minds, then, indeed, their fine forms might become peculiarly interesting, — at least to the man of sense. — But I must turn to another subject.

Being anxious to depart for the western country before the season is too far advanced, I shall intrust this report to Captain Williams, of the Electra, who, I am persuaded, will take particular care of, and deliver it safely upon his arrival. A letter to our friend M——— will go in the bag of the same ship, advising you of the present communication. Address to me at "Washington city," as I hope to be there in January, during the sitting of Congress, and after the completion of my western journey. To-morrow I intend leaving this city for Pittsburgh. Mr. Mellish tells me that the road is very good. This has relieved my anxiety; for the journey has been a source of very uneasy anticipation. As usual, I suppose, I must say something in the way of advice. In my third Report I stated, that my feelings were generally those of disappointment. My *feelings* (to use the same unphilosophical criterion) are now more favourable towards this country. Philadelphia has done much towards raising America in my estimation. But I presume that none will come out until they hear from me again. Were I proceeding no farther than this city, and felt it necessary that I should make up my mind, for or against emigration, I should feel myself most aukwardly situated; for although it occupies my attention at all times, I cannot make even an approach towards a decision. The capitalist will receive in this State legal interest of six per cent.; in the State of New York seven per cent. I think that seven, or perhaps eight, might be made upon good security. Property of all kinds is selling every day at the Exchange Coffee Rooms. There is not now any great scope for mercantile speculation. Lands can be purchased, or new and large concerns established: but either of these would be hazardous. Capital is certainly wanted throughout the country. I think a brewery could be established with sound hopes of success, and not requiring more than from ten to fifteen thousand pounds. A London shopkeeper, with a capital of from three to ten thousand pounds, and who could import his goods from the first markets, would I think succeed — not because there is a want of "dry good stores;" for I believe one-half could be spared: but there is an ignorance of good principles of business; and, I suspect, a very general deficiency of means. Lawyers, doctors, clerks, shopmen, literary men, artists, and schoolmasters, would, to use an American phrase, "come to a bad market." Mechanics can form their own judgment, from the statements in the preceding pages. Weavers, stocking-makers, and others, acquainted *only* with the cotton, woollen, hardware, and linen manufactures, would find employment very difficult to obtain. A few evenings since I saw a carpenter and his wife, who have been here but one month, from Hull, in Yorkshire. The husband stated, that in England he earned 21s. per week; that he now obtains 31s. 6d.; that he finds great difficulty in getting his money from his employer; that, "taking one thing with another," the expense of living is as nearly like that in England as possible; that had he been acquainted with every thing which he at present knows, he would not have left home; but that, having done so, he is well satisfied; and has now saved some money — a thing which he had hardly ever before effected. I state this man's information, because I consider it deserving of your confidence. It is equally free from the wild rhapsodies of some persons, and the deplorable pictures which several Englishmen in this city, and in other parts of the Union, have given me of their disappointments, and of America in general. The carpenter's success is just what would attend any other industrious man of the same business, or of several others previously enumerated. His ideas of the difficulties which he had encountered are natural, as he has not been engaged sufficiently long in other pursuits to obliterate these impressions. Could I see him in twelve months from the present time, I think his condition would be, if I may judge from others, something like the following: — saved fourteen guineas; living in two small rooms; independent of his master, and his master of him; thinks the Americans a very dirty and disagreeable people, and hates them from his soul; would be delighted to see old England again, and smoke his pipe and drink his pint, and talk politics with the cobbler, and abuse the taxes; and then he remembers that he is in America, where he cannot endure the thoughts of having his bones buried; thinks of returning to England, where his wife is also anxious to go, in order that she may drink tea and gossip with her old neighbours; then they both conjure up their former sea sickness, their fear of being drowned, the money that their passage would cost, and that when they got to Hull, his most laborious application would not more than provide them with a bare existence. He then determines to remain in America, keep the money which he has saved, add as much more to it as he can, and make himself as contented and happy as lies in his power.

The man of small property, who intends living upon the interest, and wants to remove to a cheaper country than England, should pause before the object of his choice be America. From what I have seen of large towns, living is not, *upon the whole*, lower than in English cities. In the interior it may be less than in the country parts of England. But such a man must, of necessity, have his ideas of happiness associated with many sources of comfort and gratification, which he would seek for in vain within the United States.

In conclusion, I wish to express my anxious hopes that you are all well: and that whether we remain in England or settle in the New World, we may continue to possess, and to deserve, as great a portion of enjoyment as may be consistent with our improvement in the present state of our existence.

P. S. Taxes are of trifling amount compared with the enormous drafts made upon you in that particular. A gentleman of this city, whose house is his own property, but which, if let, would be worth 130l. per annum, obliged me with his collector's receipts for three years.

"Mr. ——— Dr. to Liberty Brown, collector, No. —— Chesnut-street, for taxes in Middle Ward for 1813.

	City Tax.		County Tax.		Poor Tax.		Health Tax.		Total.	
	d.	c.	d.	c.	d.	c.	d.	c.	d.	c.
House - - -	18	12	5	79	8	70	1	81	34	42
Poll-tax - -	1	50		75		72		28	3	25
Ground on which the house stands	1	38		45		66		14	2	63
Water, to July 1814.	-		-		-		-		5	

Total amount, 45 dollars, 30 cents, or 10l. 5s. 6d."

"TAXES FOR 1815.

	Dollars.	Cents.
City Tax - -	19	38
Poor ditto - -	10	62
County - -	8	19
Dog - - -		25
Ground on which house stands - -	2	54
Total	40	98 or 9l. 4s. 3d."

"TAXES FOR 1816.

	Dollars.	Cents.
City Tax - -	18	61½
Poor - - -	10	62
County - -	8	19
Ground on which house stands - -	2	65½
Water -	5	0
Total	45	8 or 10l. 4s. 6d."

The following notice from the tax collectors is just published:

"TAXES FOR 1817.

"Notice is hereby given, that the taxes for 1817 are now due; and the owners of property and other taxable inhabitants of the city of Philadelphia, district of Southwark and townships of Northern Liberties and Penn, are required to call on the collectors hereafter named, and pay their taxes, or the law will be enforced to compel payment. The following extract from the collector's warrant, is published for the information of those concerned.

"'And if any person, charged in the said duplicate, shall neglect or refuse to make payment within 30 days from the time of the demand by you made, you are then hereby authorized and required to levy the tax due by such delinquent, by distress and sale of his goods and chattels, giving ten days' notice of such sale, by written or printed advertisements. And in case goods and chattels cannot be found sufficient to satisfy the same with costs, you are authorized and required to take the body of the said delinquent, and convey him to the gaol of the said county of Philadelphia, there to remain until the said tax with costs be paid or secured to be paid, or otherwise be discharged by the course of law. And hereby fail not at your peril.'"

I am informed that these are State, *not United States'* taxes. This distinction is essential to be borne in mind, as it is anticipated that the legislature will abolish the war taxes upon the opening of congress, and you might suppose from that fact, that all internal taxation would be done away.

FIFTH REPORT.

Leave Philadelphia for the Western Country. — Pennsylvania Farms; their Value. — Price of Stock; of Labour. — Produce. — Soil. — Taverns. — Military. — Loudon. — Landlords; their Politics. — Allegany Mountains; their Scenery. — Difficulty of crossing. — M'Connel's Ville. — Numerous Emigrants; their Mode of travelling. — Soil and Productions of the Alleganies. — Character and Pursuits of the People. — Crossing the River Juniatta. — Bad Stages. — Grensburgh. — Face of the Country towards Pittsburgh. — Improved Condition of the Inhabitants. — Pittsburgh. — Fine Situation. — Scenery. — Prices of Provisions; of Labour. — Farming. — Produce. — Price of Stock. — General Expences. — Condition of a Pennsylvania Farmer. — Coal. — Trades and Manufactures. — New Establishments likely to succeed. — Capital required. — Rapid Increase of the Western Country. — Mode of conducting Business. — Mechanics. — Theatre. — Population. — Young Watson. — Leave Pittsburgh. — State of Ohio. — Face of the Country. — Price of Lands. — State of Agricultural Knowledge. — Price of Labour. — Climate. — Wild Animals. — "Frolic." — Pursuits of Women. — Classes of Society. — Cincinnati. — Slavery. — Prices. — Rents. — Trades. — Mechanics. — Want of Capital. — Manufactures. — State of Kentucky. — Price of Lands; of Labour. — Slavery. — Rents. — Soil. — Produce. — Trades. — Manufactures. — Provisions. — Climate. — Health. — Middletown. — Louisville. — What Class of Emigrants would succeed. — Lord Selkirk. — Unfair Account of Mellish the Traveller. — Illinois Territory. — Extent. — Face of the Country. — Navigable Waters. — First Inhabitants. — Present Population. — Their Character and Condition. — Soil. — Produce. — Supposed Expense of erecting Houses. — Wild Animals. — Towns. — Considerations requiring the Attention of my Friends.

Shawnee Town, Illinois Territory, Kentucky, &c.
Dec. 1817.

PENNSYLVANIA FARMS.

OCTOBER. — Left Philadelphia for Pittsburgh. Passed through an extensive, fertile, well-cultivated, and beautiful tract of land called the "Great Valley." Farms in this district are chiefly owned by Dutch and Germans, and their descendants. They consist of from 50 to 200 acres, each acre worth 200 dollars (45l.), and are cheaper at that price than the 50 cent and dollar and half lands, which encumber other parts of the eastern States. The substantial barns, fine private dwellings, excellent breed and condition of live stock, and superior cultivation of the "Great Valley," place it decidedly in advance of the neighbouring lands, and put it fairly in competition with Old England. The proprietors are wealthy. They have the reputation of being practical opponents of the desolating system of paper money, by keeping their hard cash safely locked up in their "*old* "*country*" boxes. Be this as it may, their property, unlike that of their fellow-citizens on the sea-side, has not vanished into air by the late mighty political changes. They have been blessed by Heaven with excellent land and good markets; and although their progress in the acquirement of "this world's goods" has not been like the rise of Jonah's gourd, neither has it shared the fate of that transitory plant.

There are good farms in other districts within 20 miles of Philadelphia, which can be purchased at from 80 to 100 dollars per acre, buildings included. Limestone land will sell for 200 dollars. In a farm of 200 acres, the proportion may be estimated at 90 acres of ploughing, 50 of meadow, 10 of orchard, and 50 of wood land. The *latter*, near the city, is worth 3 to 400 dollars per acre. A farm of the above description is worth, if within five miles of the capital, 20,000 dollars; at from 20 to 40 miles' distance, 10,000 dollars. Uncleared lands, in remote parts of the State, vary in price from half a dollar to 20 dollars per acre.

The Pennsylvanian horse is a medium between our saddle and heavy cart horses, and is well suited for most purposes. They are worth from 50 to 150 dollars (11l. 2s. 6d. to 33l. 7s. 6d.). A farm waggon will cost 100 to 120 dollars (22l. 10s. to 27l.); a family ditto, 70 to 90 dollars; ditto with springs, 150 dollars; neat gig, 300; best ditto, 450; a farm cart, 50 dollars. The annual expence of keeping a family waggon and horse is about 50 dollars.

Well-improved land will produce, on an average, 25 bushels of wheat per acre (a farmer within eight miles of the city has raised 40); ditto of Indian corn, 25 to 50. Wheat is sold at from

160 to 220 cents (7s. 8d. to 9s. 11d.) per bushel; Indian corn, 80 to 100 cents (3s. 7d. to 4s. 6d.); oats, 40 to 55 cents (1s. 9d. to 2s. 5½d.): they are lighter than the English. Meadows are usually ploughed in rotation, and planted with Indian corn. Orchards are also put under the plough, grain not being considered as injurious to the fruit. A good milch cow, four years old, is worth 5l. 13s. 6d. Sheep are much smaller than ours. Half-blood Merino are 11s. 3d.: three-quarters blood, 13s. 6d.; full ditto, 22s. 6d.; rams are 4l. 10s. to 11l. 2s. 6d.; pigs four weeks old are 2s. 3d.; a sow and ditto, 1l. 11s. 6d. to 2l. 14s.; a hog of 100 pounds, 1l. 11s. 6d. to 2l. 5s.; a yoke of oxen, 15l. 15s. to 28l. 10s.

MINERALS.

A copper and zinc mine is worked about twenty miles from Philadelphia. Iron ore abounds throughout the State. Bar iron sells for 120 dollars per ton. Limestone abounds at about fifteen miles from the city. There is also a coarse grey marble in large quantities: it is used for steps and chimney-pieces. The price delivered in Philadelphia is one dollar the cubic foot.

The farmers in Pennsylvania are many of them rich: some reside in first-rate houses, and are possessed of most of the conveniences of life. Those remote from a market generally distil their grain, finding whiskey to be the most convenient and profitable form under which to carry and dispose of their stock. The great body of these men are Germans, or of German descent. They are excellent practical farmers, very industrious, very mercenary, and very ignorant. The condition of the labourer is similar to that in other parts of the United States.

The towns of Lancaster, Harrisburgh, and Carlisle, through which I passed, are all of them considerable in extent and in population. They each contain a large proportion of excellent brick buildings, and the usual erections of market houses, gaols, and churches; all evincing an extent of national prosperity, and an advancement towards European establishments truly extraordinary, when we recollect that this is a country which may be said to be but of yesterday. The German character is very prevalent throughout this State. The original language is still preserved, and there are even native Pennsylvanians who cannot speak the English language.

Arrived at Chambersburgh, 157 miles from Philadelphia, I went to the inn where the stages from Baltimore and Philadelphia to Pittsburgh usually stop. These stages are two days in arriving here from the latter, and one from the former city. I secured a place, for which I paid 14 dollars (three guineas), distance 140 miles. This town contains about 240 houses, of all sorts, two or three churches, a gaol and court-house.

October.—The stage started at three o'clock in the morning. A Mr. Flower, connected with Mr. Birkbeck, left Chambersburgh a few days previous, on his return from Illinois to England. What his views of this country are I have not learned, though I should conclude, from the reported statements of an acquaintance, with whom he conversed at Chambersburgh, that his estimation of America is highly favourable.

Arrived at eight o'clock at Loudon, at the foot of the north mountain, one of the Allegany ridges. There are here 17 log and 20 frame or brick houses. We were not allowed to breakfast at the tavern in this town, as one of the proprietors of the coach had a house at M'Connel's Ville. The tavern at Loudon is cheerless and dirty: a number of waggoners were breakfasting. The election was a topic of violent debate; bets, and as a usual accompaniment, choler, ran high. We brought the latest intelligence of the returns. All had their hopes and fears. The landlord, who is of Dutch descent, was, as a matter of course, a Hiesterite, because he was descended from a countryman. The Irish party, for similar reasons, supported Findlay. We were saluted by each at our departure, "Huzza for Hiester!" "Huzza for "Findlay!" My fellow-travellers were citizens of the world: they huzzaed for each with true philanthropic liberality. The final return throughout the State elected Mr. Findlay with a majority of 7,000. I counted thirty regular stage-waggons engaged in the transportation of goods to and from Pittsburgh. They are drawn by four strong well-fed horses, are made upon the model of English waggons, but about one-third less in size. They are from 20 to 35 days in effecting their journey. The articles sent from Philadelphia are hardware, and what are denominated "dry goods." This term includes all articles of woollen, linen, cotton, and silk. Those returned from Pittsburgh are farming produce, chiefly flour. It is necessary to understand that the road I am travelling is the only trading waggon route to the whole western country. This circumstance being taken into consideration, in addition to the fact that there is no water carriage, the number of conveyances, though great, is by no means extraordinary.

Proceeded up the north mountain, over a most excellent piece of road, which is part of the new national turnpike, proposed to extend from the head of the Potowmac to Wheeling, and when completed will be of immense importance to the western country, and indeed the whole Union, the connection of the old and new sections being at present materially impeded by excessively bad roads. At 11 o'clock, when near the summit of the mountain, we enjoyed a most extensive view of a large and beautiful valley, which must contain tens of thousands of acres that have not yet known the hand of the cultivator. The prospect, combining some grand mountain scenery, was the most magnificent I had ever beheld. The interest of the scene was also not a little heightened by the prospect of M'Connel's Ville, which we were approaching. This apparently delightful little town appeared secluded from the rest of the world, and one might have imagined it another Eden, cut off by means of woods and trackless wilds, and mountain snows, from the vices and the corruptions which, in every other quarter, visit and torment mankind. — But this is merely reverie. We entered the town, proceeded to the tavern, where we breakfasted, and a nearer inspection showed every thing around us to be merely human.

M'Connel's Ville contains 40 houses, chiefly log. — Beef is now 10 cents a pound ($5\frac{1}{4}$d.); sometimes it is only 7 ($3\frac{3}{4}$d.); mutton is not consumed: fowls are 6s. 9d. per dozen; charge for breakfast, 2s. 3d. — Passed several travellers on foot from Massachusetts, going with an intention of viewing the western country, and, if satisfied, of selecting a settlement previous to the emigration of their families: they fairly excelled our stage in expedition. Came up with 20 small family waggons; two of these were broken down, and the horses of all in very bad condition; they were chiefly from Massachusetts, Jersey, and Connecticut. One of these was the joint property of a Dutch and an American family. My companions seemed to know at first sight, from what State the emigrants travelled. The New Englanders were evidently better fitted for the great and unavoidable fatigues of removal, than the natives of Jersey and Maryland. I thought I could even discover in the white inhabitants the effects of residing in free and in slave States. The genuine Yankies (New Englanders) are ignorant of slavery; they have been necessitated to labour with their own hands; they have not been demoralized by familiarity with a system that establishes a barrier between fellow-beings on account of their colour; they have not been taught that because their neighbour's face was (to use their own phrase) a *grade* darker than their own, he was therefore of an *inferior species* (as I am sorry to see contended for even by Mr. Jefferson); they have relied on their own resources, and the consequence is, that they are more enterprising, more healthy, more enlightened, and altogether better suited to cultivate the wilderness with success, than their slave-holding neighbours. Even the women from New England were walking before their waggons, while the others were either riding or lagging behind.

These emigrants preferred travelling in companies, forming a oneness of interest, and securing an interchange of assistance when necessary. In difficult parts of this tract their progress was so slow as to be hardly perceivable. Ropes were attached to each side of the waggons, at which, while some were pulling, others were most unmercifully, though necessarily, whipping the horses, which dragged the waggons five yards at an effort. The getting these waggons and families over the mountains appeared little less than a continuance of miracles. I was prepared to expect much, but the reality has increased my ideas of the difficulty of this emigration a thousand fold.

Crossed the Juniatta — arrived at Dickenson's Tavern — proceeded to Bloody-run, where we arrived at half-past eleven, excessively fatigued — charge for supper and bed, 4s. 6d. In the latter part of this stage nothing could exceed the badness of the roads; yet the understanding between the driver and horses was so perfect, that we proceeded, though with almost broken bones, with the exactness of mechanism. A London coachman would in half an hour have dashed the strongest English stage to pieces, and probably broken the necks of his passengers.

Second day.—Started at three o'clock in the morning: thermometer ten degrees above zero: at nine arrived at *Bedford*, where we were not allowed to breakfast, as a stage-proprietor lived farther on. We all crossed over to the orchard of a farm house and stole some frozen apples, which our keen appetites caused us to enjoy.—Passed over the Dry Ridge, upon which were great numbers of family and stage waggons: some of the former were from the district of Maine, and had been out 80 days. The progress of our stage was so slow and so painful, that I preferred walking: this afforded me an opportunity of entering into the views and little histories of fellow-travellers. No person here need feel backward in asking questions, and all answer without hesitation or reserve. The women I found the most communicative: their husbands being chiefly engaged in dragging along their wretched nags. The first I conversed with was from Jersey, out 32 days: she was sitting upon a log, which served for the double purpose of a seat and a fire: their waggon had broken down the day before; her husband was with it at a distant blacksmith's: she had been seated there all night: her last words went to my heart: "Ah! Sir, I wish to God we had never left "home."

The view from the summit of Dry Ridge even exceeds the one before described. The scenery is bolder, and marked with a character of increased magnificence. The eye takes in at one glance, the various ridges called the South, the Blue, the Cove, and the more extended chain, peculiarly denominated the Allegany. The calm serenity of the numerous valleys formed a pleasing contrast with the more stupendous works of nature with which we were so profusely surrounded. Although there is here much barren country, there is a good deal of fine fertile land. The most prevalent trees are the beech, black, red, and white oaks. Clay slate appears, thus far, to characterise these mountains. — We continued to overtake emigrants' waggons from Maryland, Jersey, Pennsylvania, Connecticut, Massachusetts, and district of Maine. One of the families was that of the brother-in-law and sister of Captain Riley, whose work, detailing his shipwreck and consequent captivity in Africa, has been reprinted in England, and attracted such general and well-deserved attention. This family were in great distress.

At five o'clock in the evening we reached the top of the Alleganies. Our stage was far behind. This day I had walked about sixteen miles; and, as was the case the day before, we were not allowed to stop for dinner, there being no *coach proprietor* upon the road. "The Fountain Inn" is a miserable log-house, or what you would call a dog-hole : it was crowded with emigrants. I asked for something to eat, but could only obtain for answer, " I guess whis-" key is all the feed we have on sale." I have met with several similar instances, when I have asked, " Have you any meat?" " No." — " Either cold or hot will make no difference to " me." " I guess I don't know." — " Have " you any fowls?" " No." — " Fish?" " No." — " Ham?" " No." — " Bread?" " No." — " Cheese?" " No." — " Crackers (biscuits)?" " No." — " I will pay you any price you " please." " I guess we have only rum and " whiskey feed."

The character of the mountain inhabitants appears cold, friendless, unfeeling, callous, and selfish. All the emigrants with whom I conversed complained of the enormous charges at taverns. Log-houses are the only habitations for many miles. They are formed of the trunks of trees, about twenty feet in length, and six inches in diameter, cut at the ends, and placed upon each other. The roof is framed in a similar manner. In some houses there are windows; in others the door performs a double office. The chimney is erected outside, and in a similar manner to the body of the house. Some have clay in their chimneys, which is a precaution very necessary in these western palaces. In some the space between the logs remains open; in others it is filled with clay. The hinges are generally wood. Locks are not used. In some there are two apartments; in others but one, for all the various operations of cooking, eating, sleeping, and, upon great occasions, washing. The pigs also come in for their due share of the log residence. — By eleven o'clock at night we safely arrived at *Somerset*, 237 miles from Philadelphia.

Started at 3 o'clock on our third day's journey: thermometer 6 above zero. — Crossed Laurel Hill. A family from Massachusetts had "camped out" during the night. At five o'clock we found them cooking potatoes for breakfast: they very freely offered us a portion of their homely fare. Perhaps in Essex I should have thought this no treat — on Laurel Ridge it was a most acceptable one; so naturally does our inclination adapt itself to our circumstances. This family consisted of ten persons: an old lady, her son and his wife, with sevon children, of both sexes, from two to sixteen years of age; all in excellent health, and full of life and spirits; despising difficulties, and anticipating a rich reward when they arrived in the "land of "Canaan."

The vegetation on this ridge appears superior to that of the Allegany: it is considered to take its name from the *calmia latifolia*, which grows here profusely. The mountain called Little Chesnut Ridge, succeeds that of Laurel Hill, the difficulties of the road increasing; though those which we experienced were "light "as air," compared with those which the poor families were exposed to. The inconveniences of travelling principally arise, not from the mere height of these mountains, but from the abundance of enormous stones and of mud-holes. The road is not turnpike after the small space described previous to arriving at M'Connel's Ville. The trees on Chesnut Ridge are chiefly oak and chesnut: the soil appears chalky. This morning, after a walk of four hours, we halted for the coach to come up; though the pain of riding exceeded the fatigue of walking, yet the having it as a place of final resort was desirable: it refreshed us by *varying* the weariness of our bodies. At half-past ten at night we arrived at *Greensburgh*, a town only 36 miles from Pittsburgh. I was delighted with the near prospect of a few days' cessation from fatigue.

Started, the fourth day, at four o'clock in the morning, with the high treat of a turnpike-road; but the advantages arising from this were but of short continuance. We had to descend Turtle Creek Hill, which, in consequence of recent rains, had become, if possible, even worse than Laurel Hill. We all got out, and, up to our knees in mud, took our turns in holding up the stage. This tract bore decided evidence of being imbedded with coal. At the foot of the hill I came up with a woman and girl, with two infants in their arms, who came, to use their own language, " vrom Zomerzetzhire in Hingland." Collecting from my remarks that I had been in their country, they spoke of it with heartfelt attachment; were sorry that they had ever been persuaded to leave it; they had been told that this was the first place in the world, but they had experienced nothing but difficulties since they had set their foot upon it. The husband was behind, dragging on their little all. It was 45 days since they had left Philadelphia. I assisted them over a brook, and endeavoured to comfort them with the hopes that when they once got settled they would be well repaid for all their toil.

Passed through *M'Nair's Town*, a new log settlement; also *Eastern Liberty Town*, containing some brick-houses, an hotel, and a large steam grist-mill. At two o'clock we arrived at Hunter's hotel in *Pittsburgh*. The town was enveloped in smoke. The condition of the people from Chambersburgh to Greensburgh is that of an absence of wealth and of the conveniences of life, with, however, the means of obtaining a sufficient quantity of food. Their habitations, in our ideas, are extremely wretched; but in theirs, the contrary. The blacksmith and the tavern-keeper are almost the only occupations: the former earns from 20s. 6d. to 27s. per week: the profits of the latter must be great, judging from the high charges and bad quality. From Greensburgh to Pittsburgh, the improvement, in size and *quality* of the houses, is evident; and the cultivation and condition of the land are much superior. Many places bear the evident marks of wealth; the criterion for ascertaining which is, in this country, very tangible. Recurring to my old plan of estimation, I passed on my road from Chambersburgh to Pittsbugh, being 153 miles, one hundred and three stage-waggons, drawn by four and six horses, proceeding from Philadelphia and Baltimore to Pittsburgh, —seventy-nine from Pittsburgh to Baltimore and Philadelphia, — sixty-three waggons, with families, from the several places following: — twenty from Massachusetts, — ten from the district of Maine, — fourteen from Jersey, — thirteen from Connecticut, — two from Maryland, —one from Pennsylvania, — one from England, — one from Holland, — and one from Ireland; about two hundred persons on horseback, — twenty on foot, — one beggar, one family, with their waggon, returning from Cincinnati, entirely disappointed — a circumstance which, though rare, is by no means, as some might suppose, miraculous.

PITTSBURGH.

Pittsburgh is, in several points of view, a most interesting town; from its natural situation, being at the termination of two, and the commencement of a third river, which has a direct communication with the ocean, though at the almost incredible distance of 2500 miles; its scenery, which is truly picturesque; its exhaustless possession of that first-rate material for manufactories, coal; its original situation as an early military post, and remarkable for two defeats of the British, more especially that of General Bradock by the French and Indians, in which the great Washington first distinguished himself, though but a youth and only a militia colonel; and lastly, its present importance as being the connecting link between *new* and *old* America; and though it is not at present a "Birmingham," as the natives bombastically call it, yet it certainly contains the seeds of numerous important manufactories. The published accounts of this city are so exaggerated and out of all reason, that strangers are usually disappointed on visiting it. This, however, was not my case. I have been in some measure tutored in American gasconade. When I am told that at a particular hotel there is *handsome* accommodation, I expect that they are one remove from very bad; if "*elegant* entertainment," I anticipate tolerable; if a person is

" a *clever* man," that he is not absolutely a fool; and if a manufactory is the "*first in the world*," I expect, and have generally found, about six men and three boys employed.

PRICES.

Beef and mutton are 3d. to 4½d. per pound; pork 4½d. to 5d.; cheese, 9½d. to 14d.; butter, 10d. to 20d.; tea, 6s. 9d. to 12s. 4d.; moist sugar, 13½d.; loaf, 20d. to 2s. 1d.; coffee, 20d.; potatoes, 2s. 3d. to 3s. 4½d. per bushel; porter, 6½d. per quart; fowls, 13½d. each; ducks, 20d.; geese, 2s. 3d. to 3s. 4½d.; turkeys, 3s. 4½d. to 5s. 8d.; flour, 27s. to 31s. 6d. per barrel of 196 pounds; coal, 4d. per bushel. Mechanic's board, 15s. 9d. to 18s. per week.

FARMING.

Agricultural produce finds here a ready and an advantageous market. Farming, in this neighbourhood, is not the most profitable mode of employing capital; but it is here, as in all other parts of the Union, an independent mode of life. The farmer must labour hard with his own hands. The " help" which he pays for will be dear, and not of that kind to be relied on, in the mode of its execution, as in England. This may not proceed from a worse state of character, but a *difference in condition*, as compared with our working class. They are paid about fourteen dollars per month, and board. In many instances they expect to sit down with the master, to live as well, and to be upon terms of equality with every branch of the family; and if this should be departed from, the scythe and the sickle will be laid down in the midst of harvest. There is a class of men throughout the western country called "merchants," who, in the summer and autumn months, collect flour, butter, cheese, pork, beef, whiskey, and every species of farming produce, which they send in flats and keel-boats to the New Orleans market. The demand created by this trade, added to a large domestic consumption, insures the most remote farmer a certain market. Some of these speculators have made large fortunes.

Land in the neighbourhood of Pittsburgh is worth 100 dollars per acre. At a distance of from five to twenty miles, tracts of from 100 to 500 acres, containing meadow, pasturage, arable, and part covered with wood, have been recently sold at from 20 to 50 dollars per acre. Wheat brings a dollar a bushel; Indian corn, 75 cents a bushel. A four year old cart-horse is worth from 20 to 30 dollars; a gig ditto, 50 to 100; a saddle ditto, 20 to 150*; a farmer's waggon, 100 dollars;

* A common mode of selling horses is for the owner to gallop through the street, announcing the amount of his last bidding. I have witnessed several crying out, "twenty-five "*dallars*," "twenty-five *dallars*," "twenty-five *dallars*;"

a family ditto, from 50 to 70; cart, 50. An acquaintance of mine, from Derbyshire, gave yesterday for a cow with a calf by her side, twenty-five dollars. Sheep are from one to three dollars; live hogs from 2½d. to 4½d. a pound; a good roasting pig, 4s. 6d. Wool is but little in demand since the termination of the war. Mr. ———, of Lexington, has informed me that he purposes making a shipment of it for Liverpool; should this succeed, it will open a new source of profit to the western farmer. Clean Merino is worth here 5s. 8d. to 6s. 9d. per pound; fleece, 3s. 5d.; half-bred, 2s. 3d.; quarter, 21d. A brick house, two stories high, containing ten rooms, may be built, with good management, in the country for 4000 dollars (900l.), as the bricks can be made upon the land, and the "help" boarded in the house. In towns, a similar building will cost 6000 dollars (1350l.), exclusive of the ground, which, in particular situations, as of *all* towns that promise well, is dearer than the most choice spot in the city of London!

COAL.

In the coal hills which I have visited, the mineral is found in a horizontal position, lying

---

and after half an hour's exercise, they have been transferred, saddle, bridle, and all, to a new bidder, for twenty-five *dallars*, fifty *sants*.

at present above level. It is worked by adits or openings into the side of the hills, which draw off the water. The stream being boarded over, the coal is wheeled out in barrows, and *tripped* from an overhanging stage into one-horse waggons. The waggons are without wheels, and the horses, if blind, are preferred, the hills being so steep, that in case of the least start, nothing can save them from destruction. Labourers earn in the coal excavations 31s. 6d. to 40s. 6d. per week. — If the inhabitants of Pittsburgh are determined to call that place after some English town, I should propose that, instead of the "American Birmingham," it be denominated, with relation to the humidity of its climate, "the American Manchester;" for I remained at this place several days, during which time the rain never ceased. The smoke is also extreme, giving to the town and its inhabitants a very sombre aspect; but an English medical gentleman who has resided here some years, informs me that there is not a more healthy place in the United States. The diseases are bilious remittent fevers; rheumatic among the aged; a few cases of bronchocele which affects the theroid gland of females; and inflammatory sore-throat in wet weather. Medical aid is easy of attainment, though not always of the most valuable kind. There is of doctors, as of lawyers, too large a supply, and of course many of them very inefficient. A physician here is also a surgeon—prepares his own medicines, and practises in every department of the profession;—generally they are neither so well educated, nor in such respectable circumstances as our medical men.

TRADES AND MANUFACTORIES.

The manufacturing interest of Pittsburgh is that of the United States. Many of the manufactories originated during the late war, and all of them flourished during its continuance. At present they are generally upon the wane. A document was issued from their committee last year, setting forth their distress in the strongest language—from which it would appear to equal that of our manufacturing classes, even during the worst period of their sufferings.

Mr. Ephrim Portland, the prothonotary of this town, favoured me with the following list of manufactories up to last January, published by the authority of the committee. Mr. P. is a gentleman of information, and to whom I am personally indebted for much liberal and kind attention.

MANUFACTORIES in and near the city of PITTSBURGH, in the State of Pennsylvania, in the year 1817.

Manufacturers.	Number of Men employed.	Yearly Amount.
		Dollars.
1 Augur-maker - - - -	6	3,500
1 Bellows-maker - - -	3	10,000
18 Blacksmiths - - - - -	74	75,100
3 Brewers - - - - -	17	72,000
3 Brush-makers - - -	7	8,600
1 Button-maker - - -	6	6,250
2 Cotton-spinners and carders	36	25,518
11 Copper-smiths and tin-plate-workers - - -	100	200,000
7 Cabinet-makers - - -	43	40,000
1 Currier - - - - -	4	12,000
2 Cutlers - - - - -	6	2,400
4 Iron-founders - - -	87	180,000
3 Gun-smiths, and bridlebit-makers	14	13,800
2 Flint-glass manufacturers -	82	110,000
3 Green (window) ditto - -	92	130,000
2 Hardware - - - - -	17	18,000
7 Hatters - - - - -	49	44,640
1 Lock-smith - - - - -	7	12,000
1 Linen - - - - - -	20	25,000
7 Nail - - - - - -	47	174,716
1 Paper - - - - - -	40	23,000
1 Pattern - - - - -	21	1,500
3 Plane - - - - - -	6	57,600
1 Patten - - - - -	5	8,000
1 Rope manufacturer - -	8	15,000
1 Spinning machine - -	6	6,000
1 Spanish Brown - - -	2	6,720
1 Silver plater - - -	40	20,000
2 Steam-engine-makers - -	70	125,000
6 Saddlers - - - - -	60	86,000
5 Silver-smiths and watch-menders	17	12,000
14 Shoe and boot - - -	109	120,000
7 Tanners and curriers - -	47	58,800
4 Tallow-chandlers - - -	7	32,600
4 Tobacconists - - -	28	21,000
5 Waggon-makers - - -	21	28,500
2 Weavers - - - - -	9	14,562
3 Windsor Chair - - -	23	42,600
2 Woollen - - - - -	30	17,000
1 Wire-drawer - - -	12	6,000
1 White Lead - - - - -	6	40,000

Total number of workmen, 1280.—Ditto, amount 1,896,396 Dollars.

Some of the above manufactories may be denominated first-rate. This remark applies particularly to the nail, steam-engine (high pressure), and glass establishments. I was astonished to witness such perfection on this side of the Atlantic, and especially in that part of America which a New Yorker supposes to be at the farther end of the world.

At Messrs. Page and Bakewell's glass warehouse I saw chandeliers and numerous articles in cut glass of a very splendid description; among the latter was a pair of decanters, cut from a London pattern, the price of which will be eight guineas. It is well to bear in mind that the demand for these articles of elegant luxury lies *in the Western States!* the inhabitants of Eastern America being still importers from the "Old Country." What interesting themes of reflection are offered by such facts to the philosopher as well as to the politician! Not thirty years since the whole right bank of the Ohio was termed the "Indian side." Spots in Tenesse, in Ohio and Kentucky, that within the life-time of even young men, witnessed only the arrow and the scalping-knife, now present to the traveller articles of elegance and modes of luxury which might rival the displays of London and Paris, while, within the last half century, the beasts of the forest, and man more savage than the beast, were the only inhabitants of the whole of that immense tract peculiarly denominated the "Western Country;" which is now partially inhabited, and promises soon to be generally so by man — civilized man, possessed of the arts and the pursuits of civilized life. It is already the refuge of the oppressed from every other nation. May it become the seat of enlightenment, of private virtue and public liberty; and it may then, *but not till then*, expect to rank among the greatest, the most powerful, and the most respected of the nations of the earth!

The rapid and unexampled progress of this country, presents a valuable and an extraordinary political lesson to the world at large. It shows us what a nation *may* become when the principles of its government are *cheap* and liberal, when its resources are called forth, and its powers expanded by the means of a system emanating from the people, and not repressed by establishments whose only recommendation is their antiquity, nor compelled to contribute towards the support of a system which deprives them of the legitimate reward of their industry.—But to return to less speculative and more practical detail.

The state of trade is at present dull; but that there is a great deal of business done must be evident from the quantity of "dry goods" and "grocery stores," many of the proprietors of which have stocks as large as the majority of

London retail dealers. They are literally stuffed with goods of English manufacture, consisting of articles of the most varied kind, from a man's coat or lady's gown, down to a whip or an oyster knife. *Rents*, of course, vary according to situation: houses in the best stands for business are from 400 to 800 dollars per annum; others are from 150 to 350; — two rooms, or a very small house a short distance from town, would be 80 dollars per annum.

It is difficult to form a judgment whether there is an opening in any of the present established businesses. One fact strongly in favour of the stability of this town is, *that there has not been a bankruptcy in it for three years !!!* a singular contrast this with New York, in which the last published list of insolvents contained upwards of 400 names.

Should the establishment of cotton, linen, or woollen manufactories, be thought desirable, the want of machinists, such as you have in England, would be a most material consideration. Persons with such knowledge, and capable of repairing, as well as making *every part* of the machinery, would be necessary; and also the constant personal attendance of the proprietor would be indispensable.

I should have sanguine hopes of the success of an extensive coarse pottery. The freight, carriage, and other expences attending the import of such articles from England to Pittsburgh is now from 100 to 200 per cent. Some are of opinion that a slate quarry may be found three miles from hence; if so, and there were capital and skill engaged, it would prove a fortune. The trade of slating must be united with that of quarrying the material. — Houses are now roofed with shingles, which are dangerous, and not cheap.

Establishments might be advantageously made, in which the following articles would be of primary importance: coal, casting sands of every sort, all kinds of clays, every species of plaister of Paris, of lime, of iron, and of ochres, as they are not difficult of obtainment in Pittsburgh. — Lead is brought from Louisiana, and copper from South America.

Understanding that mechanics in every occupation met at "Carey's Porter-house," I went there several times for the purpose of obtaining information. I found them chiefly English, and all discontented with America. One remark made by the leading *grumbler*, deserves attention. It was elicited by the spirit of opposition. His friend, a stone-mason, said that there was "nothing in America but d——d Yankies and "rogues, and that it was not fit for a dog to live "in;" — "Aye, aye, Bob; you forget that you "were starving in England. Say what you will, "this, after all, is the poor man's country — "it is the poor man's country, Bob." — "Yes;

"it may be well enough for getting pork and "whiskey, and wages, and all that; but curse "the country; it would be a good country "enough if it was free from dirty, cheating "Yankies."

WAGES, &c.

Taylors earn from 31s. 6d. to 45s. per week, are now well employed; carpenter, 31s. 6d. to 40s. 6d., dull; baker, 31s. 6d. to 40s. 6d., dull; mason, 34s. to 45s., brisk; shoemaker, 31s. 6d. to 36., brisk; blacksmith, 31s. 6d. to 36s., dull; tinman, from 36s. to 45s., dull; printer, from 31s. 6d. to 36s., dull; weaver, no employment; glass-blower, 31s. 6d. to 45s., dull; glass-cutter, 31s. 6d. to 67s. 6d., dull; hatter, 31s. 6d. to 45s., brisk; brewer, 36s., dull; nail-cutter, 31s. 6d. to 36s. brisk.

I omitted mentioning that I conceive a brewery, upon an extensive scale, with adequate capital and skill, would succeed extremely well. There are at present three in the business in Pittsburgh, and none of them sell good beer. The mode is similar to that pursued by Messrs. ———, in London. The erection, or purchase of an establishment, in which there should be a steam-engine, with a malt-house and other buildings, would require a capital of not more than from 7 to 15,000 pounds.

Bottled porter is an article in considerable

demand by the emigrants, nearly all of whom take shipping for the more western States, at this place. The use of malt liquors is increasing in all parts of America. Porter in Pittsburgh is eight dollars per barrel, and 6½d. per quart.

THEATRE.

The play of "Hamlet," and the farce of "Turn Out," were acted the evening after my arrival. Upon either I have nothing particular to observe. The acting was equal to the audience, perhaps superior. A son of the celebrated Lewis performed Horatio: he was dead drunk, and extremely dirty. Mrs. Entwistle's acting in the farce, could scarcely have been exceeded by that of Mrs. Davison. Between the acts, two boys, not 14 years of age, were very solemnly discussing what the profits of the house would be monthly, if that night could be taken as an average. From this they took a view of what interest the house paid to its owner. Their calculations were made with the precision of state financiers, and their conclusions drawn with the gravity of sages. After a long dispute, whether the interest were $8\frac{3}{4}$, or $8\frac{7}{8}$ per cent, they determined that the theatre was good property. This occurrence is in perfect accordance with national character. Gain is the education — the morals, the politics, the theology, and stands in the stead of the domestic comfort of all ages and classes of Americans; it is the centre of their system, from which they derive both light and heat.

A few days after the performance of Hamlet, Mr. Entwistle, the manager, had for his benefit, that irresistibly amusing burlesque, "Hamlet "Travestie." His line of acting is a broad-farce caricature of that of Liston. He personated the modern Danish prince. The audience were solemn, serious, and dull. The affecting entrance of the deranged Ophelia, who, instead of rosemary, rue, &c. had an ample supply of turnips and carrots, did not move a muscle of their *intelligent faces*—the ladies, indeed, excepted, who evinced by the frequent use of their pocket handkerchiefs, that their sympathies were engaged on the side of the love-sick maiden. Some who had seen the original Hamlet for the first time a few evenings before, gave vent to their criticisms when the curtain fell. They thought Mr. Entwistle did not look sufficiently grave; and that, as it was his benefit, he acted very dishonourably in shaving (cheating) them out of two acts; for that they guessed when Mr. Hutton played *that 'ere* king's mad son, he gave them five acts for their *dallar*. Mr.——— assured me that on the following morning, a respectable lawyer of Pittsburgh met him, and said, "I was at the play last night, Sir, and do not "think that Mr. Entwistle acted Hamlet quite "so well as Mr. Hutton."

Upon the whole, I consider Pittsburgh, in every point of view, to be a very important town; and have no doubt, although its prosperity is now at a stand, and property if not declining, is not increasing in value, that it will *gradually advance;* and that the time must come when it will be an extensive and very populous city. The present population is 10,000, made up from all nations, and, of course, not free from the vices of each: this indeed is but too apparent upon a very short residence.

A day previous to my departure from Pittsburgh, I called at Carey's Porter-house: Mr. C. stepped forward, and pointing with his hand to a young man, said, "Mr. Watson, Sir." For some minutes I did not comprehend his meaning. The person to whom he directed my attention sat in a corner — silent, serious, and indifferent: he was short in stature and mean in appearance. Guess my surprise when I was informed that this Mr. Watson was no other than *Young Watson;* he, concerning whom, for some months, our whole country was in a general ferment. I felt some curiosity to know the history of a person so singularly thrust into premature importance. His appearance greatly disappointed me, not on account of the poverty of his dress, for that I presume results at present from circumstances beyond his controul; but I had imagined Young Watson to be a daring, bold, enthusiastic, indiscreet young man. He does not seem, however, possessed of any one of these qualities: he is reserved, not from constraint, but habit, and habit of a kind that more bespeaks an absence of talent than the attendant of mind. The ship Venus, in which he went passenger, was hauled to off Dover. Lavender and another Bow-street officer went on board, having certain information that he was there. His face was painted; he had on a farmer's frock coat, stuffed; shoes without heels, looked stouter, shorter, and younger than described in the proclamation. He went on deck upon knowing that officers were looking for him. When he was standing by their side, Miss Wilson, a cabin passenger, fainted. Lavender, ignorant of his person, told him to take care of the lady;—examined the trunks of all the passengers, not excepting that of Watson, who continued supporting Miss Wilson. The officers did not believe but that he was on board, their information being positive; they at length whispered to each other in his hearing, "he is not here;"—they departed;—the ship got under weigh;—he conversed with all concerning *Young Watson.*—Upon arriving in America, Mr. Busby, son of Dr. Busby, who was a cabin passenger, enquired of an Englishman in New York, if young Watson was in America; being answered in the affirmative, he asked by what ship. "The Venus." "No, that is impossible, for I came in "the Venus."—"He certainly came in the "Venus." "Under what name?"—"Thomas "Pearson." "Oh, I know the boy Pearson "very well, we used to call him the proud "farmer." He has got a situation in a school and receives 50l. per annum; is little known and less regarded. Americans who have heard of him either care nothing about or despise him for the political part which he has taken: in these few lines you have the particulars of a young man who has excited in no small degree the public attention. He did not express the least gratitude for the extraordinary assistance which, I presume, he must have received. I asked myself, during his conversation, is it possible that *this* is an individual, one of the foremost among those, to guard against whose mighty machinations, ministers suspended the birthright of Englishmen? But, however, so it was; and in this person we have by no means a novel instance of inexperience combined with fanaticism; neither of which qualities would perhaps ever have been called into action had it not been for the existence of an order of things which deprives a considerable portion of our population of the actual necessaries of life.

STATE OF OHIO.

Left Pittsburgh for Ohio—the State in which every emigrant I saw on the Alleganies told me he designed settling; while there the inhabitants are on "the move" for Alabama and Missouri. Emigration in this country is always in motion, and for ever changing in the points of its attraction. The usual mode of travelling hence is to float down the river, as being the easiest, most economical, and most expeditious. The land route is the most desirable for seeing the country and people. I am now fairly entered upon the western country; a tract which geographers tell us contains fifteen hundred thousand square miles, fifty thousand miles of internal navigation, one hundred thousand of river coast, with an endless intersection of rivers communicating with each other. To the contemplative politician this presents a magnificent spectacle; such an one must feel equally anxious that this almost boundless theatre for human exertion may neither be polluted by political institutions, pernicious and destructive in their own nature, nor present to the world the mockery of the best theoretical principles, which, while apparently possessed by the people, are virtually destroyed by an iniquitous perversion of their spirit.—But leaving general views of politics, I pass on to the particulars of the State of Ohio, and shall detain you with but little of minute description until my arrival at Cincinnati, a town which possesses all the features common to the principal towns of this State.

The face of the country is an uninterrupted level. Many of those tracts of land which would be desirable for our settlement, should we turn agriculturists, are pre-occupied, and cannot be bought without an advance which I think disproportionate to their actual value. The agent at the land-office informs me that there are still for sale one million of acres of United States' land, at two dollars per acre, or one dollar and sixty-four cents for prompt payment. In all the States there are government reservation lands: these are generally in the most choice situations. Some such tracts have been sold in the wild state in Tenesse, at the last auction, for the large sum of 38 dollars per acre!

Taxes on wild land are, on first-rate 2 dollars per hundred acres; $1\frac{1}{2}$ dollar on second-rate; one dollar on third-rate. There is also a county-tax of half the above amounts, as the case may be. These taxes of 6s. 9d. to 13s. 6d. on an hundred acres are certainly very small, at least with our English ideas of taxation and of produce; yet you would be astonished to witness the numerous lots of lands which are sold at auction in all the States on account of *non-payment* of taxes. I have seen lists in the newspapers, and at the taverns, which could not contain less in each than four hundred names of defaulters, whose property was to be transferred to the highest bidder.

I have been offered a lot of six thousand acres on the Little Miami, by Mr. ———, who is removing to Alabama: the terms are not particularly objectionable. Perhaps this would suit us; at least if I do not see any thing more desirable further west.

The section of country bounding on the Ohio river, from 25 miles on either side of Cincinnati, and extending back about 100 miles directly north, to the late Indian boundary line, (which, according to treaty, was extinguished a few days since,) is generally an excellent body of land, and is well settled, though but small improvements are yet made, except in a few particular places near towns. The land is closely timbered, except near the head waters of the two Miamis, where there is a beautiful champaign country. The prairies, or natural meadows, are here of considerable extent. Grazing is the chief occupation of the inhabitants. The price of land varies very much, according to situation and the proximity of townships. Farms which are called *improved* can be bought at from 8 to 30 dollars per acre: the *improvements* often consist of the erection of rough log buildings, and about from 12 to 20 acres under middling cultivation. Buildings are included in the price per acre. The next class of farms have from 20 to 50 acres under cultivation: the proportion of arable and wood is about two-thirds, of meadow and pasturage nearly equal proportions. Any of the land is here capable, by culture, of being turned into meadow. The Miamis are navigable in the spring and autumn. Limestone abounds; coal and iron have not yet been discovered, except in the eastern part of the State. Wheat sells now in the Chillicothe and Cincinnati markets for 3s. 4½d. per bushel; rye, 2s. 8½d.; Indian corn, 2s. 3d.

There are large prairies in Ross county, on the north branch of Paint Creek, near Chillicothe; these prairies are from five to eight miles square: in them there is not a shrub to be seen. They produce a grass growing thick, and about four feet high, which makes excellent fodder: it is similar to Massachusetts upland grass, and is there called English hay. These prairies are filled with herds of cattle fattening for the Baltimore and Philadelphia markets, which are sold in this State, on the hoof, for about 3 dollars per hundred weight. The chief expense of pasturage consists in a man's wages to look after the herds, twice a week, giving them salt, &c.

The principal towns are situated on the banks of the river. There are no canals, and indeed not much occasion for them, the whole State abounding with rivers and creeks, which empty themselves into the Ohio river: produce is conveyed with little expence by this means, during the freshets, or rise of the waters.

The trees produced by the best class of land are honey-locust, black walnut, and beech;—by second quality, sugar-tree, sycamore or butter-wood, and white-wood, used for building and joiners' work;—the third quality produces oak. Throughout this State there is but little under or brush-wood, caused, I presume, by the height and spreading tops of the trees, which prevent the sun penetrating to the ground, and nourishing inferior articles of vegetation. Wood for firing is sold in the towns at from 1½ to 3 dollars per cord (equal in consumption to half a chaldron of coals).

The yearly wages, I am informed, of a labouring man, is from 58l. 10s. to 65l.: of a woman, 31l. 10s.

With regard to the seasons, they are said to have severe winters of from three to four months, with a keen dry air, and cloudless sky; during summer excessive heat, (thermometer in the shade, 80° to 96°,) with heavy dews at night; springs, cold and heavy rains; autumns, fine, followed by "*Indian summer*," which is truly delightful. This I have experienced, and can say that until now I never knew what really fine weather was. Along the route I have travelled, in this State, there is scarcely an elevation which can be called a hill, with exception of slight bluffs on the margin of rivers. The dreary monotony of limited views of such endless uniformity produces sensations of the most depressing melancholy. The atmosphere, after a hot day, causes head-aches, which frequently terminate in an intermittent fever. A man's being *sick*, (the term applied to every species of illness,) is as common in this country, as being in distress is in England. In regard to healthiness of situation, there is considerable variety, as the appearance of the inhabitants will in some measure indicate; though as a general characteristic, I would say, there is a want of sound regular health, at least if our English ideas of ruddy cheeks are to be taken as a criterion. The people are of a tall, *vaulty* aspect, and seem, even during their most active occupations, to be the victims of fever and ague.

Of the existence of minerals, and to what extent and variety, at present but little is known. Judging from the beds of the rivers, and quality of the water, I should presume that coal must be abundant. Salt is found in several situations, particularly on the Kenhaway. The common order of the strata is—first sand-stone, then limestone, argillaceous schist, and coal. The wild animals are neither numerous nor troublesome; though the wolf and the squirrel are still depredators: but the sport afforded in capturing them, and the addition which the flesh of the latter makes to the family stock of provisions, compensate for their lawless invasions of the rights of property.

Land is sometimes partially cleared, by what is rather ludicrously termed a *frolic*. A man having purchased a quarter, or half section, for the purpose of *settling down*, his neighbours assemble upon an appointed day: one cuts the trees; a second lops them; a third drags them to the spot upon which a log mansion is to be erected; others cross the logs, roof the habitation, and in three days the emigrant has a "house over his "head:"—thus ends the American *frolic*. The raising of food is the next point with the new settler: in this he must rely upon his own resources. If he be *strong-handed*, (has property,) he has the trees felled, about one foot from the earth, dragged into heaps, and made into an immense bonfire. Should he be *weak-handed*, (poor,) he is compelled to be content with what is termed *girdling;* which consists in cutting the bark, thereby, of course, killing the trees; and he afterwards clears away the underwood, which is seldom considerable. These preliminary operations being effected, according to either mode, grain is sown, and the produce reaped with a fruitfulness of production, and a dexterity truly extraordinary, considering that these operations are carried on amidst stumps, (which decay in from eight to twelve years,) stones, and surrounded by entire trees. The beauty of an Indian corn crop cannot be exceeded. When cut and carried home, the neighbours assemble to assist in husking; this is called a *husking frolic.* In some parts of the country the term *frolic* admits of a different application; — the religious females present their minister with a variety of gifts, each according to their taste or means: some send a coat, others a hat, and some a goose. They are invited to the preacher's house, to partake of a supper, as a return for their liberality: this is termed a *knitting frolic.* Very little agricultural labour is performed by women. The slender means of many settlers not enabling them to purchase British goods at the high price at which they are sold, the females are therefore chiefly employed in making articles of domestic clothing.

The interior population may perhaps be divided into three classes: *First,* the squatter, or man who "*sets himself down,*" upon land which is not his own, and for which he pays nothing; cultivates a sufficient extent to supply himself and family with the necessaries of life; remains until he is dissatisfied with his choice; — has realized a sufficiency to become a land-owner; — or is expelled by the real proprietor. *Second,* the small farmer who has recently emigrated, had barely sufficient to pay the first instalment for his 80 or 160 acres of two-dollar land; cultivates, or what he calls *improves*, ten to thirty acres; raises a sufficient "feed" for his family; has the females of it employed in making or patching the wretched clothing of the whole domestic circle; is in a condition which, if *compelled by legislative acts, or by external force to endure*, would be considered truly wretched; but from being his own master, having made his own choice, from the having "no one to make "him afraid," joined with the consciousness that, though slowly, he is regularly advancing towards wealth; the breath of complaint is seldom heard to escape from his lips. *Third*, the wealthy or "*strong-handed*" farmer, who owns from five to twelve hundred acres, has one-fourth to one-third under cultivation, of a kind much superior to the former; raises live stock for the home, and Atlantic-city markets; sends beef, pork, cheese, lard, and butter to New Orleans; is perhaps a legislator, at any rate a *squire* (magistrate); is always a man of *plain business-like sense*, though not in possession, nor desirous of a very cultivated intellect; understands his own interest, and that of his country; lives in sufficient affluence, and is possessed of *comfort*, according to the American acceptation of the term, but to which we "*old country*" folks must feel inclined to take an exception: but in conclusion, and a most important conclusion it is, the majority of this class of men were, ten or fifteen years ago, inhabitants of the eastern States, and not worth, upon their arrival in Ohio, twenty dollars.

Well-prepared land in this State produces, per acre, 30 bushels of wheat; 50 to 75, of Indian corn; 50 to 75, of rye. Horses are worth from 40 to 100 dollars (9l. to 22l. 10s.) Cows, (four years old,) 12 to 20 dollars (54s. to 90s.)

The management of farms is full a century behind that of England, there being here a want of improved machinery for the promotion of economy in time and labour, and no regular attention to the condition of live stock, while the mode of culture in general appears slovenly and unsystematic. Cows are milked sometimes twice, sometimes once a day: at others four times a week. Barns are erections which you would not know by that name, and which must materially deterioriate the annual receipts; — upon the whole, Bowles's rude but delightful picture of "The Farm Yard" would be as unintelligible to an Ohian, as it is to the Cockney, whose ideas of a country life are limited to a Sunday's excursion to Chalk-farm and Highbury-barn.

CINCINNATI.

My arrival in the interesting town of Cincinnati was at 10 o'clock at night. I put up at the Cincinnati hotel, on the banks of the Ohio.

When I had remained here half an hour, the bar-keeper informed me that all their beds were engaged. This, at so late a period in the evening, and with the rain pouring in torrents, was not the most agreeable reception, particularly as I had not rested upon a bed for the four previous nights. A gentleman whom I had seen when in Pennsylvania endeavoured to procure me a share in that of his friend, his own being already *doubly* engaged. The negotiation failing, I applied to the bar-keeper to be allowed to remain in the house, though without a bed. To this he assented, and placing some chairs against the wall, with saddle-bags for my pillow, I enjoyed a comfortable night's rest.

Many persons in this State have coloured people, which they call *their property*. The mode in which they effect this perpetuation of slavery, in violation of the spirit of the Ohio constitution, is to purchase blacks, and have them *apprenticed* to them. Some are so base as to take these negroes down the river at the approach of the expiration of their apprenticeship, *and sell them at Natchez for life!*

Yet the first article of the Ohio constitution is, " All men *are born equally free and independent.*"

PRICES.

I visited the public market before the sun had appeared above the horizon. The whole town presented a scene of life and activity. The market-house is an excellent building, and under judicious regulations; but the supply on this occasion was neither various nor profuse. Beef and mutton are from 2d. to 3$\frac{1}{2}$d. per pound; veal, 4d.; pork, 2$\frac{1}{2}$d. to 4$\frac{1}{2}$d.; potatoes, 2s. 3d. a bushel; flour, 27s. a barrel of 196 pounds; fowls, 10d. each; geese, 2s. 3d. each; turkeys, 3s. 4$\frac{1}{2}$d. to 4s. 6d.; moist sugar, 13d. a pound; loaf ditto, 20d.; porter, 27s. to 31s. 6d. per barrel of 32 gallons, 6$\frac{1}{2}$d. per quart; cider, 11s. 3d. per barrel; gin, 5s. 7$\frac{1}{2}$d. per gallon; whiskey, 2s. 8d.; brandy, 13s. 6d. to 18s.; rum, 11s. 3d.; shoes, 13s. 6d. to 15s. 9d. per pair; Wellington boots, 36s. to 40s. 6d.; Hessian ditto, 49s. 6d. to 54s.; superfine blue cloth, 2l. 18s. 6d. to 3l. 7s. 6d. per yard; making a coat, 27s.; hats, of American manufacture, 31s. 6d. to 45s.; rent of two small rooms, 18l. per annum; ditto, of a small house in a third or fourth-rate situation, from 33l. 15s. to 67l. 10s. The general average of houses, in good business situations, is from 90l. to 137l. 10s. per annum: taxes trifling, indeed I could not ascertain their amount; a good evidence that they cannot be oppressive. Women-servants are paid 20s. 3d. to 29s. 3d. per month; men ditto, 63s. to 72s. Mechanic's board and lodging per week, 13s. 6d.; respectable ditto, 18s. to 22s. 6d.; ditto at the best inns, 47s. 3d. These charges are enormously disproportionate to the rate of provisions; although large rents, dear clothing, and high price of labour, are items of no small importance in the hotel and boarding-house keepers' calculations, and for which allowances should fairly be made. The wages of mechanics, in all trades suited to the present condition of the country, vary from 36s. to 45s. per week. Tailors, shoemakers, carpenters, blacksmiths, masons, and saddlers are good trades, and at present are in full employ: these I would distinguish by denominating first-rate; tinmen, bakers, and hatters, second-rate; printers, third-rate; for the weaver there is no employment. A watchmaker, as such, could not obtain a subsistence, watches not being manufactured in America; such a mechanic possibly could get a living by mending watches, and attending to every department of silversmiths' work. It is thought there is an opening for a dyer, there being but one in the town, — an old woman.

You are aware of the sudden rise and improvement of this place; the present population is said to be 10,000; though Mr. Williams, editor of "The Western Spy," told me that he considers it does not exceed eight, including blacks, who are rather numerous. The town is built upon the model of Philadelphia; and should it ever become as large, which I think not improbable, its whole appearance will be more pleasing. There are five churches belonging to Methodists, Episcopalians, Presbyterians, Quakers, and Baptists: two others, large in size, and handsome in appearance, are now erecting.

EDUCATION.

The School-house, when the whole plan is completed, will be a fine and extensive structure. In the first apartment, on the ground-floor, the Lancasterian plan is already in successful operation: I counted 150 scholars, among whom were children of the most respectable persons in the town; or, to use an American phrase, "of the first standing." This school-house is, like most establishments in this country—a joint stock concern. The terms for education, in the Lancasterian department, are, to share-holders, 11s. 3d. per quarter; others, 13s. 6d. There are in the same building three other departments (not Lancasterian); two for instruction in history, geography, and the classics; and the superior department for teaching languages. Males and females are taught in the same rooms, but sit on opposite sides. The terms for the historical, &c. department are—to share-holders, 22s. 6d. per quarter; others, 27s.: there were present 21 males and 19 females. In the department of languages, the charge is —to share-holders, 36s. per quarter; others, 45s.

Teachers are paid a yearly salary by the company: these men are, I believe, New Englanders, as are the schoolmasters in the western country generally.

I also visited a poor half-starved, civil schoolmaster: he has two miserable rooms, for which he pays 22s. 6d. per month: the number of scholars, both male and female, is 28: the terms for all branches 13s. 6d. per quarter: he complains of great difficulty in getting paid; and also of the *untameable insubordination of his scholars.* The superintendant of the Lancasterian school informs me, that they could not attempt to put in practice the greater part of the punishments as directed by the founder of that system.

NEWSPAPERS.

This town produces two newspapers, "The "Western Spy," and "Liberty Hall." The impression of each is said to be 1200 per week. As the terms upon which they are sold are an index to the want of capital, though not of property, in this country, I extract the following statements *verbatim* from the XIVth volume of "Liberty Hall," Nov. 10. 1817.

" The price of this paper is three dollars and fifty cents for
" 52 numbers; but which may be discharged by the pay-
" ment of three dollars *within* the year, or two dollars and
" fifty cents in ADVANCE.

"Subscribers must pay the postage of their papers.

"*Payments in advance being to the mutual interest of both "parties, that mode is solicited.*

"A failure to notify a discontinuance at the expiration of "the time subscribed for, will be considered a new engage-"ment.

"When subscribers wish to discontinue, all arrearages "must first be paid.

"Letters to the Editors must be POST-PAID.

"TERMS OF ADVERTISING: 12 lines, or less, for three "insertions, one dollar: each continuance 25 cents.

"Longer advertisements in the same proportion.

"When a customer's advertising amounts, in the course "of a year, to $ 12 and not exceeding $ 25, a deduction of "20 per cent. will be made; and 25 per cent. on all sums "above $ 25."

Terms from the "White Water Gazette."

"Wheat, Rye, Corn, Oats, Whiskey, Pork, Bacon, "Sugar, Linen, Flax, Feathers, Wool, Beeswax, Tallow, "Candles, Furs, Rags, or CASH (*notes*), at market prices, "and delivered at such places as may be agreed upon, will "be taken in payment for subscriptions."

The type and general execution of the above-named papers are superior to those of Philadelphia; but, in common with all American newspapers, they are extremely uninteresting, relying almost entirely for matter upon advertisements and English news, the latter being always made their leading article. From the paper mentioned above ("Liberty Hall"), and of the same date, I take the following, which is a fair sample of the general contents of every news publication in the United States: —

LATEST FROM ENGLAND.

New York, Oct. 22.

" By the schooner Weymouth, Benedict, in 33 days
" from Liverpool, the editors of the Mercantile Advertiser
" received, at a late hour last evening, the papers of that
" place to the 17th, London to the 15th; and by the Maria
" Theresa, from Havre, French papers to the 13th ultimo,
" all inclusive. They contain no news of moment.

" Accounts from Ireland state, that the typhus fever had
" begun to subside.

" The Prince Regent was landed at Brighton on the 13th,
" having been at sea four days and three nights, during
" which time he visited the coast of France.

" Mrs. Cobbett, with her two sons and three daughters,
" sailed from Liverpool, on the 16th, in the Aurora, for New
" York.

" The papers speak of the universal revival of trade in all
" parts of the kingdom, and particularly of the rise of cotton
" and linen goods.

" Paris papers to the 13th contain nothing of interest.
" Desbands and Chayoux, who plotted the assassination of
" Monsieur and son, had been shot in the plain of Grenoble.

" Lord Wellington had been non-suited in his prosecu-
" tion of the printer of the Ghent Journal, and adjudged to
" pay the costs. It is said the duke had appealed from this
" decision."

TRADE AND MANUFACTURES.

The woollen manufactory, the steam grist-mill, and a glass-house, are on a tolerably large scale: the two former are said not to pay the proprietors. In the main street, *English goods abound in as great profusion as in Cheapside.* A first-rate shop sells every thing; keeps a stock of from 20 to 30,000 dollars; annual returns may be 50,000 dollars, upon half of which they give from 6 to 18 months' credit. Some of their goods they import direct from England, but more commonly purchase at Philadelphia; their journey for which purpose, to and from that city, occupies them three months: goods average 50 days in arriving. A house at Pittsburgh advances money in payment of carriage, and attends to the receipt of the goods by waggon and their shipment by boats, for which the dealer here pays 5 per cent. commission. The credit which they receive at Philadelphia is from six to seven months, but they can seldom pay at the specified time, and are then charged 7 per cent. interest. Shopkeeping has been very profitable, but it certainly is now very much over-done: all complain that trade is extremely dull. I remark what appears to me an universal and most important error in all the stores — too large a stock: by this means tradesmen, in every country, are exposed to lose as much as by bad debts. I find much difficulty in deciding whether any manufactures in which our Yorkshire and Leicestershire friends could engage would be successful: English ascendancy is so strongly established, that America must be tributary for many years to our country. Some of the best-informed inhabitants are of opinion that cotton, woollen, linen, and stocking-making would succeed, if large capital, with competent and varied skill, were employed; but in these opinions I place little confidence.

The imports are — nearly every description of English goods, and some French and India: these are received *via* New Orleans, Baltimore, or Philadelphia; chiefly the two latter cities. The exports are flour, beef, pork, and butter. The town contains two chartered banks and one unchartered, all in respectable credit; a branch of "The United States' Bank" is also just established there; the paper money system has gone beyond all bounds throughout the western country. Specie of the smallest amount is rarely to be seen, and the little which does exist is chiefly *cut* Spanish dollars, which are divided into bits of 50, 25, and 12½ cents. Notes of 3¼d., 6¼d., 13d., and 2s. 2d. are very common; indeed they constitute an important part of the circulating medium. I purchased Cincinnati notes in Pittsburgh at 5 per cent. discount, and Louisville notes at 7½. This does not proceed from want of faith in those banks, nor are the latter esteemed less safe than the former: the increase of discount arises from Louisville being 150 miles farther distant. The same principle applies to every other town, and operates *vice versâ* upon Pittsburgh. The paper of banks which are not chartered, or which are deficient in reputation, can be bought, at similar distances from the place of its first circulation, at from 10 to 40 per cent.

discount: had I sufficiently understood this *trade* when I landed in America, I think I could have nearly paid my expences by merely buying in one town the notes of that to which I was going. There is no difficulty in obtaining them, as there is always a stock on hand at the shavers (brokers) and lottery offices. Had I brought pistoreens (10d. pieces) from Philadelphia, I should have made 25 per cent. by them: they pass here, in consequence of the want of specie, for thirteen pence. Before I leave Cincinnati, let me say, that I think it a very handsome town; a town, in fact, that must astonish every traveller when he recollects how recently it has been established. Mr. Piatt is building a house here which would not disgrace the very first London squares. The number of moderate-sized, well-built brick buildings is considerable; the three markets are excellent establishments; the churches are neat and elegant; the post-office would bear a comparison in its arrangement and management with that of London; some of the streets are paved, others are now paving; ground for building in the town is enormously dear; Mr. Piatt (banker and merchant) informs me that one particular spot, which cost when he first settled here (18 years ago) 30 dollars, is now worth 20,000.

The next consideration is, does this town offer substantial inducement to settlers? I think not; it has advanced rapidly, but it cannot continue to do so; the future progress is certain, but it must be gradual. Property is as high here as in Philadelphia, and all occupations are filled. On the road, every emigrant tells you he is going to Ohio; when you arrive in Ohio, its inhabitants are "moving" to Missouri and Alabama; thus it is that the point for final settlement is for ever receding as you advance, and thus it will hereafter proceed and only be terminated by that effectual barrier — the Pacific Ocean.

KENTUCKY.

Being in the neighbourhood of Kentucky, I felt anxious to see a State that forms so very important a part of the "Western Country;" and although I knew it was a slave State, yet having seen so much of *practical slavery* in those States denominated *free*, I did not anticipate that one in which this deplorable order of things is legalized, could be really worse. In addition to this, I had received an impression that the genuine Kentuckian had many excellent traits of character. Mr. Mellish says that "they resemble "the Irish; are frank, affable, polite, and hos- "pitable in a high degree; they are quick in "their temper, sudden in their resentment, and "warm in all their affections." A variation of character was evident in a trifling occurrence at the first tavern at which I put up: six gentlemen were seated at the dining-room fire drinking wine, and engaged in varied and rational conversation; this was an instance of *sociality* which, common as it may appear to you, *I had not witnessed in my previous western travels.*

I proceeded into the interior with the intention of seeing Lexington and then proceeding to Louisville, but found the roads so excessively bad, winter rapidly approaching, and my objects not half effected, that I relinquished that design. This at the time was a source of regret, as I had imagined Lexington from its high reputation to be a Paris in miniature.

A gentleman, who is a resident of Lexington, had the politeness to forward me the following particulars of the prices of lands in its vicinity.

LANDS, &c.

LANDS depend on a variety of circumstances, such as the distance from the town, the convenience of shipping produce, the contiguity of the same to some populous town, the quality of the land, its water privileges, and the permanency of such streams. A general estimation may be made as follows:—Those within five miles are from twenty to forty dollars per acre; five to ten miles, ten to twenty dollars; ten to fifteen miles, from five to fifteen dollars. This statement supposes *no improvements* to have been made on the land. Such land is computed to produce from fifty to seventy-five bushels of Indian corn per acre, and very frequently one hundred bushels when well tilled. As wheat requires land not so rich, its produce is less, being from twenty to thirty bushels per acre; thirty to forty of oats; twenty to thirty of rye; one thousand to fifteen hundred pounds of tobacco, and about the same quantity of hemp, may be taken as fair averages, although frequently a much greater quantity is produced. "The price of good field negroes is now about "eight hundred dollars. The annual expense of "such hands may be estimated at from seventy-"five to one hundred dollars; ditto for clothing, "at from twelve to fifteen more;—say together, "eighty-seven to one hundred and fifteen, or an "average of one hundred dollars per annum. "Their provisions differ but little from hired "white servants." In general, farmers command a ready cash sale for their produce. The old custom of carrying it to the New Orleans market is nearly superseded by the creation of a new order of tradesmen, who are a medium between the western farmer and the Orleans merchant.

The state of education is improving. The terms are various: the best is 45l. per annum, including board. Schoolmasters of talent and respectability are in demand in Kentucky. Instances exist of their realizing from seven hundred to fourteen hundred dollars per annum.

Rents may be said to be high in Lexington: there are so few persons really poor, that all houses command great prices. Even buildings of mean appearance let for from fifty to five hundred dollars per annum; and stores and shops for *double* these amounts.

The trees of this State are various, and some which I have seen are of a very enormous size. The black oak and honey locust denote the richest lands: they grow thirty feet in height. The white and yellow poplar, and cucumber tree, measure in circumference twenty feet. The general character of the soil is chalk, covered with a stratum of vegetable earth from eight to twelve feet in depth. A want of water in the summer season is much felt, except in the vicinity of great rivers and their principal dependent streams. Indian corn is raised here in vast abundance, and almost without labour. Stock of various kinds is raised for the New Orleans, southern, and Atlantic markets. Thirty thousand hogsheads of tobacco were shipped from this State last season, and eighty thousand barrels of flour; the price of which latter experiences great fluctuation, varying from four to eight dollars per barrel: at present it is six to seven. Pork is well fed, and of excellent quality: the present price is three to four dollars per cwt. Beef is also of good quality, and the stock has received considerable attention by the mixture of English breeds. Whiskey is an extensive article of manufacture: the export of last season was one million of gallons. Cordage, yarn, and bagging, have been important businesses; but European competition has materially decreased their consumption. The following statement of exports for the last season may be considered correct. Such a statement is useful, as aiding us to form an estimate of the productions and wealth of Kentucky.

		Dollars.
Flour and Wheat - - -	amount of	1,000,000
Pork, Bacon, and Lard - - - -		350,000
Whiskey - - - - -		500,000
Tobacco - - - - -		1,900,000
Wool and fabrics o fWool and Cotton - -		100,000
Cordage, Hemp, and fabrics of Hemp - -		500,000
Cattle - - - - - - -		200,000
Horses and Mules - - - - -		100,000
Salt-petre and Gun-powder - - -		60,000
White and Red Lead - - - -		45,000
Soap and Candles - - - - -		27,000
		4,782,000

Being at *Middletown*, in my way to Louisville, I met with Mr. —— and Mr. ——, of Liverpool, together with Dr. B—— and Col. B——, who were going to New Orleans. They had been two days and nearly two nights coming in the stage from Lexington, a distance of about fifty miles. We all went to "Lawes'

Hotel," the following charges and rules of which are posted up in the public-room.

	Dollars.	Cents.
Board for Horse, per year	120	
Ditto, per week	3	
Ditto, per night	0½	
Ditto, single feed	0	18¾
Dinner for Man	0	37
Supper	0	25
Bed	0	12½
Breakfast	0	25
Board, per year	120	
Ditto, per week	3	
Ditto, per day	1	

Rules to be observed by all Gentlemen who choose to board at Lawes' Hotel, Middletown, Kentucky:

1st. All Gentlemen to give in their names to the Bar-keeper.

2d. No Gentleman shall enter the Dining-room until the second bell rings.

3d. No Gambling allowed in the Bed-rooms.

4th. The doors closed at ten o'Clock, except on the night of public amusement.

5th. No Gentleman shall take the Saddle, Bridle, or Harness of another Gentleman without his consent.

TREATMENT OF NEGROES.

A few minutes before dinner, my attention was excited by the piteous cries of a human voice, accompanied with the loud cracking of a whip. Following the sound, I found that it issued from a log barn, the door of which was fastened. Peeping through the logs, I perceived the bar-keeper, together with a stout man, more than six feet high, who was called Colonel ——, and a negro boy about 14 years of age stript naked, receiving the lashes of these monsters, who *relieved* each other in the use of a horse-whip: the poor boy fell down upon his knees several times, begging and praying that they would not kill him, and that he would do any thing they liked: this produced no cessation in their *exercise*. At length Mr. Lawes arrived, told the valiant Colonel and his humane employer, the bar-keeper, to desist, and that the boy's refusal to cut wood was in obedience to his (Mr. L.'s) directions. Colonel ——— said, that "*he did not know what the niggar had done,* "but that the bar-keeper requested his assistance "to whip Cæsar; of course he lent him a hand, "being no more than he should expect Mr. "Lawes to do for him under similar circum-"stances." At table Mr. Lawes said, "that "he had not been so vexed for seven years." This expression gave me pleasure, and also afforded me, as I thought, an opportunity to reprobate the general system of slavery; but not one voice joined with mine; each gave vent in the following language to the superabundant quantity of the milk of human kindness, with which their breasts were overflowing:—

"I guess he deserved all he got."

"It would have been of small account if the "*niggar* had been whipt to death."

"I always serve my b——d *niggars* that way; "there is nothing else so good for them."

It appeared that this boy was the property of

a regular slave-dealer, who was then absent at Natchez with a cargo. Mr. Lawes' *humanity* fell lamentably in my estimation when he stated, "that whipping *niggars*, if they were his own, "was perfectly right, and they always deserved "it; but what made him mad was, that the boy "was left under his care by a friend, and he "did not like to have a friend's *property* in- "jured."

There is in this instance of the treatment of a negro, nothing that in this State is at all singular; and much as I condemned New York, Pennsylvania, and Ohio, when in those sections, I must now give them the character of enlightened humanity, compared with this State, in which such conduct as that I have described is tolerated and approved, and where such public notices as the following, extracted from a newspaper, are of every-day occurrence :—

"20 DOLLARS REWARD.

"RAN AWAY on the 27th instant, a NEGRO MAN "named JACK, about 5 feet 6 or 7 inches high, very stout "made, of a dark complexion, and has several of his fore "teeth rotten or out, about 25 years of age. He was brought "from Lexington, Kentucky, by Messrs. Jacoby and Stone, "*negro traders*, where I think it is likely he will try to get "to. The above reward will be paid on his being appre- "hended and lodged in any gaol, so that I may get him, "together with all reasonable expenses, if brought to the "subscriber. BASIL LAMAR."

Is it possible to read and to hear of these things, without exclaiming, in the indignant language of the poet, who, after describing the miseries of war, adds,

> "Thus man devotes his brother, and destroys;
> "And worse than all, and most to be deplored,
> "As human nature's broadest, foulest blot,
> "Chains him, and tasks him, and exacts his sweat
> "With stripes, that Mercy, with a bleeding heart,
> "Weeps when she sees inflicted on a beast.
> "Then what is man? *And what man seeing this,*
> "*And having human feelings, does not blush*
> "*And hang his head to think himself a man?*"

LOUISVILLE.

Louisville, at the falls of the Ohio, is daily becoming a most important town, being the connecting link between New Orleans and the whole western country. It must soon take the lead of Lexington in extent of population, as it has already done in the rapid rise of town property, the increase of which during the last four years is said to have been two hundred per cent. Rents, prices of provisions, nature of employment, and earnings of mechanics, prices of land in the neighbourhood of the town, &c. do not possess a *difference* of sufficient importance to those given in the previous part of this report, to require minute detail. Mechanics can have immediate employment, and are paid 40s. 6d. to 54s. per week. Shoes that are very inferior in wear, though not in make to English, are from 15s. 3d. to 18s. a pair. Best hats, 36s. to 45s. each; and every other article of clothing in proportion. The population of this town is from 4 to 5,000. Good brick buildings are fast increasing. One of the hotels (Gwathway's) is said to be rented at 6,000 dollars per annum: from 150 to 200 persons dine at this establishment daily. About every tenth house in the main street is a doctor's.

Louisville is said to be improving in health: the prevalent diseases are fever and ague; besides which, the common disorders of this State are consumption, pleurisy, typhus, remittent and intermittent fevers, rheumatism, and dysentery. I do not feel myself competent to confirm or deny the general claim of the Kentuckians to generosity and warmth of character; of their habits I would wish to speak with equal diffidence; that they drink a great deal, swear a great deal, and gamble a great deal, will be apparent to a very brief resident. The barbarous practice of *gouging*, with which they are charged, I have not seen occur, though I have good reason to believe in its existence. They have also another practice, nearly akin to this, called "gander-pulling." This *diversion* consists in tying a live gander to a tree or pole, greasing its neck, riding past it at full gallop, and he who succeeds in pulling off the head of the victim, receives the laurel crown. I think I have heard of a similar *pastime* as practised in Holland; but these are not to be taken as *unmixed* characteristics.* Society is unquestionably improving, and Lexington probably already possesses inhabitants who are polished and refined.

* American newspaper advertisements have frequently the character of singularity, at least to an English conception: as the following one from the "Kentucky Reporter," published at Lexington, possesses, in addition to this quality, a partial illustration of Kentucky society, I copy it for your perusal: —

"TAKE NOTICE,

"And beware of the swindler JESSE DOUGHERTY, who "married me in November last, and some time after mar- "riage informed me that he had another wife alive and be- "fore I recovered, the villain left me, and took one of my "best horses — one of my neighbours was so good as to fol- "low him and take the horse from him, and bring him back. "The said Dougherty is about forty years of age, five feet "ten inches high, round-shouldered, thick lips, complexion "and hair dark, grey eyes, remarkably ugly and ill-natured, "and very fond of ardent spirits, and by profession a noto- "rious liar. This is therefore to warn all widows to beware "of the swindler, as all he wants is their property, and they "may go to the devil for him after he gets that. Also, all "persons are forewarned from trading with the said Dough- "erty, with the expectation of receiving pay from my pro- "perty, as I consider the marriage contract *null* and *void* "agreeably to law: you will therefore pay no attention to "any lies he may tell you of his property in this county. "The said Dougherty has a number of wives living, per- "haps eight or ten, (the number not positively known,) and "will no doubt, if he can get them, have eight or ten more. "I believe that is the way he makes his living.

"MARY DODD.

"Livingston county, Ky. Sept. 5, 1817.—38 at (ch. W. G.)"

In drawing towards the conclusion of my remarks upon Kentucky, I wave the usual important consideration, whether or not emigration here would be desirable; because I am sure that were gold to be obtained in countless quantities for the mere asking, that there is not a man or woman among you who would leave England to become citizens of a slave State; but as Kentucky is perhaps the strongest member of the western body, and must, of necessity, influence its growth and healthfulness, and as in this State the vitally interesting subjects of agriculture and manufactures have received a considerable degree of attention, I forward you an estimate which has been just made by some very judicious men of the state of manufactures in Lexington:—12 cotton manufactories, employing a capital in the whole of 67,500l.; 3 woollen ditto, 32,600l.; 3 paper ditto, 20,250l.; 3 steam grist-mills, 16,875l.; gun-powder mills, 9,000l.; lead factory, 14,800l.; founderies for casting iron and brass, connected with a silver-plating establishment, 9,000l.; 4 hat factories, 15,000l.; 4 coach ditto, 12,600l.; 5 tanners and curriers, 20,000l.; 12 factories for cotton bagging and hempen yarns, 100,400l.; 6 cabinet-makers, 5,600l.; 4 soap and candle factories, 12,150l.; 8 tobacco factories, 11,450l.; sundry others, 120,000l.; total amount of capital employed in the manufactories of Lexington, 467,225l.

I believe that the capitalist could employ his money to much advantage in Kentucky. Perhaps, in the way of manufacturing, hat-making might be suggested. Farming is lucrative, as is also distilling. A good woollen dyer is wanted. Oil crushing mills are established, but upon principles which are susceptible of great improvements; the part which affords what is termed the oil-cake is thrown away. Flax and hemp seed sell from 2s. 3d. to 2s. 8½d. per bushel. The price of boating goods from New Orleans to Louisville (distance 1412 miles), is from 18s. to 22s. 6d. per hundred. The freight to New Orleans from hence, is 3s. 4½d. to 4s. 6d. per hundred. The average period of time which boats take to go to New Orleans, is about 28 days; that from New Orleans, 90 days. Steam-vessels effect the same route in an average of 12 days down, and 36 days up, when their machinery does not meet with an accident.

HOTELS.

Having been twice at Louisville, I boarded at both the hotels (Allen's, Washington Hall, and Gwathing's, Indian Queen): they are similar establishments, both upon a very large scale, the former having an average of 80 boarders per day, the latter of 140: their charges are—breakfast, 1s. 8d.; dinner, 2s. 3d.; supper, 1s. 8d.; bed, 13d.; if fire in room, an extra charge of $6\frac{3}{4}$d. per night; board and lodging, per day, 6s. 9d.; ditto per day for three months certain, 4s. 6d. Such charges, with an immense extent of business, must insure a man, moderately careful, a large fortune. These hotels are conducted differently from those with which you are acquainted. A person desiring to put up at one of them, applies to the bar-keeper, and he must not feel disappointed should he be refused admittance from want of room. The place for washing is in the open yard, in which there is a large cistern, several towels, and a negro in attendance. The sleeping-room commonly contains from 4 to 8 bed-steads, having mattrasses, but frequently no feather-beds; sheets of calico, two blankets, a quilt (either a cotton counterpane, or made of patchwork); the bedsteads have no curtains, and the rooms are generally unprovided with any conveniences. The public rooms are — a news-room, a boot-room, in which the bar is situated, and a dining-room. The fires are generally surrounded by parties of about six, who gain and keep possession. The usual custom is to pace up and down the news-room in a manner similar to walking the deck at sea. Smoking segars is practised by all without an exception, and at every hour of the day. Argument or discussion in this part of the world is of very rare occurence; social intercourse seems still more unusual; conversation on general topics, or the taking enlarged and enligmened views of things, rarely occurs; each man is in pursuit of his own individual interest, and follows it in an *individualized* manner. — But to return to the taverns: at half past seven, the first bell rings for the purpose of collecting all the boarders, and at eight the second bell rings; breakfast is then set, the dining-room is unlocked, a general rush commences, and some activity, as well as dexterity, is essentially necessary to obtain a seat at the table. A boy, as clerk, attends to take down the names, in order that when bills are settled no improper deduction should be made. The breakfast consists of a profuse supply of fish, flesh, and fowl, which is consumed with a rapidity truly extraordinary; often before I had finished my first cup of tea, the room, which when I had commenced was crowded to suffocation, had become nearly empty.

At half-past one, the first bell rings, announcing the approach of dinner; the avenues to the dining-room become thronged. At two o'clock the second bell rings, the doors are thrown open, and a repetition of the breakfast scene succeeds. At six, tea, or what is here called supper, is announced, and partaken of in the same manner. This is the last meal, and usually affords the same fare as breakfast. A billiard table adjoins the hotel, and is generally well occupied. At ten o'clock, nearly all have gone to bed, or what they call "*turned in.*" At table there is neither conversation nor yet drinking; the latter is effected by individuals taking their solitary "eye openers," "toddy," and "phlegm dispersers," at the bar, the keeper of which is in full employ from sun-rise to bed-time. A large tub of water, with a ladle, is placed on the bar, to which customers go and help themselves. When spirits are called for, the decanter is handed, and you take what quantity you please; the charge is always 6¼d. It is never drunk *neat,* or with sugar or warm water. The life of boarders at an American tavern, presents the most senseless and comfortless mode of killing time which I have ever seen. Every house of this description that I have been in is thronged to excess, and there is not a man who appears to have a single earthly object in view, except spitting and smoking segars. I have not seen a book in the hands of any person since I left Philadelphia. Objectionable as these habits are, they afford decided evidence of the prosperity of that country, which can admit so large a body of its citizens to waste in indolence three-fourths of their lives, and would also appear to hold out encouragement to Englishmen with *English habits,* who could retain their industry amid a nation of indolence, and have sufficient firmness to live in America, and yet bid defiance to the deadly example of its natives.

When at Gwathway's hotel, I had the pleasure of meeting with Lord Selkirk: he was on his return from his unsuccessful expedition in the north-western territory. I procured for him, from the respectable house of Vernon and Blake, some Boston papers which were only two months old: they contained, as usual, English news. He had not heard any intelligence from Europe for nine months, and was therefore much pleased with the novelty. During my first visit to this town, I addressed a letter to Mr. Birkbeck, at either Princeton or Vincennes, not having determined at that time to visit Illinois. On leaving Kentucky, I have to regret that so much remains to be done for the habits of the people, and to feel from my soul the most sincere sorrow, that men who can form a theoretic constitution, in which it is declared, that "men when they form a social "compact are equal; that no man or set of men "are entitled to exclusive, separate public "emoluments or privileges from the community, "but in consideration of public services; that "all men have a natural and indefeasible right "to worship God according to the dictates "of their consciences;" I cannot, I say, but feel sorrow that men who can in theory lay down such principles, can in their practice continue, and even boast of the most demoralizing habits, treat their fellow-creatures worse than brute beasts, and buy and sell human beings like cattle at a fair.

In quitting this State, I can by no means coincide with Mr. Mellish, when he says "The "*only* serious evil that I had to complain of in "my journey through this country, arose from "the proneness of many of the natives to "swearing." If this be a fact, I cannot envy Mr. Mellish his feelings, although his love for universal liberty is so great, that he could neither remain in England, nor bear to set his foot in Canada. Neither can I agree with this *profound* philanthropist, that "these sad doings "are outdone every day by transactions in "the capital of a nation *who think themselves* "*the most polished on earth*, and some of these "even supported and encouraged by the "Corinthian capitals of polished society." Mr. Mellish calls Mr. Ashe "*a hireling*." When I find a writer at times thus blindly glossing over the most glaring faults, and at others enlarging and exaggerating, and finding excellencies and signs of prosperity which only exist in his own imagination, I confess I am inclined to suspect that he is himself a candidate for an occupation by no means dissimilar to that which he thus attributes to his rival traveller.

ILLINOIS TERRITORY.

After a long and fatiguing journey, I have at length reached the Illinois territory, which in all probability will soon become the twentieth State of this flourishing Republic. In my report from Philadelphia, sent in the Electra, and which I calculate you will receive by about the 12th December, I forwarded all the information of which I was then in possession. Though I have seen a large portion of this interesting continent, my mind is by no means yet made up concerning it. I have in fact come to no decision, and can as yet, at least, make no final report of the country, or its inhabitants. I feel that my residence here has been too brief to enable me correctly to form a judgment upon what is, in more senses of the expression than one, "a new world," or fully to comprehend a land and a people essentially different from those I have been accustomed to contemplate. Acting under this impression, therefore, I would wish, at least for the present, to give you, as far as lies in my power, facts from which you may form your own judgment, and be enabled hereafter, perhaps, the better to see the propriety of mine: I shall proceed, therefore, as before, in giving extracts from my journal, which I have kept with minute exactness from Philadelphia to this place.

Although it was not a part of our original views that I should have visited the Illinois territory; yet conceiving the practicability of a comfortable settlement in the eastern States extremely questionable, and finding that the *old* settled States, even on this side of the mountains, offered not much greater encouragement, property in all the towns which are possessed of reasonable advantages having attained the full amount of Philadelphian value, and, in the country, speculators having laid their hands upon a vast number of fine tracts, I thought it best to seek elsewhere; not that in the States of Ohio, &c. there was no land yet to be purchased at government prices; but it appeared to me, that if a removal from England should become, under all circumstances, our duty, and if, as was by no means improbable, we should be induced to mark out a new channel for our exertions, by becoming agriculturists, it would be no great addition to our privations to proceed a little farther west than Ohio, where, if we could not find cheaper lands, we should at least have a greater variety for selection, and possess all the advantages enjoyed by the first proprietors of well-chosen sections. With these impressions I have advanced thus far, and am now anxious to close this report in time for the post, previous to the farther pursuit of my objects. As it is written close, and on very thin paper, I trust the postage will not be extravagant. It will go by way of New York, inclosed to the care of Messrs. ——— of that city. I pass over Indiana, a State to which there exist some strong objections that may be detailed in my next. The territory of Illinois, though but very thinly populated, has been inhabited at Kaskaski, and a few other places, for many years, originally, I believe, by the French from Canada.

The mean breadth of the territory is said to be 200 miles, length 350, lying between N. latitude 36° 30′ and 42°. The Ohio river is its southern boundary, extending from the mouth of the Wabash to the junction of the former with the Mississippi, a distance of 150 miles. The Mississippi forms the western boundary, stretching from the above junction to the rocky hills, a distance of 600 miles, following the course of that river, but the windings are so great that the real distance is much less. The Wabash river separates Illinois from Indiana: an imaginary line, which it is proposed shall extend due east from the Rocky Hills, will separate it from the north-western territory. The number of acres is calculated to be 35,000,000; that of square miles, 50,000. Exertions are now making to have this territory admitted into the Union, and you will join with me in praying that slavery may not form a part of its constitution, as, should it do so, that, I conceive, will form an insurmountable barrier to the emigration of every man possessed of a humane or independent mind. The population, I am informed, is at present chiefly on the Wabash, below Vincennes, and on the banks of the Kaskaski, Ohio, and Mississippi rivers. The means of internal navigation, without the expence of cutting canals, are truly extraordinary; added to which, the facilities of export afforded by those "fathers of waters," the Ohio, Mississippi, and Missouri, present a picture of future greatness dazzling to conceive — impossible to estimate.

The estimated courses of the waters of this territory are, in length,

Wabash,	-	230 miles.
Mississippi,	-	600
Ohio,	-	150
Illinois,	-	300
Kaskaski,	-	300
Various tributaries,		1400
		2980 miles.

Amount of internal navigation, 2000 miles; ditto of frontiers, 1000; the distance from Shawnee Town *by water* to Buffalo, through the lakes, 1200 miles; ditto from the same place to New Orleans, 1130: thus securing a most immense *internal* water communication, as well as a direct one with the ocean; the face of the country must, in so large an extent, possess considerable variety. The general surface of the lands in the Shawnee Town and Kaskaski districts, and in the neighbouring parts of the Illinois, is more than ordinarily level, though to this there are some exceptions. The alluvial lands of both the Ohio and Mississippi rivers occasionally terminate in bluffs, in some places high and craggy, in others more gradual in their rise, and easy of ascent. There are throughout the State a vast number of *prairies*, of boundless extent, and presenting a most delightful contrast to the sombre character of an American wilderness. The soil is infinitely more varied than the face of the country. It has been classified by some as follows: 1st. Hills of a barren soil, and covered with pines and small oaks. 2d. Moderately hilly land, and well watered. 3d. Wet prairies, which are remote from streams, the soil cold and barren, abounding with swamps, ponds, and covered with a tall coarse grass. 4th. Dry prairies, bordering the rivers, lie, on an average level, higher by 60 feet, are from three to fifteen miles wide, and possess a rich soil, well adapted for cultivation. These natural meadows are generally destitute of trees, except where crossed by streams. Some have clusters of trees, which may be denominated, what they very much resemble — islands, though upon *terra firma*. The prairies of this territory are said to cover more than a million of acres. The soil in some places assumes the hue of iron rust, interspersed with a light sand. 5th. Unripe alluvial, which bears sycamore, water-maple, ash, and willow. This land is generally found at the mouths and confluences of rivers, and, as a place of residence, in the present uncleared state of the country, is considered as highly injurious to health. 6th. Ripe alluvial. This land is of the best quality, and is found in various degrees of extent on all the rivers. It bears honey locust, pecan, black walnut, and sugar maple trees. In autumn, the fruit and leaves of the black walnut are said to produce an agreeable flavour. This land is considered to be remarkably fertile, in proof of which some part of it is asserted to have been cultivated to profit without manure, for the last hundred years.

Squirrels, racoons, foxes, deer, wolves, and bears abound; as do wild turkeys and quails; geese and ducks partially; hawks, buzzards, and pigeons in tolerable quantities; the rivers contain several species of fish; in the prairies there are rattle-snakes; the woods supply grapes, pecan nuts (similar to our walnut), and hickery nuts; hops, raspberries, and strawberries grow wild; there are several salt ponds — the produce is sold at the saline works, 26 miles below the Wabash, for 3s. 4½d. per bushel. The annual produce of this establishment is from one to two hundred thousand pounds. Copper and lead have been found. The French, when in possession of this territory, procured mill-stones near the Illinois lake. Coal has been discovered; and also white clay.

ILLINOIS TOWNS.

Kaskaski, the seat of the territorial government, contains about 150 houses, built on a plain; some of them are of stone. This town is 150 miles from Vincennes, and 1000 from Washington. The inhabitants are chiefly French: their principal occupation is raising stock. This town has been settled more than a century.

Shawnee Town (from which I now am writing), about 30 houses (log). The chief occupation of the inhabitants is the salt trade. There is here a "United States' Land-office," and a log bank is just established. The chief cashier of this establishment was engaged in cutting logs at the moment of my arrival.

Wilkinson Ville, a miserable settlement, takes its name from General Wilkinson, who, in 1801, established a station here for the American troops; it then prospered, but has since fallen into complete decay. The other towns of this territory are—*Cahokia*, containing 150 small houses, chiefly inhabited by French. *St. Philip*, fifty miles from Cahokia, is smaller but more pleasant. *Prairie du Rochers*, containing 60 French families : this is a fine prairie. There are also three very small places, called Belle Fontaine, L'Aigle, and Edward's Ville.

The lands belonging to the Indians lie chiefly between the Wabash and Illinois rivers. They have considerable reservations north of the Illinois river. The United States have lately obtained a cession of six miles square, at the end of Peoria lake. The aborigines now remaining are the Soukies, who have three villages; — their number is about 3000. The Kaskaskians, Cahokias, and Peorias, are much decreased in numbers, in consequence of their wars with the Soukies and Foxes.

Private sales at the Land-office are here, as in all other parts of the Union, fixed at 2 dollars, or 1 dollar 64 cents, for prompt payment. The public sales by auction have not, for the most choice tracts, exceeded six dollars per acre: the old French settlements are from one to fiftty dollars per acre. The land-tax is levied on the same principle as described in Ohio. The military bounty lands in this State amount to 3,500,000 acres. They are appropriated to the soldiers who were engaged in the late war, and are frequently sold by them in the eastern States, for a quarter and a half dollar per acre. Indian corn (maize) is the leading article of produce. There are some fields of 500 acres, cultivated in common by the people of a whole settlement. Wheat is abundant, except where the soil is too rich. Flax, hemp, oats, potatoes, and cotton are also productive, giving very considerable crops. The French have made excellent wine from a wild grape, which grows here luxuriantly. Indian corn, I am informed, produces, with moderate care, and in a favourable soil, 50 to 70 bushels per acre; wheat, 20 to 30; barley, 20 to 30; oats, 30 to 50; tobacco, 10 to 13 hundred. Indian corn sells from 13d. to 16½d. per bushel; wheat, 3s. 4½d.; oats, 19½d.; tobacco, 20s. 3d. per hundred. The price of horses is from 13l. 10s. to 18l.; cows, 4l. to 5l.; a good sow, 2l. 14s.; beef is sold at 22s. 6d. per hundred; pork, 15s. 9d. to 18s. Labourers are paid 2s. 3d. per day, and board. Clothing and groceries are extremely dear. Indian corn is gathered in November. Wheat is cut in June, and housed in July. Pork for export is killed in December. Freight from this place *to* Louisville (distance 307 miles) is 5s. per cwt; *from* Louisville, 1s. 8d.; *from* hence *to* New Orleans, (distance 1130 miles,) 4s. 6d.; *from* New Orleans, 20s. 3d.; hence *to* Pittsburgh, (distance 1013 miles,) 15s. 9d.; *from* Pittsburgh, 4s. 6d. This vast disproportion in charge of freight is produced by the difference in time, in navigating *up* and *down* the streams of the Ohio and Mississippi.

I have not had sufficient experience in these

back woods, to feel confidence in the following estimate of expences for erecting a residence; it is, however, the most authentic that I have been enabled to procure. A log cabin of two rooms can, I am informed, be raised for 11l. 5s. to 16l.; a frame house, 10 to 14 feet square, for 130l. to 150l.; a log kitchen, 7l. to 8l.; a log stable, 7l. to 9l.; a barn, 18l. to 22l.; fencing, 13d. per rood; ditching, in prairie land, 16d. to 2s. per rood.

INHABITANTS OF ILLINOIS.

The inhabitants of Illinois may, perhaps, be ranked as follows: First, the Indian hunters, who are neither different in character or pursuits from their ancestors in the days of Columbus. 2d, The "Squatters," who are half-civilized and half-savage. These are, in character and habits, extremely wretched: indeed, I prefer the genuine *uncontaminated* Indian. 3d, A medley of land-jobbers, lawyers, doctors, and farmers, who traverse this immense continent, founding settlements, and engaging in all kinds of speculation. 4th, Some old French settlers, possessed of considerable property, and living in ease and comfort.

Concerning the state of society, my experience does not allow me to say much, or to speak with confidence. Generally, I suspect that the powers of the legislature are, as yet, weak in their operation. Small provocations insure the most relentless and violent resentments. Duels are frequent. The dirk is an inseparable companion of all classes; and the laws are robbed of their terror, by not being firmly and equally administered. A general character of independence, both as to the means of living and habits of society, appears universal. Here, no man is either thought or called " master;" neither, on the other hand, is there found any coarse vulgarity. A cold, selfish indifference is the common characteristic of the labourer and the judge; and I should hope that Illinois-State constitution will not, when formed, authorize and legalize slavery; yet the Ohio practice will, I have no doubt, continue as it *now is* in Illinois, — *indenturing negroes for a term of from* 10 *to* 15 *years.* This baleful practice promises a perpetuation of *practical* slavery throughout America.

Of the *climate* I know but little from personal experience. The mornings and evenings, at this time, are extremely cold. In July and August Fahrenheit ranges from 85° to 105°. In the winter (which is not long), from 10below to 20 above zero. The wildness of the country implies an *unformed* climate. The disturbance of a great body of surplus vegetable matter, upon the first settling of land, together with the dampness arising from stagnant waters, frequently produce bilious fevers and agues.

My mind continues undecided concerning our removal. When in England I had hoped, in common with yourselves, that the old settled States of America, which must be so much better suited to our habits and pursuits than an uncultivated wilderness, would have afforded sufficient inducement to emigration, particularly as our objects are the continuance in well-established habits of industry, and not rapid fortune-making. With the means of forming a judgment on this subject, I have endeavoured, as far as lies in my power, to supply you in the course of my preceding reports.

Should your minds be favourable to a western country settlement, I should wish to press upon your deliberate re-consideration the following ideas:

First,—Is it essential to your prosperity and happiness that you should leave England?

Second,—Do the habits and character of the American people afford you rational grounds for desiring to become their fellow-citizens?

Third,—Have all of you the dispositions requisite in order to become cultivators of a wilderness?

Fourth,—Assuming that you have those dispositions, are you fitted for such an entire change of pursuits, and can you endure the difficulties and dangers necessarily attendant on such a situation?

If, after cool, deliberate, and rational consideration, with your minds as free from enthusiastic expectations connected with this continent, as they well can be under the existence of the present order of things in England, you can answer in the affirmative, then I have little doubt of the propriety of recommending to your attention the Illinois territory.

P. S. Should I resolve upon taking New Orleans in my route to Washington, I shall most likely address you from the former city.

SIXTH REPORT.

Leave the Territory of Illinois for New Orleans. — City of Natchez. — Boat-Loads of Negroes for Sale. — Prevalence of British Goods. — Habits, and State of Morals. — Embark on board Steam-Boat " Orleans." — Mississippi River; its Scenery. — Arrival at New Orleans. — Vast Importance to the Western Country. — Habits, Character, Morals, Amusements. — The Mayor's barbarous Proclamation concerning Negroes. — Leave New Orleans for the City of Washington. — A Review of the Western Country. — Character of Tradesmen. — Mode of employing Capital. — Arrival in Washington. — Its Situation. — Fine Scenery. — Capitol and President's House. — British Crusade. — Effects in increasing the Prosperity of this City. — Aristocratical Absurdity of the original Plan of the City. — Population. — George Town and Alexandria. — Price of Provisions. — Rents. — Mechanics. — Prevalence and Price of British Goods. — Paper almost the only Currency. – The " Virginian Dynasty." — English Ambassador. — Mr. Clay. — Presdent's Drawing-Room. — Habits. — Customs. — The Theatre. — Incledon. — Indian Juggler. — Cobbett and his Friend of Philadelphia. — His ill Treatment by the Legislature of Pennsylvania, and his Statement of their political Corruption. — American Manufactures; their present ruinous State. — Capital employed during the late War. — Veterans of the Revolution. — General St. Clair. — Attend both Houses of Congress. — Their Forms; Members; Subjects discussed. — Corruption in Caucus *Election of President. — General Harper's and Mr. Rufus King's Speeches upon the Subject. — Poet Moore. — Opposition to Napoleon. — — European Politics of Washington. — Mr. Birkbeck's Letter to myself.*

State of Virginia, and Washington City,
February and March, 1818.

At the date of my last, in December, I had not left the Illinois. Since my departure from that territory to the present time, I have travelled a vast distance, and I lament to say that there is little of it which I, or indeed any man among you, could be induced to make a permanent settlement. The white population are the victims of demoralizing habits. The native Indians present, of course, nothing but a picture of mere savage life; and the poor negroes suffer even more than commonly falls to the lot of their oppressed and degraded condition. What a foul stain upon the republic, professing, as it does, the principles of liberty and equal rights, that, out of twenty States, there should be eleven in which slavery is an avowed part of their political constitution; and that in those *called free* (New England excepted) the condition of blacks should *practically* amount to slavery! Like the Greeks of old, they talk of freedom, while the degraded Helot is within their doors.

Previous to entering into details concerning this city, I would wish to call your attention to two others, certainly not under any idea of their being suitable places for emigration, but in consequence of their immediate and important connection with the whole western country. First,

NATCHEZ, in the State of Mississippi; and second, NEW ORLEANS, on the Mississippi River, one hundred miles above its entrance into the Gulph of Mexico. *Natchez* stands on a bluff, about 250 yards above the level of the river; a situation, from what I have seen, very unusual on the Mississippi, the greater part being level, and often overflowing its banks. The landing-place is on the river edge, about half a mile from the town. At this place there are about thirty houses, the greater part of which are whiskey shops, gambling and other houses, in which there is a degree of *open* profligacy, which I had not before witnessed in the United States. While contemplating this melancholy scene, my attention was directed to the number of boats which were then in port. They consisted of twenty-five flats, seven keels, and one steam-vessel. The flat, I should explain, is a square, covered vessel, of considerable capacity, used for carrying freight from Pittsburgh, and other places below that town, down to New Orleans; their construction is temporary, and of slight materials, being broken up at New Orleans, as not sufficiently strong to be freighted *up* the river. The keel is a substantial, well-built boat, long, and in form resembling the floating bath at Blackfriars Bridge.

Observing a great many coloured people, particularly females, in these boats, I concluded that they were emigrants, who had proceeded thus far on their route towards a settlement. The fact proved to be that fourteen of the flats were freighted with human beings for sale. They had been collected in the several States by slave-dealers, and shipped from Kentucky for a market. They were dressed up to the best advantage, on the same principle that jockeys do horses upon sale. The following is a specimen of advertisements on this subject: —

" TWENTY DOLLARS REWARD,

" Will be paid for apprehending and lodging in gaol, or de-
" livering to the subscriber, the following slaves, belonging
" to JOSEPH IRVIN, of *Iberville*: —

" TOM, a very light Mulatto, blue eyes, 5 feet 10 inches
" high, appears to be about 35 years of age, an artful fellow
" — can read and write, and *preaches* occasionally.

" CHARLOTTE, a black wench, round and full faced,
" tall, straight, and likely — about 25 years of age, and wife
" of the above-named Tom.

" These slaves decamped for their owner's plantation, on
" the night of the 14th September inst.

" WILLIAM KENNER & Co."

The treatment of the negroes throughout these States is as villainous as can be well imagined; and although they are themselves not insensible to the evils of their condition, they do not seem to feel it so acutely as might be anticipated, or as the man of common humanity would feel on their account. This, however, is natural enough, and easy to account for. As the body is enslaved, the mind becomes degraded, and loses a sense of its own dignity, and of the value of independence.

I observe that there are a few native Indians who raise cotton, *and hold slaves;* others (but only women) are hired to pick the cotton, their fathers or husbands receiving their wages. No male Indian would submit to the supposed degradation of being in the employ of any one. — A man possessed of from 2 to 10,000l. capital, with a pliable conscience, above the common feelings of humanity, and whose only object is gain, would soon realize, by the culture of cotton in this district, a very large fortune.

There are here numerous stores; three-fourths of the stock of every one consist of British goods. Shopkeeping is profitable. Mechanics are very highly paid, and at this time much wanted, in consequence of their having, more than the other classes of society, fallen victims to the late contagious disorders. — "Packwood's "razor strops" have even penetrated into this remote quarter of the globe: the negro barbers do not omit making that circumstance a leading point of attraction.

Lotteries are as prevalent here as in the eastern States; the one carrying on at this time is for *building a Presbyterian church!* The "scheme" is preceded by a long address upon the advantages of religion, and the necessity of all citizens supporting Christianity by purchasing tickets in this *holy* lottery ! !

The church-yard is opposite to Irvine's hotel (at which I stopped). Two young men that were standing at the door had been warmly engaged in a debate ; one was a resident in Natchez, the other not so ; their subject of controversy was the healthiness of the city ; the latter contended that it was sickly ; his friend could not endure so foul an aspersion upon his native town ; the other explained that he did not mean any thing personal, but he considered Natchez was sickly, and as a strong proof that his opinion was correct, he pointed to the church-yard, in which one-fourth of the late population had been entombed in the course of five weeks. This explanation was of no avail — he should *call him out* for daring to say that *his* city was sickly ; to be sure, five hundred people *had* died in a short time, but men did not live for ever, even among the Yankies (New England). " I say, " Sir, that there is not a more healthy place in " the world than Natchez." — I find it indeed a universal trait of character, that no American will allow any place to be so healthy as the one in which he resides. — Upon the whole I leave Natchez with little knowledge of its inhabitants indeed, but with an impression of its comparative prosperity exceeding any town which I have ever seen. The streets are literally crammed with cotton bales for the Liverpool market, they are carried to the water-side in carts drawn by two mules, horses being little used,—in consequence, it is said, of the severe chastisement usually inflicted upon them by negro drivers; thus these much-injured men revenge upon the dumb animal the wrongs they themselves receive from their common owner. During my residence at this town I twice visited the State legislature, which is composed of men who appear any thing but legislators. Their place of meeting was in a kind of superior hay-loft. The imitation of the forms of the British parliament was rather ludicrous:—the only business transacted during my stay was the election of a sergeant-at-arms!

NEW ORLEANS.

Viewing this city as intimately connected with the considerations of a western country colony, I felt desirous of seeing it. I was aware, besides, that this would be desirable to assist my judgment in forming a correct estimation of the whole American people; for I feel persuaded, that for myself I could not make up a final judgment without personal acquaintance with the entire "body politic." The steam-boat "Orleans" being upon the point of departure, I engaged a place for New Orleans—fare, including board, 3l. 7s. 6d.; distance 300 miles; time 56 hours.

The scenery of the Mississippi in the immediate neighbourhood of Natchez is interesting: till within a few miles of that city it becomes extremely dull, being a dead flat, with banks overflowed; for 150 miles, until we came near Point Caupee church, we were moving through an immense and dreary forest, without openings or breaks of any kind, destitute of variety, and only producing by its sombre monotony the most melancholy sensations.

Approaching to New Orleans, a more civilized country than I had previously seen presented itself, though there were (according to the old story) no men hanging in chains. The banks were cultivated, settlements multiplied, good houses were not uncommon: while numerous extensive sugar plantations bespoke wealth and population. Upon my arrival at *New Orleans*, it is hardly possible to conceive the delight which I experienced; after a tedious and dreary journey, even the masts of ships afforded me pleasure, as recalling by association what I should now denominate the *comforts* of New York and Philadelphia. The increase of this city since it has become a part of the United States is truly extraordinary, affording another proof of the advantages possessed by a people who are unshackled. Originally its trade was conducted by men who purchased the right of monopoly from the parent country, or the viceroys and governors. While this enriched the few, it of course impoverished the many, and was wholly inconsistent with general prosperity. Trade is a plant that can only luxuriantly flourish in a free soil. Under the government of America, every man is left to pursue the bent of his own inclination, and to go to the full extent of his means; — there exists no monopoly, except that which superior talent or property always must, and always ought to confer. The consequence of this state of things is, that the United States are making unprecedented strides towards substantial wealth and national greatness, though cursed, as I am sorry — mortified to the heart to be obliged to confess, with a population undeserving of their exuberant soil and free government.

The French language is still predominant in New Orleans. The population is said to be 30,000; two-thirds of which do not speak English. The appearance of the people too was French, and even the negroes evinced, by their antics, in rather a ludicrous manner, their connection with the natives of that nation.

The general manners and habits are very relaxed. The first day of my residence here was Sunday, and I was not a little surprised to find in the United States the markets, shops, theatre, circus, and public ball-rooms open. Gambling houses *throng* the city: all coffee-houses, together with the exchange, are occupied from morning until night by gamesters. It is said, that when the Kentuckians arrive at this place, they are in their glory, finding neither limit to, nor punishment of their excesses. The general style of living is luxurious. Houses are elegantly furnished. The ball-room, at Davis's hotel, I have never seen exceeded in splendour. Private dwellings partake of the same character; and the ladies dress with expensive elegance. The sources of public amusement are numerous and varied; among them I remark the following:

" INTERESTING EXHIBITION.

" On Sunday the 9th inst. will be represented in the place " where Fire-works are generally exhibited, near the Circus, " an extraordinary fight of *Furious Animals.* The place " where the animals will fight is a rotunda of 160 feet in cir- " cumference, with a railing 17 feet in height, and a circular " gallery well conditioned and strong, inspected by the " Mayor and surveyors by him appointed.

" 1st *Fight* — A strong Attakapas Bull, attacked and " subdued by six of the strongest dogs of the country.

" 2d *Fight* — Six Bull-dogs against a Canadian Bear.

" 3d *Fight* — A beautiful Tiger against a black Bear.

" 4th *Fight* — Twelve dogs against a strong and furious " Opeloussas Bull.

" If the Tiger is not vanquished in his fight with the Bear, " he will be sent alone against the last Bull; and if the latter " conquers all his enemies, several pieces of fire-works will " be placed on his back, which will produce a very enter- " taining amusement.

" In the Circus will be placed two Manakins, which, not- " withstanding the efforts of the Bulls to throw them down, " will always rise again, whereby the animals will get " furious.

"The doors will be opened at three and the Exhibition "begin at four o'clock precisely.

"Admittance, one dollar for grown persons, and 50 cents "for children.

"A military band will perform during the Exhibition.

"If Mr. Renault is so happy as to amuse the spectators "by that new spectacle, he will use every exertion to diver- "sify and augment it, in order to prove to a generous "public, whose patronage has been hitherto so kindly be- "stowed upon him, how anxious he is to please them."

I visited the theatre: it is an old building, about two-thirds the size of the little theatre in the Haymarket. The play was "John of "Calais," well performed by a French company to a French audience. At a tavern opposite I witnessed a personal conflict, in which I suppose one of the parties was *dirk'd.* These things are of every-day occurrence; and it is not often that they are taken cognizance of by the police.

I was present at a criminal trial: the pleadings were a mixture of French and English. The jury consisted of ten French, and two Americans. The counsel were equally divided, being two of each language: the judge was American. The French counsel requested leave to quote the code Napoleon, which was granted, on condition that he should explain to the French part of the jury that it was not law, and that he adduced it on the same principle that he would the works of a poet, merely to illustrate his ideas. The English law is the law of Louisiana, with such additions as local circumstances have rendered necessary; one of which that was cited upon this occasion, is a law against "biting "off the ear, the nose, tearing out the eyes," &c. I was proceeding to remark upon the condition of negroes in Louisiana, but an official document lying before me upon the subject, I prefer forwarding to you, without note or comment, except to observe that such regulations as these exist *in spirit* throughout *nine* at least, if not *eleven* more of the State republics!

"CITY COUNCIL OF NEW ORLEANS.

"*An ordinance in relation to slaves in the city and suburbs "of New Orleans, as also in the neighbourhood thereof, "and to no other persons herein mentioned.*

"The City Council ordains as follows:

"Art. 1. No slave or slaves within the city and sub-"urbs of New Orleans, and the neighbourhood thereof, shall "have, hold, occupy, reside or sleep in any house, out-"house, building or enclosure, other than his or her "owner's, or his or her owner's representatives, or of the "person whom he is or they are serving for hire, without "first obtaining a ticket or tickets from his, her, or their "owner or owners, expressly describing the place which "such slave or slaves is or are allowed respectively to oc-"cupy, reside, or sleep in; and specifying also the time "during which the aforesaid permission or permissions is or "are granted; and every slave holding, occupying, resid-"ing or sleeping in any house, out-house, building or en-"closure, without obtaining the permission aforesaid, shall "be committed to the gaol by any officer of police, or any "other white person, *there to receive twenty lashes*, on a "warrant from the mayor, or from a justice of the peace, "*unless the owner or owners of such slave or slaves shall pre-*

"*viously pay a fine of five dollars for each of them, with all*
"*costs and charges.*

"Art. 6. The assemblies of slaves for the purpose of
"dancing or other merriment, shall take place only on
Sundays, and solely in such open or public places as shall
"be appointed by the Mayor; and no such assembly shall
"continue later than sunset; and all slaves who shall be
"found assembled together on any other day than Sunday,
"or who, even on that day, shall continue their dances
"after sunset, shall be taken up by the officers of police,
"constables, watchmen or other white persons, and shall
"be lodged in the public gaol, where they shall receive from
"10 to 25 lashes, on a warrant from the mayor or a justice
"of the peace; the clauses specified in the preceding article
"against all owners or occupants of houses or lots, forming
"or tolerating such assemblies on their premises, being in
"full force against them.

"Art. 7. *No person giving a ball to free people of*
"*colour shall, on any pretext, admit or suffer to be admitted*
"*to said ball any slave, on penalty of a fine from* 10 *to* 50
"*dollars; and any slave admitted to any such ball shall re-*
"*ceive* 15 *lashes.*

"Art. 8. Every slave, except such as may be blind or
"infirm, who shall walk in any street or open place with a
"cane, club, or other stick, shall be carried to the police
"gaol, where he shall receive 25 lashes, and shall moreover
"forfeit every such cane, club or other stick, to any white
"person seizing the same; and every slave carrying any
"arms whatever, shall be punished in the manner pre-
"scribed by the *Black Code* of this State.

"Art. 9. If any slave shall be guilty of whooping or
"hallooing any where in the city and suburbs, or of making
"any clamorous noise, or of singing aloud any indecent
"song, he or she shall for each and every such offence, re-
"ceive at the police gaol, on a warrant from the mayor, or
"any justice of peace, a number of 20 lashes or stripes;
"and if any such offence be committed on board any vessel,
"the master or commander thereof shall forfeit and pay a
"sum of 20 dollars for each and every such offence.

" Art. 10. *Every slave who shall be guilty of disrespect*
" *towards any white person, or shall insult any free person,*
" *shall receive* 30 *lashes*, upon an order from the mayor,
" or justice of the peace.

" Art. 13. The present ordinance shall be printed in the
" usual Gazettes, and shall moreover be published by drum-
" beat, within the city and suburbs twice a week during fif-
" teen days, and once every month, after that time.

J. SOULIE, Recorder.

" Approved, October 15th, 1817.

" AUG. MACARTY,

" Nov. 3. Mayor."

Provisions are of very bad quality, and most enormously dear. Hams and cheese from England, potatoes, butter, and beef from Ireland, are common articles of import. Cabbages are now ten-pence per head; turkeys, three to five dollars each. Rents are also very extravagant. Yet to all men whose desire only is to be rich, and to live a short life but a merry one, I have no hesitation in recommending New Orleans.

Proposing at once to transport you to the city from which part of this is written, that of Washington, I have only now to take a general retrospect. With regard, then, to the western country generally, let me first observe upon the strong evidence which it affords of increasing national wealth, strength and population. This, indeed, is striking to a degree which has been the subject of astonishment in various ways. The rapid ratio of its increase, the maturity of its establishments, the ignorance of *real freedom* among the people, the immense advantages resulting from an enlightened political constitution, and the probable future condition of this part of the American continent, are all themes calculated to excite speculation, and each affords abundant sources for reflection. Throughout the western country, there are many men of real, but more of fictitious capital. In their occupations they are not confined to any one particular pursuit, the same person often being farmer, store and hotel-keeper, land-jobber, brewer, steam-boat owner, and slave-dealer. In their characters they bear evidence of this diversified, though, I think, but in few instances able application of talent. They talk much of *American genius*, persuading themselves that because they were born on this continent, there is prepared for them, in every department of knowledge, a royal road. All are speculators; and each man anticipates making a fortune, not by patient industry and upright conduct, but by "a lucky "hit." Should he be disappointed, the consequences must, of course, fall upon his creditors; but neither those who suffer by his failure, nor his neighbours, nor himself, attach to him any kind of disrespect for the transaction. I witnessed some whose success had been astonishing, both as to amount, and the rapidity with which it had been collected; as, indeed, must ever be the case with a speculating people in a *new* country, particularly in one unburthened with taxes, and in which the habits of trade are yet unsettled. Merchants and tradesmen bear little or no similitude to those of England: their diversified pursuits, and migrating character, cause them to possess more *general* but less *particular* and *substantial* knowledge. The impression which they convey on first acquaintance, is that of being well-informed, and comparatively enlightened: but this wears off upon more intimate acquaintance, if, at least, by the expressions *well-informed* and *enlightened* we should imply men of reading or of thought, men possessed of sound information, who take large views, who feel liberally towards men of opposite sentiments, and attached to the general cause of human happiness: looked at in this point of view, they are, in truth, any thing but enlightened. This order of men, the merchant and tradesman, here generally compose the second, some of them rank in the first class of society. Though residing in a republic, they are, in fact, more really aristocratic than Englishmen similarly circumstanced. The mechanic in this country is naturally an important character, the more so if the town or settlement in which he resides be of recent establishment. If industrious and economical, his earnings soon place him on an equality with the second-rate tradesmen; and should he feel disposed for agriculture, and be willing to forego the comforts of a town life, he may purchase a tract of land, which, if judiciously selected, will in the course of twenty years make him a rich man. I saw many families in this part of the Union in rags and wretchedness: but there is this peculiarity about American poverty—it seems free from anxiety, exhibiting a total carelessness about the future, and apparently leaving the morrow to provide for itself.

Towns which are of any importance, are not what we understand by "*country towns:*" they are *miniature cities,* containing numerous first-rate brick buildings, all new, very neat in their exterior, and always high rented. Town property is as high as in Philadelphia, and more so than in London. The tide of emigration, it should be observed, is eternally changing its course. The attractions of Ohio are now lost in those of Missouri, Alabama, and Illinois. Lexington was, a short time since, the general magnet: its advances towards prosperity have now, however, ceased to be rapid, and property there has become stationary in value, whilst at Louisville it is rising prodigiously. This last-mentioned place, with St. Louis on the Missouri, promise to be ranked among the first towns in the western States. Provisions in the country are cheap, and groceries and clothing enormously high in price. In towns, 25 per cent. may be added to the former, and the same, perhaps, deducted from the latter; though, at the lowest market, you would be surprised at the charges, arising from the high price of labour, combined with the extraordinary fact, that the crockery, hardware, linens, cottons, and woollens, which fill the log-stores of even the most remote parts in the wildernesss, are imported from Great Britain.

Banks, as I have before remarked, are extremely numerous. They afford, to an unlimited extent, all the facilities within the possible capacity of an immense paper currency. But still even this species of capital is rarely employed in agricultural pursuits: it is engrossed by town lots, building, steam-boats, and mill-seats; in any of which occupations there is certainly a profitable opening for the European capitalist.

Without further dwelling on this country, or on my journey, I shall now at once take you to

WASHINGTON.

It has been so fashionable with natives, as well as foreigners, to ridicule the federal city, that I had anticipated the reality of Moore's description of

> "This famed metropolis, where fancy sees
> "Squares in morasses, obelisks in trees."

But in this I was pleasingly disappointed.

The river Potowmac, at this place, is only navigable for small craft near its banks. Besides the Potowmac, the River "Tiber" runs through the city; its stream is about the width of the Paddington canal. The ridiculous, though characteristic vanity displayed in altering it from the original name of "Goose Creek," to that of the Tiber, has been happily exposed by Moore.

The President's palace, and the Capitol, situated on opposite hills, are the chief public buildings, both of which were nearly destroyed by the buccaneering incursions of our countrymen, who acted, perhaps, agreeably to their orders, but certainly in opposition to the feelings, judgment, and character of the British people. These buildings are now rapidly rising into increased splendour. The Capitol, in which are both houses of the legislature, and several public offices, stands on a bank of the Potowmac, seventy feet above the level of that river: it as yet consists of but two wings, intended to be connected by a centre, surmounted by a dome. The architect is Mr. Latrobe: In the internal construction of this building, he has not evinced even a common knowledge of what contributes to convenience, and still less to elegance of appearance. The apartments are small, crowded, and without unity of design: the exterior, when completed, will, however, produce a really grand effect. Some of the pillars are of a native marble, of a peculiarly novel and beautiful description, bearing some resemblance to the finest specimens of mosaic. The Americans, however, are not content with the productions of their own country: they have made large imports from Italy of its most expensive marble; and so anxious is even the President himself for "foreign ornament," that he has imported chairs at one hundred dollars each, though the cabinet-makers of Baltimore would have equalled, and I believe surpassed them in every particular, at the price of sixty dollars!

The President's house is at the opposite end of "Pennsylvania Avenue," commanding a most beautiful prospect. On each side of it stands a large brick building; one of which is the treasury, the other the war and navy offices. These are to be connected with the palace, which, when completed, would form an ornament even to St. Petersburgh itself. Upon a second visit to the Capitol, I explored nearly all its recesses. Marks of the late conflagration are still very apparent, while the walls bear evidence of public opinion in relation to that transaction, which seems to have had the singular fate of casting disgrace upon both the Americans and British. Some of the pencil drawings exhibit the military commander hanging upon a tree; others represent the President running off without his hat or wig; some, Admiral Cockburn robbing hen-roosts: to which are added such inscriptions as, "The capital of the Union lost by cowardice;" "Curse cowards;" "A —— sold the city "for 5000 dollars;" "James Madison is a ras-"cal, a coward, and a fool;" "Ask no ques-"tions," &c.

The post-office is a large brick building, situated at about equal distances from the President's house and the Capitol. Under the same roof is the patent-office, and also the national library, for the use of members of congress. In the first of these departments, I witnessed upwards of nine hundred specimens of native mechanical genius. This would appear to afford decisive proof, that Americans are not deficient in inventive talent, though it cannot be extensively, or with profit, called into action, until your little island ceases to be the universal workshop. The library is small, consisting of but 3000 volumes; but it is select and well chosen, and includes various classes of literature, having been the property of Mr. Jefferson, for which he obtained from the United States 20,000 dollars. The former library, containing from 7 to 8000, was destroyed by our *enlightened* countrymen. So great has been, at some periods, the depreciation of property in this city, that in 1802, what had originally cost 200,000 dollars, was sold for 25,000. This decay continued to go on, until the visit of General Ross, and the subsequent signature of peace: since that time it seems to have risen, like the phœnix from the flames, and is once more partially increasing in prosperity. There are now a number of two and three story brick buildings, none of which are uninhabited; and also some small wooden houses, though, according to the original plan, none were to be built less than three stories high, and all to have marble steps. But the childish folly of this scheme was soon subverted by the natural course of events; and though the existence of "*lower orders,*" even in the capital of the republic, may not accord with the vanity of its legislators, they ought to be told, that neither prosperity nor population can be possessed by any nation, without a due admixture of the *natural classes* of society.

The population of Washington city is stated to be about 9000; of Georgetown, 6000; of Alexandria, 8000; and of all other parts of the district of Columbia, 7000; making a total of 30,000. *Alexandria,* which is seven miles from the city, may be considered the sea-port. *Georgetown* is the residence of shopkeepers, and *Washington* the depôt for office-holders, place-hunters, and boarding-house keepers, none of whom would appear to be in possession of too much of this world's goods. Between these three divisions of this district there exists considerable jealousy.

PRICES, &c.

There are three market-houses in Washington, and I believe, four market days per week. Negroes are the chief sellers. The supplies at this time are neither good nor various. Beef is from 3½d. to 6½d. per pound; pork the same; potatoes, 3s. 4½d. per bushel; bread, 2d. per pound; beer, 6½d. per bottle; milk, 5½d. per quart; tea, 4s. 6d. to 13s. 6d. per pound; coffee, 12¾d. to 16d.; sugar, from 54s. to 90s. per hundred. Rents are as high as elsewhere. Mechanics are fully employed, and well paid. Shopkeepers are too numerous, and none of them remarkably successful. British goods abound, as in every other part of America. When I had been here a few hours, I went to a store to purchase a pair of worsted gloves: they were of the commonest kind, such as are sold in London at 8s. 6d. per dozen. The price was half a dollar per pair. I presented a Philadelphia one dollar note; it would not be taken without a discount of 2½ per cent. I then tendered a Baltimore bank, of the same amount. This being one hundred miles nearer was accepted. The store-keeper had no silver change; to remedy which, he took a pair of scissors and divided the note between us: I enquired if the half would pass, and being answered in the affirmative, took it without hesitation, knowing the want of specie throughout the country, and being previously familiarised with Spanish dollars cut into every variety of size. I now find that demi-notes are a common circulating medium. Capital is generally wanted, though my enquiries do not lead me to believe that it can be employed here with any thing more than ordinary advantage. The increase of the federal city cannot be rapid. Here is fine natural scenery, but no decidedly great natural advantages; little external commerce, a barren soil, a scanty population, enfeebled too by the deadly weight of absolute slavery, and no direct means of communication with the western country. For the apparently injudicious selection of such a spot, upon which to raise the capital of a great nation, several reasons are given. Some have even gone so far as to attribute to Gen. Washington, the influence of pecuniary interest, his property being in the neighbourhood. But the most common argument adduced in support of the choice is that it is central, or rather that it *was* so; for the recent addition of new States has removed the centre very far west, so much so indeed, that the inhabitants of Lexington affirm, that *their* town must on that ground soon become the capital; and even the people of St. Louis, in the Missouri, put in their claim, that city being said to be geographically the exact centre of the Union. But assuming that Washington were central, I do not see much validity in the argument;—at least if we are to be influenced in our judgment by any country in the old world—where is the important nation, whose capital is placed exactly in the centre of its dominions? Spain is perhaps the only country which can be adduced, and no very favourable conclusion can be drawn from such an instance: though unquestionably if rivers and soil, if roads and canals, all united to recommend that situation, it would be in some other respects extremely convenient; but this not being the case, the knowledge of Euclid must be dispensed with for something of more practical, though perhaps more vulgar utility.

There may be other objections to this capital: among them I would venture to suggest, that the legislators, and rulers of a nation, ought to reside in that city which has the most direct communication with all parts of their country, and of the world at large; they ought to see with their own eyes, and hear with their own ears, without which, though possessed of the best intentions, they must often be in error. Newspaper communications, letters and agents, are but substitutes, and sometimes very poor ones; besides which, I conceive that mere expedients should not be admitted in national legislation. Unless this city increases with a rapidity unsanctioned by the most sanguine anticipation, the American law-makers will be half a century behind what they would become by a residence in New York or Philadelphia. Another objection to Washington may suggest itself to some minds, in its neighbourhood to Virginia. The "Virginian dynasty," as it has been called, is a subject of general, and I think very just complaint throughout other parts of America. This State has supplied four of the five presidents, and also a liberal number of occupants of every other government office. The Virginians very modestly assert, that this monopoly does not proceed from corrupt influence, but is a consequence of the buoyancy and vigour of their natural talent. Without entering into the controversy, whether or not seventeen States can supply a degree of ability equal to that of Virginia single-handed, I must express my want of respect for a State in which every man is either a slave-holder, or a defender of slavery— a State in which landed property is not attachable for debt—a State in which human beings are sold in the streets by the public auctioneer, are flogged without trial at the mercy of their owner or his agents, and are killed almost without punishment;—yet these men dare to call themselves democrats, and friends of liberty! — from such democrats, and such friends of liberty, good Lord deliver us!

The customs of society at this season differ, I presume, in some degree, from those portions of the year when congress is not sitting. Tea parties, and private balls, are now very frequent. Mr. Bagot, the English ambassador, and his lady, are particularly assiduous in their attentions to all classes, and maintain a strict conformity with the habits of the place. Their cards of invitation are left at my boarding-house for different gentlemen every day. The speaker (Mr. Clay) gives public periodical dinners. A drawing-room is held weekly at the President's house: it is generally crowded. There is little or no difficulty in getting introduced on these occasions. Mr. Munroe is a very plain, practical man of business. The custom is shaking, and not the degrading one of kissing, hands. Conversation, tea, ice, music, chewing tobacco, and excessive spitting, afford employment for the evening. The dress of the ladies is very elegant, though that of the gentlemen is too frequently rather ungentlemanly.

The theatre is a miserable building. I have attended several representations in it by the same company which I saw when in Pittsburgh. Incledon has been here — the Washington critics think him too vulgar, and also an indifferent singer!

In this city I witnessed also the exhibitions of *Sema Sama*, the Indian juggler, from London. My chief attention was directed to the audience; their disbelief of the possibility of performing the numerous feats advertised, and their inconceiveable astonishment at witnessing the actual achievement, appeared extreme, — approaching almost to childish wonder and astonishment.

The few private families to which I have had introductions, do not evince a more accurate knowledge of that English word *comfort* than I have remarked elsewhere; indeed, I would class them a century inferior to Boston and half a century behind New York. The boarding-houses and inns partake of the same characteristics. I first applied at the chief, which is Davis's Indian Queen tavern: most of the door-handles are broken; the floor of the coffee-room is strewed with bricks and mortar, caused by the crumbling of the walls and ceiling; and the character of the accommodations is in unison with this unorganised state of things: the charges are as high as at the very first London hotel.

Mr. Law, brother of Lord Ellenborough, resides here, and is the owner of numerous houses. Mr. H——, a Lancashire cotton-bleacher and friend of Mr. Cobbett, has lately emigrated to this country, and has been recently here, endeavouring to induce this government to lay double duties on all British goods; what his success has been I have not learned.

Observing the following statements in the Philadelphia Aurora, I forward them to you, as shewing Mr. Cobbett's impressions of the Pennsylvanian government.

" FROM THE HARRISBURG ORACLE.

" THE CASE OF WILLIAM COBBETT.

" While the subject was before the senate on Tuesday " and Wednesday last, considerable discussion took place, " advocated chiefly by Mr. Lowrie, and opposed by Messrs. " Reed of Westmoreland, C. Smith, Reed of Philadelphia, " and B. R. Morgan. And on the question of agreeing to " the resolution, it was negatived. — Ayes 9. Nays 20.

" Immediately after this decision, Mr. Cobbett, who was " present during the debate, walked up to the speaker's " chair and handed the following to the speaker, which was " read and laid on the table.

" *To the Honourable the Senate and House of Represent-" atives of the Commonwealth of Pennsylvania, in Gene-" ral Assembly met.*

" The Petition of William Cobbett, an Englishman, this " 19th day of February, 1818,

" MOST RESPECTFULLY SHEWETH:

" That your petitioner has heard with inexpressible sur-" prise that the senate of the commonwealth has rejected " the petition lately presented to that honourable body by " your petitioner; that seeing the flagrant enormity of the " injustice of which he complained, he confidently hopes " that such rejection has arisen from some great misunder-" standing as to the circumstances of the case; that he, " therefore, most respectfully, but most earnestly, prays that " the honourable senate will, without loss of time, be " pleased to permit him to appear in person at the bar of " their honourable house, there to support the prayer of his

" said petition; that he feels the more confidence in the " making of this respectful request, since it appears that his " petition has been opposed upon arguments drawn from the " laws and usages of England, where similar requests, under " similar circumstances, are never refused; and he finally " begs leave to be permitted to state (which he does with " the most profound respect) that a sense of duty towards " his beloved country and his sovereign, his love of truth " and justice, his attachment to real *and his hatred of sham* " *freedom*, are the principal motives of this his most re- " spectful petition.

" Wm. Cobbett."

" TO THE EDITOR OF THE AURORA.

" *Philadelphia*, 23*d February*, 1818.

" Sir,—I have read, in the *Democratic Press* of this day, " an article, purporting to be an 'extract of a letter from " Harrisburg;' in which extract it is said, that, after that " most honourable body, the senate, had refused to hear me " at its bar, in support of my petition, another petition was " presented by me to the house of representatives; that this " petition was, by some of the members, thought 'to *cast a* " *reflection* on the *political institutions*' of this country; but " that, the subject was an *important* one, and that, 'if the " *individual* could be *forgotten*, it would, perhaps, be *viewed* " *in a different light*.'

" This, Sir, is a pretty sort of shuffle indeed! So, because " I complain of great and shocking injustice, suffered by me, " under these institutions, I am to be accused of casting re- " flections on the institutions themselves, and, *on the ground* " *of that accusation*, my claim is to be rejected!—This mode " of arguing is a *finisher* as to all petitions for redress of " grievances. No, no, Sir! It is not the 'individual con- " cerned' that needs to be '*forgotten*.' Say, rather, the " *six thousand three hundred and seventy three dollars*. If " these could be forgotten, the writer of the extract would, " I fancy, view the matter in the right light in a moment.

" It is impossible, Sir, for this stain on the government of

" the State to be wiped away without the doing of complete
" justice. I can perceive, clearly enough, what some per-
" sons *think* will do. They are gently preparing the way for
" hushing the people by recommending an act *to prevent the*
" *like in future;* and thus, to *keep the dollars*, and, at the
" same time, as they imagine, to *remove the odium*. You
" remember, I dare say, the story of La Fontaine's Nun,
" who, having had *one bastard*, became a *virgin* for the rest
" of her life!

" I am, Sir,
" Your most humble,
" And most obedient servant,
" WM. COBBETT."

Mr. H. informs me that he was with Mr. C. at Harrisburg; that Mr. C. declares that during the several years which he resided near the Treasury in London, he did not witness so much bribery, corruption, and place-hunting as he had seen in one week in Pennsylvania; that the members of the legislature were engaged in little except smoking, drinking, and gambling; and that he could certainly have carried his point had he condescended to bribe. In all these opinions Mr. H. joins his friend.

Although I cannot go the length of Mr. H. and Mr. Cobbett in their wholesale censures, perhaps from not having had the same opportunities with them of forming a judgment, yet I have become acquainted with facts in Washington which no man could have induced me to believe without personal observation.

MANUFACTURES OF THE UNITED STATES.

The object of Mr. H.'s visit to the capital is one of high national importance, and in which I should have individually felt much interested at an earlier period of my acquaintance with this country ; but I am now, after the most deliberate examination, convinced, that our Yorkshire and Leicestershire friends could not profitably succeed as manufacturers. This opinion is amply borne out by memorials to Congress from various parts of the Union, and in these documents it is essential to remark that the request is not for Government to erect new establishments, *but to protect those which are in existence from utter ruin.* The memorial from Oneida county, in the State of New York, contains the following striking passages :

" *A Memorial presented to the Senate of the United States,*
" *January* 7. 1818.

" To the Honourable the Senate and House of Representatives of the United States, in Congress assembled, the Petition of the Inhabitants of the County of Oneida, in the State of New York, as well Manufacturers as Others,

" RESPECTFULLY SHEWETH :

" That the above county contains a greater number of manufacturing establishments, of cotton and woollen, than any county in the State, there being invested in said establishments at least 600,000 dollars.

" That although the utmost efforts have been made by

"the proprietors to sustain those establishments, their "efforts have proved fruitless, *and more than three-fourths of* "*the factories remain necessarily closed, some of the pro-* "*prietors being wholly ruined, and others struggling under* "*the greatest embarrassments.*

"In this alarming situation, we beg leave to make a last "appeal to the Congress of the United States. While we "make this appeal, at the present crisis, the extensive em- "barrassments in most of the great departments of industry, "as well as the peculiar difficulty in affording immediate re- "lief to manufacturers, are fully seen and appreciated. Yet "your petitioners cannot believe that the legislature of the "Union will remain an indifferent spectator of the *wide-* "*spread ruin of their fellow-citizens*, and look on, and see a "great branch of industry, of the utmost importance in "every community, prostrated under circumstances fatal to "all future attempts at revival, without a further effort for "relief. We would not magnify the subject, which we now "present to Congress, beyond its just merits, when we state "it to be one of the utmost importance to the future interests "and welfare of the United States.

"We hope to find excuse in the importance of the sub- "ject, for submitting to the consideration of Congress the "following principles of political economy, which have been "adopted by the most enlightened governments, and are "deemed not altogether unapplicable to the United States.

"*That the public good requires of government to restrain,* "*by duties, the importation of articles which may be pro-* "*duced at home, and to manufacture as much as possible of* "*the raw material of the country.*

"*That the branches of industry particularly necessary or* "*useful to the independence of the community ought to be* "*encouraged by government.*

"*That the most disadvantageous commerce is that which* "*exchanges the raw material for manufactured goods.*

"*That any nation who should open its ports to all foreign* "*importations, without a reciprocal privilege, would soon be* "*ruined by the balance of trade.*

"The policy of Great Britain, in support of which, no

" wars, however bloody, no expense, however enormous, " are too great a sacrifice, ought never to be lost sight " of by the United States. That nation assumes to *manu-* " *facture for all nations, but will receive the manufactures of* " *none.*

" *But let no one imagine that a general system of manu-* " *factures is now proposed to be introduced into the United* " *States. We would be understood as limiting our views to* " *the manufactories already established; to save those which* " *have not already fallen, from the ruin which threatens them.*

" It might have been expected, that the present fallen " condition of manufactures would have soothed prejudice " and disarmed hostility. With all their alleged war profits, " there are now none so poor. Is it not seen, that the " destruction of the present manufactories must inevitably " produce the same evils of extravagant prices in the event " of a future war, as were experienced in the last.

" It is objected, that the entire industry of the country " may be most profitably exerted in clearing and cultivating " our extended vacant lands. But what does it avail the " farmer, when neither in the nation from which he purchases " his goods nor elsewhere, can he find a market for his abun- " dant crops. Besides, the diversion of labour from agri- " culture to manufactures, is scarcely perceptible. Five or " six adults, with the aid of children, will manage a cotton " manufactory of two thousand spindles.

" From the gloomy condition of the manufacturers, the " mind, turning to another quarter, is cheered with the " brightest prospects to others. In the more southern " States, it is believed, that the amount received, during " the last year, from the export of two or three articles " of agricultural produce only, exceeds forty millions of " dollars."

The manufacturers of Baltimore use not dissimilar language.

The amount of capital, real or fictitious, said to have been employed (though I suspect erroneously) in manufacturing establishments previous to the late peace, is the following:

Hats, - - - - -	£2,000,000
Iron, - - - - -	2,500,000
Leather, - - - -	4,000,000
Cotton and Wool, - - -	10,000,000
Spirituous Liquors, -	3,000,000
Wood, - - - -	500,000
Soap, Candles, Tallow, Oil, Sugar, &c.	600,000
	£22,600,000

Total amount of capital employed in all the manufactories of the United States 22,600,000l. At present this must be greatly reduced; perhaps even two-thirds would not be too large a deduction. Fine sites for cotton and woollen factories exist in every State which I have visited: the Falls of Pasaic, near New York, cannot, for such purposes, be exceeded. Mr. Casey, lately of Liverpool, is endeavouring to form a cotton twist establishment at that place.

Much diversity of opinion exists amongst Americans as to the policy which it would be desirable their government should pursue with regard to domestic manufactures; and it would still appear to remain an unsolved question among them, whether the strong arm of government should or should not, in the present infant stage of the republic, be held out to protect and encourage those establishments, by the usual means of bounties on the one hand, and duties or prohibitions on the other? Mr. Jefferson originally took the negative side of this question: he wished Americans to remain a nation of agriculturists, deprecating the time when that people should be changed from "robust "and virtuous farmers, into deformed, sickly, "and profligate manufacturers:" but it should now seem, from his letter to the "American "Society for encouraging Manufactures," and also from another letter of his, inserted by Mr. Mellish in a pamphlet he has recently written at, I am informed, the dictation of Mr. Hulme, that he (Mr. J.) has changed his opinions.

The general arguments against manufactures are, that their encouragement will enhance the price of clothing: that this will operate as a heavy tax upon the whole community, for the benefit of but a few: that the revenue of the United States would be materially injured, as its chief supply is from duties on imports: that in an extensive country, with but a scanty population, it is most beneficial to direct the mass of labour to the clearing of new lands, and other agricultural pursuits: that by so doing they will make greater and more rapid advances in extent of population and amount of national wealth, than by drawing off a part of their capital and labour, and devoting it to purposes of manufacture; more especially while most of the articles wanted can be imported from England 30 to 50 per cent. cheaper than it is possible for them to be produced within the Union: that as labour is so high and land so cheap, there is an ever-existing inducement for men to leave factories, and free themselves from masters, to become lords of their own domain: and that this has been uniformly found to be the case, — the slow advance of manufactures, and the consequent high price of the articles having been a natural result of the situation of the country: that, in a word, it is the true interest of America to continue supplying Europe with raw material and with agricultural produce, both of which find there a certain market, while labour is from 25 to 50 per cent. higher than in England, and from 50 to 75 more than on the European continent.

On the manufacturers' side of this truly great national question is Mr. De Witt Clinton, governor of New York: in a speech which has had few equals in comprehensive and philosophic views, addressed to the legislature, he makes the following able reflections:

"The excessive importation of foreign fa-
"brics was the signal of ruin to institutions
"founded by enterprising industry, reared by
"beneficial skill, and identified with the ge-
"neral welfare. The raw materials of iron,

"woollen, and cotton manufactures are abundant, and those for the minor and auxiliary ones, can, in most cases, be procured at home with equal facility. Nothing is wanting to destroy foreign competition but the steady protection of the government, and the public spirit of the country. High duties, and prohibiting provisions applied to foreign productions, afford the most efficient encouragement to our manufactures: and these measures appertain to the legitimate functions of the national government.—But much may be done by the State government, by liberal accommodations, by judicious exemptions, and by the whole weight of its influence; and much more may be accomplished by the spirit of the community. For I am persuaded, that if every citizen who adopts the fabrics of other nations, would seriously consider that he is not only paying taxes for the support of foreign governments, but that he participates in undermining one of the main pillars of our productive industry, he would imitate the honourable practice which you have this day evinced in favour of American manufactures."

Mr. Mellish stands forth prominent in this discussion: his picture of present distress, if well founded, would be truly deplorable. For myself, I have seen nothing in the district of Philadelphia, or indeed throughout America, which justifies his calculation, "that nearly one-"fourth of the whole population are engaged in "unproductive labour;" but as I wish to put you in possession of the materials from which I draw my conclusions, I forward you Mr. Mellish's ideas in his own words:

"Failures," he says, "innumerable have "taken, and are taking, place; and the com-"mercial character of the country is sunk and "degraded in consequence. The surplus wealth "of the country is drained off, to support our "rivals in Britain; and, in many districts of "the country, a great portion of the citizens "are at a loss for employment! Yes, in this "very country, this industrious population are "absolutely at a loss for something to do. It "is really painful to contemplate the picture; "but contemplate it we must; for in no other "way can we do justice to the subject.

"This melancholy picture pervades the coun-"try throughout, less or more; but it is very "prominent on the Atlantic coast, and parti-"cularly in and about the great commercial "cities. It is calculated that, in Philadelphia "city and county, at least 15,000 people, all "able and willing to work, are either idle, or "occupied in unproductive labour. The pro-"portion along the seabord is probably equal to "this, through its whole extent; and half this "proportion may be the estimate for all the "other parts of the country.

" This will give, along the Atlantic coast, about	150,000
" And in other parts - - - - -	350,000
" Making a population, in all, who have either " nothing to do, or are engaged in unpro- " ductive labour, of - - - - -	500,000
" Now, by looking at the last census of the " U. S. we will see that the whole popula- " tion is - - - - - - -	7,239,903
" Of these, the free white males, between 16 " and 45, amount to - - -	1,119,944
" Females - - - - - - -	1,105,824
Total	2,225,768

" This we may assume as the number of in-
" habitants in the U. S. fit for productive labour;
" and we find, that if the estimate of those who
" are rendered unproductive by existing cir-
" cumstances be correct, it amounts to nearly
" one-fourth part of the whole!"

How these statements of want, of ruin, and of unproductive labour, can be reconciled with a romance in two volumes, called, "Travels in "America," by the same author, I am at a loss to conjecture. It is not to be denied, that there may be individuals unprofitably employed, but, I believe, there is no person in health, and disposed to labour, but what may, at this moment, obtain advantageous work in America. To conclude—upon this subject of manufactures, as far as I have been enabled to form an opinion, I should incline to think that it is not now the interest of the United States, artificially to encourage their growth, by granting them peculiar advantages. It appears at any rate certain, that in the present state of things, none of our friends could engage in the cotton or woollen establishments without a certainty of loss.

DOMESTIC EXPENDITURE.

Perhaps some useful information upon the important subject of domestic expenditure may be derived from the two following statements. The first is a list of household furniture, which was sold by auction in Chesnut-street, Philadelphia, by order of the sheriff, for the payment of rent, at the sale of which I was present. None of the articles were very old, but nearly all were in bad condition. The second is a statement of Mr. H——'s expenses for six months, ending the first of March 1818. This gentleman is an English emigrant; the account he allowed me to copy from his petty ledger, and is, I presume, correct.

SHERIFF'S SALE IN CHESNUT-STREET.

Amounts in English Currency.

	l.	*s.*	*d.*
12 Chairs, (wood, painted,) each - - -	0	5	10
A small writing-desk - - - -	1	0	3
A lady's work-box - - - -	0	9	0
2 Plated candlesticks and snuffers - -	0	13	6
A bed-room looking-glass - - -	0	18	0
A small toilet table - - - -	0	4	9
A mahogany wash-hand stand - - -	0	14	8
4 Pair linen sheets, (Irish,) per pair - -	1	1	4½

	Amounts in English Currency.		
	l.	s.	d.
Cotton counterpane, (12 quarters square,)	2	2	3
Marseilles quilt, (ditto,)	2	2	3
Bed curtains, lined with blue, for a small four-post bedstead	6	1	6
(The furniture print was by John Low, calico-printer, of Manchester, and worth, in England, 15½d. per yard. The lining worth about 14d. per yard.)			
A large and good hair mattress	5	4	0
A straw ditto,	1	0	6
A breakfast-table	2	0	6
A card-table	2	0	6
An English Brussels carpet and rug	7	8	0
A feather-bed, at per pound	0	2	6
2 vols. Edgeworth's Patronage, Scott's Lady of the Lake, Byron's Childe Harold, and Curran's Speeches	0	3	4½

No Auction duty.

MR. H——'S EXPENSES FOR SIX MONTHS.

This family consists of thirteen: Mr. H——, Mrs. H——, three Misses H——, sixteen years of age and upwards, two ditto, younger, four boys, four to twelve years of age, one woman-servant, one girl.

They occupy the whole (store excepted) of an excellent house in Market-street, Philadelphia; in it there are 13 rooms, kitchen included, and three cellars. The rent is 500 dollars per annum. The following account is for the first six months of their residence in the United States It includes rent, and what little clothes the females may have found necessary to purchase, in consequence of the difference of American fashions; also about one hundred dollars for travelling expenses. Their style of living is extremely plain, respectable, and economical.

1817,		Dollars.	Cents.
Sept. 1st to 8th	One week's board and lodging at a boarding-house	80	0
Sept. 8th.	Wood, (for firing)	19	76

	Dollars.	Cents.
Wine and spirits - - - -	9	50
Other expenses - - - -	199	6
Wood, (firing) - - - -	21	18
Other expenses - - - -	149	2
Wood, (firing) - - - -	39	39
Shoes - - - - -	25	50
Other expenses - - - -	221	36
Schooling, (for two boys) - - -	15	65
Wine and spirits - - - -	15	0
Aurora newspaper - - -	5	0
Schooling, (eldest boy) - - -	21	50
Wood, (firing) - - - - -	50	0
Ditto ditto - - - - -	39	50
Other expenses - - - - -	388	37
Schooling, (for two boys) - - -	12	0
Total, 1st Sept. 1817 to March 1818,	1313	79

This account does *not* include the expenditure for household furniture: they have paid for Scotch carpeting, yard wide, (commonest qualities) 170 cents per yard; stair carpeting, narrow, strong, and common, of domestic manufacture, 100 cents per yard; oil-cloth, yard wide, 175 cents per yard; Windsor chairs, 216 cents each; fancy rush bottoms, light and genteel, 375 cents each.

VETERANS OF THE REVOLUTION.

I have been highly interested upon several occasions, by being in company with some of the veterans of the revolution. There is a something in the associations connected with that immortal cause, which attracts insensibly towards those who were engaged in it feelings of respect — almost of reverence. The attention of the government has lately been directed towards these men in consequence of discussions which have taken place in congress relative to what is called "Revolutionary Claims:" these claims are for monies advanced, or services rendered, which have never been repaid or recompensed. The leader of this poor but sacred band of national creditors, is General St. Clair. This respectable veteran is now 80 years of age; he was the companion of Washington, engaged in his country's service at the gloomiest periods of the revolution, fought and bled in the cause of liberty; when the national finances were bankrupt he advanced 1800 dollars of his private property for the common defence: this sum has never been repaid; and in consequence of the scanty amount of his annual income, he has been compelled to take up his abode in the wilderness. This aged patriot, with clothes which might seem from their appearance to have felt the effects of all the seasons for the last ten years, with flaxen hair, tottering limbs, a care-worn countenance, deeply dejected from supposing his country ungrateful, and with one foot in the grave, is now a petitioner to that people in whose service he spent his youth, his treasure, and his blood, aiding them in their emancipation from external dominion, and in raising them into a great and an independent nation.

CONGRESS.

Congress being sitting, I have several times attended their debates. Their present place of meeting is a temporary one: it was designed, I believe, for an hotel, and is in the immediate neighbourhood of the Capitol.

My first visit to congress (which assembles at 11 o'clock in the morning, and adjourns at 4 in the afternoon) was to the senate. This body is at present comprised of forty members, the States having increased from their original number of thirteen to that of twenty, and each State, regardless of its population, sending two. The gallery is open to all, *without orders from members, or half-a-crown to the door-keeper*: the only form to be observed, is taking off the hat in obedience to a public notice to that effect. The chairman's seat is central, under a handsome canopy; the members are placed on rich scarlet cushions, some at double, and some at single desks. There are two large fires. The room is carpeted, as is also the gallery. The forms of business are taken from those of our parliament, with a few minor exceptions. One point of variation, at least, from the British senate, is, that every speech is apparently listened to, and all, whether good or bad, whether marked by superior excellence or by unequalled dullness, seem regarded with equal apathy and complete lifeless endurance, neither applause nor censure being allowed; and it would not be an easy task to discern which were felt, judging from the countenance. I have heard nearly all their usual speakers. Mr. Otis, of Massachusetts, is an eloquent man, but not remarkable for solidity of reasoning. Mr. Rufus King is a true gentleman, and one whom I should conceive has not many superiors among the public men of any country. Mr. Barbour, called Governor Barbour, of Virginia, is a speaker who, perhaps, violates all the rules of theoretic oratory, but who, notwithstanding, possesses an irresistible charm from his evident sincerity, and the manliness of his deportment, which, while it rivets the attention of his audience, compels them to love the object of their admiration. His countenance is one of that kind which, in a few minutes, enlists in its favour all the social affections, and you insensibly feel anxious and predisposed to take that side of the argument of which so apparently kind and able a man professes himself the advocate. A friend from Boston replied to some observations of mine concerning him, "I entirely agree with "you in relation to Mr. Barbour,—he is a man "in whom you cannot be deceived, he carries "his heart in his hand." There are, in the senate, a great proportion of men of experience, of sound ability, and who would do credit to any nation upon earth.

The *Representative* chamber is in the same building, and of about twice the extent. An admission to the gallery is equally easy, and is also open to both sexes. This assembly consists of nearly two hundred. They want in appearance the age, experience, dignity, and respectability which we associate with the idea of legislators, and which are possessed by the superior branch of the congress. The interior decorations of this room are marked by an inferiority to the senate, which is rather anti-republican. The members sit on very common chairs, at unpainted desks, which are placed in rows, the whole resembling a Lancasterian school, though without its regularity. Some two or three speakers regularly command attention; others talk on as long as they please, the members being occupied in writing letters, and in reading or folding up newspapers. This is carried to such an extreme, that it appears fully to justify the charge of Mr. Randolph, that "the House of "Representatives consisted only of a large col-"lection of printers' boys." Spitting boxes are placed at the feet of each member, and, contrary to the practice of the Upper House, at once members and visitors wear their hats. I have been present at numerous discussions, among which were the subjects of "Revolu-"tionary claims," "a General Bankrupt Bill," and "General St. Clair's Claim." The latter was the topic when I first entered the gallery of this assembly. The fact of his having advanced 1800 dollars of his private property for national purposes, was proved by a receipt, attesting it at the time, given by the next in command. I was surprised to find the question of repayment of this sum could be made a subject of debate, naturally concluding that this powerful nation would not have suffered itself, even for a moment, to remain debtor to poor individuals; and that the mere fact of a revolutionary general having fallen into distress, only required to be known in order that he should be relieved. To my extreme surprise and regret, however, I was speedily undeceived. General St. Clair's claim was so strongly opposed, that I concluded it would necessarily be lost. The arguments advanced by its advocates were, first, that the money was due to him, and if not paid, the country were neither more nor less than swindlers; and, secondly, that having been one of their political saviours, they ought to go hand and heart to pour oil and wine into his wounds, and not to suffer his grey hairs to descend with sorrow to the grave. These reasons met with the following mercenary, cold-blooded arguments, in the way of reply: — "General "St. Clair certainly has claims upon our grati-"tude; and if we could be directed by our "wishes, we should assent to the bill: but we

" were not sent here by our constituents to be " governed by, or to legislate according to our " feelings. The obtainment of our liberties, " also, was certainly a valuable acquisition: " but those are arguments foreign to the pre- " sent discussion. We have now *got* our con- " stitution, and *how it was obtained* is, at this " time, a matter of little moment. We are not " eternally to be looking at the past: we *are* " *now free*: that is our main consideration: " our duty and true policy is to look at the fu- " ture." The prominent leader of this side of the question was a man gifted with great volubility of speech, much self-importance in delivery, considerable occasional violence of manner, and who seemed to command much attention, rather from the strength of his lungs, however, than the solidity of his reasoning. This gentleman I found to be Mr. Henry Clay, speaker of the House of Representatives, an active man of business. He is said to understand the forms of the house better than any other member. His manners are not exactly gentlemanly. His natural talent I should suspect to be good, though but little cultivated, at least by present application. His mode of speaking possesses strength, but is totally destitute either of pathos or of logical arrangement. His arguments against Gen. St. Clair I thought ably refuted. It was proved to demonstration, that, although gratitude ought not to be overlooked, this claim was not of that class. It was a demand upon their *justice;* and if they did not pay the money, principal and interest, they were actually robbing their creditor. Upon a division the original motion was lost, and an amendment carried, allowing him, *on the ground of national gratitude*, 13l. 10s. per month. I believe there is not a man in Washington who would insure the General's life for a year and a half.

The claims of some of the private soldiers of the revolution were met in a similar spirit. A great number were rejected altogether. Those whose claims were admitted, received, after numerous discussions, the *liberal allowance of 13s. 6d. per week* during life. Two of the Philadelphia federalist newspapers, in reporting this debate, were printed in deep mourning, considering the honour and character of the country compromised by such a mean provision for men towards whom the nation was deeply indebted. Nearly all the members of the representative chamber are young men; and out of the 190 members, 150, at the least, are lawyers, a class of men whose minds, here, as elsewhere, appear moulded and contracted by their profession, and not possessed of that general knowledge, or not taking those large and equitable views of things, which should be the distinguishing characteristics of the legislators of a great and a commercial people. Last session the member from Baltimore, who is a merchant, introduced the late "tariff." While giving the details, and necessary statements on this most important subject, he perceived that nearly the whole assembly, Mr. Speaker included, were inattentive or slumbering. Stopping in the midst of his speech, he apologised for his own deficiency of ability, stating "that he perceived the subject he was speak-"ing on was not understood by the body he was "addressing. The exact cause of this he could "not pretend to determine: but of this he felt "quite confident, that there was not a boy in his "counting-rooms but would comprehend the "subject perfectly." This roused the "learned "gentlemen;" and throughout the remainder of the subject they put on, at least, the aspect of attention.

The State-legislatures are equally infested with lawyers. They occupy, in fact, eight-tenths of all the public situations in America. This is a great and a crying evil, and being one that is more likely to increase than diminish, may naturally give rise to some melancholy forebodings concerning the *practical* continuation of this excellent constitution.

In relation to the laws of the United States, I have remarked, on a previous occasion, the *dependence* of judges upon the counsel. I have been present in courts where this has been strikingly injurious to the cause of justice, though this is not to be understood as an universal feature of judicial proceedings; at least I saw no evidence of it in the Supreme Court at Washington, where Judge Washington is among those who preside. He is nephew to the late General, and resides at Mount Vernon.

Some of the judges are, doubtless, men of superior legal knowledge, and high standing in society; but there are others who certainly are not in possession of the former, though they may be of the latter qualification; as, for instance, the Chief Justice of the Common Pleas at Newark, who, I am informed, is a butcher — not a butcher retired from business, and become a lawyer, but he attends to both trades, even on the same day, selling at seven o'clock in the morning a leg of mutton, and at eleven supplying his customers with a slice of Blackstone. Much evil must necessarily result from this heterogeneous admixture of ignorance with learning. Although we might hail the appointment of plain men of business, and possessed of good solid understandings, to award justice to their fellow-citizens as an important benefit conferred on society, in substitution of the legal quibbling and learned oppression of the bar and bench; yet if such men are not permitted to follow the plain dictates of their own understanding, but are tied down by legal forms, by ancient precedents, and by the laws and practice of a country with which they are entirely unacquainted, then, indeed, the appointment of such men becomes an evil instead of a benefit to society; and it would be better to place individuals on the bench, who, — whatever may be their characters in other respects, — their arrogance of deportment or their political subserviency, — yet, at any rate, understand the business upon which they are employed.

Although there may be, and doubtless are many members of the legal profession who are honourable men, yet from all I have seen, or have been able to understand, the lawyers of this country do not seem to merit a particularly high character. My impression of them is, to use an American mode of estimation, at least thirty-three and a third per cent. lower than of their brethren in England. There are various causes which may have produced this deterioration. In the first place, deep and solid research *in any occupation* is neither so much wanted, so much esteemed, nor is it so "*marketable*" a commodity as in Great Britain; further, the greater equality of society, which renders men more independent of each other; the non-classification of the profession of the law, which prevents either portion from being deeply studied, while the ease with which even legal gentlemen can and do alter their mode of obtaining a livelihood, naturally weakens the motives to exertion, and lessens too that strong impression of having at once a reputation, and the very means of existence at stake; — these latter causes we know to be powerfully operative in England. The vast number of lawyers also, as compared with the amount of American population, divides the business into so many channels, that when a job is obtained, no means can be *afforded* to be left untried to render it profitable. These causes, aided by that prolific source of chicanery, our statute book, may account for that of which Americans complain so loudly — the expense of law proceedings, and the want of principle in their professional men.

ELECTIONS.

To pass to another subject. — In all the electioneering addresses which I have seen, it is deserving of remark, that the defeated party complain of the corrupt influence of "Caucus." I have often enquired the meaning of this term, or the nature of the power exercised, but have not received any very satisfactory information. An American writer says that it is "a cant "term for those private meetings which are "held by the political parties, previous to elec-"tions, for the purpose of agreeing upon can-"didates for office, or concerting any measure "which they design carrying at the subsequent "public meeting." The other day I called upon a resident of this city, a person of some political importance. Aware that the subject is already and very variously discussed throughout the States, I casually enquired, "Who do you "think, Sir, will be your next president?" He gave no reply, except by a significant nod. I followed up my enquiry by, "Do you "think, Sir, Mr. Adams will be selected?" To which he answered, with decided confidence, "No; I guess not, Sir; we have the man, we "have the man, we know our man.—Crawford "(the present secretary of the treasury) had it "in *caucus* last time, within a few." I enquired what he meant by having it in caucus; for that Mr. Munroe was elected by an overwhelming majority. His answer was, "Ah! I guess you "don't understand our modes; when you have "been here a few years, you will comprehend "these things. Only mind, I tell you Adams "never can be president; for he will not be "able to do any thing with caucus." From minute enquiry, I understood that this thing called caucus, was *practically* invented by Mr. John Adams, during his presidentship; and that it is now universally practised in the election to every office in America. Since the first choice of Mr. Jefferson, the presidential elections are managed by private meetings (or *caucus*) of the democratic members of congress, previous to elections: they settle among themselves who shall be president. This is what is called getting "the appointment in caucus," and *an instance never occurs of the votes being in opposition to caucus.* When they have determined upon who they wish to be president, they send circulars to their different States, pointing out, by a kind of *congé d'élire*, who they have resolved should be elected: and as the right of voting for presidents is confined to a very limited number, there is no instance of the caucus being *disobeyed.* Mr. Munroe being a democrat was, as a matter of course, voted for by the democratic States; and those of New England being federal, would not, I believe, give a vote upon the occasion It appears that the members of the Washington caucus were almost equally divided between Mr. Crawford and Mr. Munroe; but that some accommodation being agreed upon, the latter got "*the appointment.*" Had his rival obtained this, he and not Mr. Munroe would have been voted for by the democratic States, *as a matter of course.* These are alarming facts; for thus we see that the very men (the members of congress) *who are directly excluded by the constitution from voting*, become, by means of a secret something unknown to that constitution, and at variance with both its letter and spirit, *the real electors to the presidentship.* How necessary are the most unceasing vigilance, and the greatest degree of public principle and public virtue, to preserve even the best institutions from gross perversion! No oligarchy can be more dangerous than this, which deludes the people with a belief that they are all-powerful, and the electors of their chief magistrate, while virtually they are the mere tools of a faction, and have not a voice in the matter. By a reference to the proceedings of congress, it would appear that this vitally important subject was brought under their public consideration in 1816; upon which Mr. Rufus King, and General Harper, made the following observations, every syllable of which deserves your most marked attention :—

Mr. King said, " If there was any part of " the constitution, deemed by its framers and " advocates to be better secured than any other " against the enterprises which have since oc-" curred, it was the very provision on the sub-" ject of election to the *presidency*. The idea " was, that the action of *that particular agency,* " *which has since controlled it,* was as much " displaced by the constitutional plan of elect-" ing the President and Vice President, as could " possibly be devised. *We all know the course* " *which this thing has taken. The election of a* " *President of the United States is no longer that* " *process which the constitution contemplated. In* " *conformity with the original view of the authors* " *of that instrument, I would restore, as tho-* " *roughly as possible, the freedom of election to* " *the people. On the contrary, our progress in* " *government is not for the better ; it is not*

" *likely, hereafter, to be in favour of popular*
" *rights.* It was with the people, the constitu-
" tion meant to place the election of the chief
" magistrate; that being the source the least
" liable to be corrupt. *But if, under the name*
" *of the liberty of the people, we put this power*
" *into other hands, with different interests, we*
" *place it in a situation in which the rights of the*
" *people are violated. Men now live, who will*
" *probably see the end of our government, as we*
" *now go on; terminate when it will, the termin-*
" *ation will not be in favour of public liberty.*
" *For five years past, I have seen a character*
" *developing itself, the predominance of which*
" *I fear.*"

General Harper said, " As to the main propo-
" sition, he was decidedly in its favour; for this
" general reason, that its adoption would tend
" to make the election of President *less a matter*
" *of juggle and intrigue than it now is.*

" He would not say that it would have the ef-
" fect of wholly excluding intrigue; of placing
" this great election on the footing, on which the
" great men who framed the constitution vainly
" imagined they were placing it, of a free, un-
" biassed expression of the public will; but it
" would bring it nearer than at present. *Party*
" *arrangements and bargains would not be so*
" *easy. Bargains could not be so readily struck*
" *with one State for this great office, with another*

"*for that; as according to the present mode of* "*election.* Districting the States for electors, "would have a tendency to render the presi- "dential election more free and independent; "to remove it more from the grasp of party "arrangements; *to prevent bargains between* "*profligate agents, and the selling of the nation* "*for offices to the highest bidder.*"

The motion to remedy these evils was lost by a large majority.

The prevailing American politics of Washington at this time are, what is here called democratic. Previous to what they consider the piratical attack of the English government, some among them were strong federalists. The conduct of our soldiers, with the exception of destroying the public buildings, is said to have been exemplary; private property, and individuals, receiving the most complete protection. Anecdotes are related of English officers assisting the ladies—the male population having all run away, leaving their homes to the protection of the women and children.

The children, particularly in Alexandria, have a dread of the name of "Admiral Cockburn," similar to that I used to entertain of Bonaparte and the Devil. General Ross is an universal favourite, from being, I presume, more humane, and enforcing the orders of his government with less rigour than that exercised by the naval commander. General Lacock, senator from Pennsylvania, who boarded at the same house with myself, and with whom I had the pleasure of a slight acquaintance, amused me one evening by a humourous detail of what foreign travellers have said against America, especially the celebrated poet Thomas Moore, who had visited America in 1803. With the following epistle, dated from Washington, the General was particularly familiar: —

" The lover now, beneath the western star,
Sighs thro' the medium of his sweet segar;
The weary statesman * for repose hath fled
From halls of council to his negro's shed,
Where, blest, he woos some black Aspasia's grace,
And dreams of freedom *in his slave's embrace.*
In fancy now, beneath the twilight gloom,
Come, let me lead thee o'er this modern Rome,
Where tribunes rule, where dusky Davi bow,
And what was Goose Creek once is Tiber now.
This fam'd metropolis, where fancy sees
Squares in morasses, obelisks in trees,
Which travelling fools and gazetteers adorn
With shrines unbuilt and heroes yet unborn;
Though nought but wood and —— they see,
Where streets should run, and sages *ought* to be.
Oh, great Potowmac! Oh, you banks of shade,
You mighty scenes! in nature's morning made;
Say, were your towering hills, your boundless floods,
Your rich savannahs, and majestic woods;
Oh! was a world so bright but born to grace
Its own half-organised, half-minded race

* Supposed to refer to a charge made by the federalists against a celebrated politician of Virginia.

Of weak barbarians, swarming o'er its breast
Like vermin gender'd in the lion's crest?
Were none but brutes to call that soil their home,
Where none but demi-gods should dare to roam?
O'er lake and marsh, through fevers and through fogs,
'Midst bears and Yankies, ——— and frogs,
Thy foot shall follow me; thy heart and eyes
With me shall wander, and with me despise."

The old general laughed at Moore's conceit; and observed, that foreigners were commonly disappointed with this country, more particularly those that were, in Europe, friends of liberty. He thought, however, that such a publication was discreditable to our poet, only *because he had received while here much personal attention.* This same argument was adduced to me by the son of Colonel Boyd, with whom I dined at New Orleans, concerning Moore, and other writers, who told unpleasant truths of their country, or did not view it as the great and faultless political Elysium. That a distinguished individual receiving attentions in a foreign land is a proof of the existence of the common habits of civilized society is unquestionable; but that that should be the criterion by which he is to judge of the whole mass of a country, requires no refutation. Yet I have generally found this to be the standard by which Americans themselves estimate the different parts of their own continent, as well as of Europe: it is not what they saw, but how they were personally treated, which forms the burden of their song; as though in describing a country, either for our friends or the public, we are not bound by every moral tie to speak the truth of that country, and its inhabitants too, whatever may have been the personal conduct of individuals towards ourselves. There can be, surely, in this no breach of hospitality; on the contrary, the man who tells the honest truth of a nation is, as I should conceive, its best friend. Seeing it with the eye of a stranger, he discerns defects which, perhaps, custom has rendered invisible to the eye of the native, and by candidly pointing them out, he affords an opportunity of amendment which would not otherwise be gained.

EUROPEAN POLITICS.

What the European politics of Washington are at this time, I should feel some difficulty in ascertaining: what they were in 1813, may be judged by the following extracts from a small pamphlet which has just fallen into my hands: it is entitled "The celebration of the Russian "victories, in Georgetown district of Columbia, "5th June 1813, including the oration of Mr. Cus- "tis and the address of Mr. Harper.—Printed by "James B. Carter." After describing in glowing language the "*second Lucifer*" (Bonaparte), who, like his archetype, was envious and jealous of the poor remains of human happiness — who

spread devastation with his sword, and meditated the banishment of all true religion; the writer adds,—" In the redemption of the world
" by the arms of Russia, all nations must re-
" joice! And the heart that would not join in
" the " *Te Deum*" which religion and huma-
" nity shout for the deliverance of mankind,
" must be already attuned to the fell discord
" of fiends howling in frantic despair. Can
" it then excite surprise that, in America,
" among a people enjoying the blessings and
" happiness of a government of their own choice,
" the news of BONAPARTE'S DEFEAT was re-
" ceived with a burst of joy and gratitude, such
" as a virtuous and humane people would dis-
" play upon the downfall of tyranny, and the
" promised restoration of peace and prosperity
" to an EMANCIPATED WORLD? Could they con-
" template, without emotions of sympathy,
" any portion of the human family, hunted
" down by the ' *dogs of war*,' and panting un-
" der a load of oppression, extortion and cruelty?
" While you rejoiced at the successes of Russia,
" you evinced a sympathy known only to vir-
" tuous hearts. Then glory in the example
" you have set the world—shew the parasites
" of power, and the creatures of ambition, that
" freedom and virtue expand and warm your
" hearts with general benevolence to mankind
" —and teach a TYRANT and his MINIONS, that

" when the *grand destinies of the United States* " are most *beautifully developed*, they will be " seen in sympathy with those who suffered by " *his* wrongs, and exulting in his OVERTHROW.

" Influenced by such considerations as are " here briefly and faintly described, it was pro- " posed at a meeting of the citizens of George- " town, in the district of Columbia, to testify " their gratulation, and to evince their gra- " titude to the Dispenser of all good, by a suit- " able COMMEMORATION OF THE LATE RUSSIAN " VICTORIES.

" Saturday, the 5th of June, was fixed upon " for the celebration; and John Peter (Mayor), " Robert Beverly, William Marbuary, Thomas " Peter, Washington Bowie, Francis Dodge, " John I. Stull, and John Lee, Esquires, were " appointed a COMMITTEE to prescribe and su- " perintend the arrangements for the day.

" NARRATIVE OF THE CELEBRATION.

" The celebration of the Russian victories commenced on " Saturday, the 5th of June, at the hour of 2 o'clock, P. M. " The company principally assembled previously, at the " Union Hotel, where the committee of arrangement an- " nounced the following as the

" *Order of the Day.*

" In procession to the church — 1st. Ladies. 2d. *Pre-* " *sident of the United States* (Madison), *and Heads of De-* " *partments!!* 3d. Senators and representatives in Congress. " 4th. Members of the Maryland legislature. 5th. Strangers " of distinction. 6th. Citizens. The assembly seated — " 7th. The Russian minister, with his lady, and suite.

" 8th. Foreign consuls. 9th. Reverend clergy and orator
" of the day. 10th. Committee of arrangement. Exercises
" in church — 1st. Solemn music. 2d. Introductory prayer.
" 3d. Music. 4th. Oration. 5th. Music. 6th. Concluding
" prayer. 7th. Grand Russian march, and adjournment to
" the hotel.

" This order was punctually observed, and " contributed much to the regularity and so- " lemnity of the occasion. Agreeable to its " terms, a vast crowd assembled in the Presby- " terian church at the hour appointed. At half " past two the Russian minister, his lady, coun- " sellor of legation, and secretary, reached the " place in his carriage of state. They were " received by the committee of arrangement, " and escorted to a large pew appropriated es- " pecially for their accommodation. At the " same time the foreign consuls, accompanied " by the president and vice-president of the " day, were conducted to another large pew " adjoining that occupied by the Russian le- " gation. The reverend clergy and the orator " of the day, (Mr. Custis,) were next introduced " by the committee.

" The hearts of all in sympathy being suit- " ably tranquillized, the Rev. Mr. Balch, in a " pathetic and reverential strain, addressed the " throne of heaven, imploring the blessing of " God upon the assembly. Mr. Custis, after a " short interval of music, then delivered an " highly interesting, historic, and didactic ora-

" tion, in a style peculiar to his oratory, and re-
" flecting warm and sympathetic encomiums
" upon Russian valour. The scene in the church
" was closed with prayer, when the lady of
" the Russian minister was conducted to her
" carriage, the band playing a fine exhilarating
" Russian march. The Russian legation, suc-
" ceeded by foreign consuls, and other persons
" of distinction, including senators and repre-
" sentatives in Congress, were escorted to the
" Union Hotel.

" At four o'clock the company entered the
" dining rooms, and was seated in the most
" perfect order — the Russian Legation and
" foreign consuls ranged on the right, the
" Orator of the day on the left, of the Pre-
" sident. The whole entertainment was sump-
" tuous, and beautifully ordered, to which a
" company of near three hundred gentlemen
" sat down.

" After the cloth was removed the President
" announced the following toasts :

" *The United States of America* — May justice
" be her guide, neutrality her policy, and liberty
" the essence of her national existence.

" [Music — Hail Columbia.

" *The Empire of Rusisa* — May this Northern
" Star break the power of attraction that has
" fastened the Continent of Europe to the mag-
" net of France. [Grand Russian air.

" When the fourth toast was to be given, the
" President called on Mr. Harper of Baltimore,
" who gave " ALEXANDER THE DELIVERER."

" (This toast was accompanied by a course of
" remarks made by Mr. Harper, that excited
" bursts of applause highly descriptive of the
" feelings which animated this patriotic as-
" sembly.)

" *Moscow in Flames* — This is the holy confla-
" gration, that lights the nations of the earth to
" independence and peace. [Solemn Russian air.

" *The Memory of Washington*—Oh! that thy
" canonized form, hearsed in death, could burst
" its cearment and raise a drooping empire!
" [Washington's March.

" *The Heroes of the Revolution* — Alas! the
" fruits are fast withering of your patriot toils.
" [Solemn Dirge.

" *The American Navy* — This is the cradle of
" our rights, here let us cherish, foster and
" honour those heroic spirits, who are destined
" to punish the aggression of hostile powers.
" [Tars of Columbia.

" *Capts. Hull, Jones, Decatur, Bainbridge,*
" *and Lawrence;* ' and ye too have scattered
" thunderbolts.' — Columbia, these thy chosen
" sons, outstrip the world in deeds of valour.
" [Decatur's March.

" *The native Tars of America* — Eternal war,
" when necessary, for their essential rights.
" [Freedom and our Native Land

" *Agriculture mourning—Commerce in tears—*
" You have our sympathies, we can do no more.
" [Guardian Angels.

" *The Fair of America*—With what Roman
" matron may we not compare?
" [Sweet Passion of Love."

OFFICIAL COMMUNICATION FROM THE LAND-OFFICE.

Having been invited to visit the tomb of the great Washington, which is about 10 miles from hence, I hasten to a conclusion; and shall leave my own reflections to my next and last report, which I design shall follow this in about three weeks, when I shall have seen Baltimore, and also visited some of the smaller eastern towns.

By a private letter to my friend R—— you are aware of an application which I have made to the land-office, concerning a tract of 40,000 acres; I inclose you Mr. Meigs's reply.

" Sir, General Land-Office.

" In reply to your letter: I have to say, that
" the public lands north-west of the river Ohio
" are sold at two dollars per acre, payable one-
" fourth cash; one-fourth in two years; one-
" fourth in three years; one-fourth in four
" years. A discount of eight per cent. per
" annum for prompt payment reduces the cash
" price to one dollar sixty-four cents per acre.
" If the instalments are not all paid within five

" years, the land is offered at public sale, if it " brings more than the principal and interest " due to the United States, the surplus is paid " to the original purchaser; if the principal and " interest is not bid, the land reverts to the " United States, and the monies paid on account " are forfeited.

" These are the terms of sale without respect " to persons or quantity.

" I am very respectfully,

" Sir,

" Your obedient servant,

" JOSIAH MEIGS."

" MR. HENRY FEARON,
" At Mrs. Lindsay's, Washington."

The present report will go by the British packet free of expence, the English ambassador having acceded to my application in the following polite note, though I had not an introduction to him:

" Mr. Bagot presents his compliments to Mr. " Fearon, and has the honour to inform him " that if Mr. F. will send the papers alluded to " in his letter to Mr. Bagot's house in the " course of Friday next, he will endeavour to " transmit them to England in his bag, should " they not prove voluminous."

" Washington,
" MR. HENRY FEARON, Pennsylvania Avenue."

Wishing health and happiness to you all, and indulging the anxious hope that I shall soon see you either on this or the other side of the Atlantic, I for the present take my leave.

P. S. I break open the package to inclose a letter from Mr. Birkbeck, in reply to mine when I *first* visited Louisville; it is addressed to me at Baltimore.

" Sir, Princeton, Nov. 29. 1817.

" It would give me much pleasure to afford " you satisfactory information on the several " particulars you mention, but I am, like your- " self, a stranger in this country, and can there- " fore only communicate to you my opinions in " answer to your inquiries.

" To the first, as to the most eligible part of " the United States for obtaining improved " *farms*, or uncultivated lands for Englishmen, " &c. I reply, that with a view to the settlement " of the number of families you mention, it will " be vain to look for improved farms in any " part that I have seen or heard of. Probably " a single family might be suited in almost any " large district, as the changes which are con- " tinually occurring in human affairs, will occa- " sionally throw eligible farms into the market " every where. But you can have no *choice* of " cultivated lands, as those you would prefer

" are the least likely to be disposed of; and it
" is altogether unlikely you should meet with
" a body of such lands, for the accommodation
" of thirty or forty families; considering, too,
" that, by travelling a few days' journey farther
" west, you may have a *choice* of land of equal
" value at one-tenth of the price, where they
" may settle contiguous, or at least near to each
" other, I have no hesitation in recommending
" you to do as I have done; that is, to head
" the tide of emigration, and provide for your
" friends where the lands are yet unappro-
" priated.

" After traversing the States of Ohio and
" Indiana, looking out for a tract suited to
" my own views, and those of a number of
" our countrymen who have signified their in-
" tentions of following our example, I have
" fixed on this spot in Illinois, and am the
" better pleased with it the more I see of it.

" As to obtaining *labourers*. A single settler
" may get his labour done by the piece on
" moderate terms, not higher than in some
" parts of England; but if many families settle
" together, all requiring this article, and none
" supplying it, they must obtain it from else-
" where. Let them import English labourers,
" or make advantageous proposals to such as
" are continually arriving at the eastern ports.

" *Provisions* are cheap of course. Wheat three

"and four-pence sterling per bushel. Beef and "pork two-pence per pound, groceries and "clothing dear, building moderate, either by "wood or brick. Bricks are laid by the thou-"sand, at eight dollars or under, including "lime.

"*Privations* I cannot enumerate. Their "amount depends on the previous habits and "present disposition of individuals: for myself "and family, the privations already experienced, "or anticipated, are of small account compared "with the advantages.

"Horses, 60 to 100 dollars, or upwards; cows, "10 to 20 dollars; sows, 3 to 5 dollars.

"*Society* is made up of new-comers chiefly, "and, of course, must partake of the leading "characters of these. There is generally a "little bias of attraction in a newly settled "neighbourhood, which brings emigrants from "some particular state or country to that spot; "and thus a tone is given to the society. Where "we are settling, society is yet unborn as it "were. It will, as in other places, be made "up of such as come; among whom English "farmers, I presume, will form a large pro-"portion.

"*Roads* as yet are in a state of nature.

"*Purchases* of land are best made at the land-"offices: payments, five years, or prompt; if "the latter, eight per cent. discount.

" Mechanics' wages, 1 dollar to 1½. Carpen-
" ters, smiths, shoemakers, brickmakers, and
" bricklayers, are among the first in requisition
" for a new settlement: others follow in course;
" —tanners, saddlers, tailors, hatters, tin-work-
" ers, &c. &c.

" We rely on good *markets* for produce,
" through the grand navigable communication
" we enjoy with the ocean.

" *Medical aid* is not of difficult attainment.
" The English of both sexes, and strangers in
" general, are liable to some bilious attacks on
" their first arrival; these complaints seem,
" however, simple, and not difficult to manage
" if taken in time.

" The *manufactures* you mention may here-
" after be eligible; cotton, woollen, linen,
" stockings, &c. Certainly not at present.
" Beer, spirits, pottery, tanning, are objects of
" immediate attention.

" The *minerals* of our district are not much
" known. We have excellent limestone; I be-
" lieve we have coal: wood will, however, be
" the cheapest fuel for some years.

" *Implements* are cheap till you commence
" with the iron. A waggon, 35 or 40 dollars,
" exclusive of tier to wheels. A strong waggon
" for the road complete will amount to 160
" dollars or upwards.

" The best *mode of coming* from England to

" this part of the western country is by an " eastern port, thence to Pittsburgh, and down " the Ohio to Shawnee town. Clothing, bed- " ding, household linen, simple medicines of " the best quality, and sundry small articles of " cutlery and light tools, are the best things for " an emigrant to bring out.

" I can hardly reply to your inquiry about " the *manner of travelling*; it must be suited to " the party. Horseback is the most pleasant " and expeditious; on foot the cheapest: a " light waggon is eligible in some cases; in " others the stage is a necessary evil. I see I " shall render you liable to double postage, but " I wished to reply to each of your inquiries as " far as I could.

" To serve you or your friends will be a plea- " sure to, Sir,

" Yours, &c. &c.

" MORRIS BIRKBECK."

" To MR. H. FEARON,
" Post-Office, Baltimore."

Note.—In preparing these pages for the press, I observe that this communication of Mr. Birkbeck's forms a part of his recent publication, called " Letters from Illinois." Aug. 1818.

SEVENTH REPORT.

Leave Washington. — Arrive in Baltimore. — Character of the People. — Churches; their Architecture. — Religious Sects. — Mode in which Capital could be advantageously employed. — New York Forum. — Politics of Americans in relation to Europe. — Their Feelings towards Citizens of foreign Birth. — Public Resolutions upon this Subject. — My Friends commission Mr. Flower to purchase Land in Illinois. — Review of the Character and Condition of Americans. — The first Settlers. — Progressive Advancement towards the Comforts and Intelligence of Europe. — The Colonial Government. — The Revolution; its Cause. — Mr. Jefferson's Statement concerning the Effect of Paine's "Common Sense." — Effect of Revolution upon Moral and National Character. — Disorder of the Government. — Revision of the Constitution. — Rise of the Parties called Democrats and Federalists; their adverse European Politics. — Administration of Mr. Adams. — Rise of Mr. Jefferson. — Indolent Character of Americans; its Cause. — The War of 1812. — *Depreciation of Government Security. — National Laws.*

New York, April 21. 1818.

Having now again arrived at the point from which I set out in the summer of last year, I have determined to take up my residence in this city, at least until I receive the long-wished-for letters of my friends ——, ——, and ——, which will, of course, govern my future proceedings, and inform me whether to prepare for your reception, either in this city or that of

Philadelphia, or return to the western country, and make a final arrangement concerning some lots in either Ohio or the Illinois; or recross the Atlantic, making Liverpool the port of my destination, in order to visit our friends in Yorkshire and Leicestershire, previous to my arrival in London. — — — — —
— — — — — — —
— — — — — — —

BALTIMORE.

On leaving Washington for this place, I took Baltimore in my way, and resided there some time. It is a commercial city of great importance; and, though not at present of the first rank, is rising with a rapidity almost unparalleled.

The *substantial features* of the American character appear here to be the same as throughout the Union, although the "Baltimorians" themselves lay claim to a superior reputation for hospitality, enterprise, and bravery. Taking my own experience as a sample of the first, I most willingly bear favourable testimony to their character; but then it must be understood comparatively, and not in the English sense of the word. In regard to the second, they appear entitled to it, judging from their shipping, much of which is engaged in hazardous pursuits, together with the speculative improvements of their town, and their having, by superior activity, supplanted Philadelphia in part of the western country trade; yet the merchants of this city are said to be deficient in capital. Of their bravery, history will speak when recording their gallant and successful defence of their city, though attacked by the combined naval and military forces of England.

Dancing and music are the prevailing amusements.

The ladies dress gaily and expensively.

Rents, occupations, price of labour, clothing, employment for, and wages of mechanics, are here so precisely similar to those of the other Atlantic cities, that a detail is unnecessary.

Some idea may be gained of the rapid progress of certain parts of the United States, from the fact, that 70 years ago Baltimore consisted of 10 houses: it now contains 60,000 inhabitants.

The principal street runs east and west, parallel with the river, and is intersected by numerous others, containing many excellent buildings. North and east of the town the land rises, affording beautiful views of the city and bay.—Steam-boats proceed from here to Norfolk in Virginia, and to New London in Connecticut, by way of New York. In the winter months this delightful mode of travelling is interrupted: miserable stages and bad roads are then its substitute.

There are several religious sects, the most numerous of which are Roman Catholics. Episcopalians, Baptists, Presbyterians, Methodists, and Quakers, have each a respectable number of partisans; and an Unitarian Church is now building. In connection with churches, let me observe, by the way, that the architecture of several displays first-rate talent; and it seems not a little surprising, that such ability should have been overlooked by the conductors of the national buildings at Washington.

The most accurate information which I can obtain, causes me to believe that capital could be profitably engaged here, in importing dry goods from Great Britain; that mechanics, in the usual businesses, can get ready employment, will receive 40s. 6d. to 45s. per week, and pay for their board and lodging 15s. 9d. to 18s. In politics, Baltimore is a singular exception to all other American sea-port cities, in being anti-federal, or what is here denominated democratic. It lies, however, in a slave State, and seems by no means deficient in all the horrors of that barbarous system. This city also occupies the foremost ranks in deadly animosity towards England.

Having returned through many parts of my former route, I have no new facts to communicate, but can say that my impressions of America are generally confirmed.

NEW YORK.

There is a highly respectable public assembly occasionally held in New York, called "The Forum:" I have attended twice — the place of meeting is in the ball-room of the city hotel. In the centre a sort of stage is erected, from which the orations are delivered. The charge is 6¾d., with free admission for ladies. The receipts are appropriated to charitable purposes. The speakers, as I understand was once frequently the case in London, are young lawyers, who practise as an assistant to their more profitable exercises. Though the speaking is extemporaneous, inasmuch as it is not written, yet it appears by no means spontaneous, bearing decided evidence of previous rehearsal and hard labour. The number of orators upon those occasions, when I was present, was six. To each side of both the questions was allotted an equal number of advocates; who, though following each other with the regularity of mechanism, did not even risk a glance at the line of argument pursued by their predecessors, each having got his task by rote: and when their memories failed them, immediate recourse was had to the written speech, carefully deposited in the pocket. Although the talents of these young gentlemen for public display do not rank in the first class of American oratory, yet they may be regarded as presenting a fair average sample of the elocution of both the bar and senate; an elocution which, though said to be founded upon the English and French models, is so essentially different from either, that it deserves to be regarded as a distinct species. It is chiefly distinguished by a set logical arrangement with regard to matter, but expressed in inflated language, unaccompanied by correspondent action; strong expressions are used to express minor ideas; words of six syllables are substituted for deep thought or sound argument; and there is evidently a constant labour after allusions and simile, which are often thread-bare and broken. The manner of their speakers is generally marked by an equal absence of modest diffidence and manly boldness: they show little evidence of possessing a literary mind; their train of argument and their choice of language are, in their general effect, cold, measured, legal, and bombastic.

The question discussed upon the first evening of my attendance was the following: "Is the "present peace of Europe likely to be of long "continuance?" The number of the audience was about 700, full one-half of which were ladies, and all highly respectable in their appearance. The place of assembly is not surpassed by any ball-room which I have seen in London. The native political views of all the speakers were the same, though they took opposite grounds in this debate upon foreign affairs.

The following is a summary of their principles: America, the greatest country in the world; republics, the best form of government in the world; the revolution, the most important epoch since the establishment of Christianity; war, occasionally necessary; a state of perpetual peace would be a perpetual curse; Russia, the greatest country in Europe,—will soon be enabled to contend with England at sea; Napoleon, a fiend—the French, a nation of athiests who do not deserve peace; English government, very excellent—English people, the contrary; Alexander, the deliverer, the most virtuous and magnanimous monarch ever known; evil necessary in society—a long digression to prove its origin; missionary societies of incalculable benefit, particularly those which were sent to the wild parts of Kentucky and Indiana; death of the Princess Charlotte must entail upon England dire calamities; the holy league, a wise, pacific, and humane combination; liberty and happiness of all parts of Europe rapidly *progressing*.

The next subject which I heard spoken upon was, "Is it necessary for the interests of the "United States, that its government should be "in the hands of a party?" This elicited similar trains of ideas to those delivered upon the previous evening. There was the same strange, incongruous mixture of republican and anti-republican sentiments, mixed up in the speech of every orator. The advocates of reform in England were ridiculed with the same breath that praised their own revolution: popular meetings censured, and the United States' constitution, founded upon the rights of the people, extolled to the skies. Lord Cochrane was abused, the American navy flattered, the rights of man and the excellence of the Emperor Alexander insisted upon, dangers of parties and cabals exposed, and popular meetings execrated.

This being the close of the season, a valedictory address was delivered by Mr. Fessenden, a gentleman of very middling talent, and extravagantly conceited in his manners. He laid down as the basis of good government, a variety of axioms favourable both to liberty and tyranny. "The first qualification for *all offices*, from the "president down to the lowest constable, ought "(he said) to be, that the candidates were *natife* "*born* citizens." This sentiment was frequently repeated, and always tumultuously and unanimously applauded! I was previously well aware of the firm hold which this feeling possesses in the minds of all native Americans; but I did not anticipate its fearless avowal in a large and mixed assembly. Throughout the States, I have remarked that there is a strong line of distinction drawn between *citizens of native and of foreign birth*; and, in some cases, where the latter have professed principles of republicanism in Europe, (a sin which might, at least, one should suppose, be forgiven them *in the United States of America,*) they are *treated with scorn*, as out-casts, who ought to have remained in their own country, and have submitted to whatever form of despotism it chose to exert over them. So deeply rooted, indeed, are these sentiments in the American mind, that they give some colour to, though they can hardly justify the address which I find unanimously voted in the year 1809, at a meeting in New York of five hundred adopted citizens, from which the following are extracts:

" At a respectable meeting, consisting of about five hundred " Adopted Republican Citizens of the city of New York, " held at Lyon's Hotel, Mott-Street, —*Mr. Archibald* " *Taylor* being unanimously called to the chair, and *Dr.* " *Stephen Dempsey* appointed secretary, the subjoined " address was unanimously adopted, and ordered to be " published.

" *To the Adopted Republican Citizens of the City of* " *New York.*

" FELLOW CITIZENS,

" A long train of disagreeable circumstances have called us " together, and induced us to address you upon a subject " which, for years, we have acutely felt and deeply deplored. " Some of you, groaning under oppression in your native " land, have voluntarily emigrated from it, whilst others, " more afflicted by despotism, and less favoured by propi- " tious events, find yourselves in the condition of involuntary " exile. All, however, have chosen, as a resting-place in " the journey through life, this ' asylum for the oppressed " of all nations.' Here, perhaps, mistaking the character

" of human nature, we pleasingly anticipated, from those " who avow themselves the friends of freedom, exemption " from that religious persecution and civil tyranny, whose " inexorable reign had forced us from our native country. " Alas! *how greatly were we mistaken! how egregiously have " we been disappointed! Our constitutions and governments " are indeed free, but between these admirable institutions and " ourselves a tyranny is intervened, much less tolerable than " that from which we fled.* We have made permanent set- " tlements in the land of our forefathers; we admire and we " are attached to our republican institutions; we have " complied with the injunctions of the constitutions and the " laws, and we will support them upon equal terms, with " our lives and our fortunes. *But how are we treated? " What has been our reception? Has good faith been observed? " Have the promises been performed? Are not we, who are " citizens by all the solemnities and obligations of law, treated " as aliens—stigmatized as foreigners.* We complain not " of the constitutions and the laws; they are liberal in prin- " ciple and benign in operation. They enjoin an abju- " ration of former allegiance: have we not with alacrity " complied with the injunction? They require an oath of " fidelity to the Union and to the States: devoted in spirit " and in truth to both, we have eagerly taken it. What more " is required? What more can be expected? The laws re- " quire no more. *Shall an under-plot, a counter operation, " individual jealousy, and pale-faced cabal, frowned upon by " the very elements of the state, subvert the law—put it at " defiance—trample it under foot?* The law places upon " the same undistinguishable level, the citizen of native and " the citizen of foreign birth. Are we to be told, in this " enlightened age, that the *law* is *not* to govern; that the " essence of well-ordered society is *not* a government of " laws, but a government of the worst passions? Go back " then to a state of anarchy; tear out the bowels of society; " revert to the rude condition of untutored nature, and let " the strongest govern. We have never ceased to cherish " and to inculcate those opinions which are most consonant " to the civil and social state. We have remonstrated against

" *distinctions, at once impolitic and unjust, between native*
" *and adopted citizens;* but have not our remonstrances and
" efforts been in vain? No zeal, no exertions, no services,
" however disinterested, unremitted, or great, have been
" sufficient to shield us from an epithet which, while it
" poisons the social and impairs the enjoyment of political
" life, must ultimately terminate in the ruin of the repub-
" lican party in this city. Alas! has our republic turned
" upon itself, and in the short period of a few years from
" the adoption of the constitution?"

" Resolved unanimously, that 500 copies of the above
" address and resolution be printed in hand-bills for the
" benefit of our fellow republican adopted citizens.

" ARCHIBALD TAYLOR, Chairman.
" S. DEMPSEY, Secretary."

24th April. — Upon my return from an excursion to New Jersey, I received a letter from my friend C——, dated " Hertford, Jan. 30." brought by Mr. W. Walford of Bishopsgate-street, who came in the " Minerva, Smyth," and is immediately proceeding on to Mr. Birkbeck. I am much concerned to hear, that even at that date, my first was the only report which had reached you. Of the accident which occurred to the " Electra of Philadelphia," and the melancholy catastrophe of Captain Williams, I was apprised by Lloyd's list; but as she was taken safely into St. Maloes, I had indulged the hope, that before the date of the above letter, you had safely received my communications: they were accompanied by a large packet of newspapers, pamphlets, and some curiosities. Had I been so thoughtful as to have mentioned to Mr. ——, of Philadelphia, that I wished a parcel taken to England, he assures me that Mr. Rush, the ambassador, who sailed in the Franklin, seventy-four, would have most willingly conveyed it to London; — however, this knowledge is now unavailing, but I trust that my several reports, including the last from Virginia and Washington, dated in March, are, by this time, in your possession. Your commission to Mr. Flower, Mr. Birkbeck's associate, to purchase 9,000 acres in the Illinois, is certainly a bold measure; but as you desire my immediate return, I shall defer the discussion of its merits until I am blessed with the pleasure of meeting you all face to face, and once more enjoying the indescribable delight of your society and an English fire-side. I shall, in all probability, embark by about the middle of next month. Captain H.—— sails in a few days, and I am sure will take particular care of this communication.

The remark is now an old one, "That "Americans have no national character." Half a century ago the observation was probably correct; but I think a personal acquaintance will show its utter want of foundation at the present period. Their national character, in my judgment, is broadly and distinctly marked; and, as is common with that of other nations, partakes of a mixture of wisdom and folly, of virtue and vice, of some excellences and of great defects.

Although I cannot go the whole length of *Moore*'s description of them, yet with a mind constituted, as I presume his to be, and with the disappointments which his strong prepossessions in favour of America must have given rise to, I can easily conceive that he would not find much difficulty in concluding that — "The rude fa-
" miliarity of the lower orders, and indeed the
" unpolished state of society in general, would
" neither surprise nor disgust, if they seemed to
" flow from that simplicity of character, that
" honest ignorance of the class of refinement,
" which may be looked for in a new and inexpe-
" rienced people. *But when we find them arrived*
" *at maturity in most of the vices, and all the pride*
" of civilization, while they are still so remote
" from its elegant characteristics, it is impossible
" not to feel *that this youthful decay, this crude*
" *anticipation of the natural period of corruption*,
" represses every sanguine hope of the future
" greatness and energy of America."

National, like individual character, must be in a great measure formed or controlled by the circumstances in which men are situated. For the creation of a valuable standard of character, Americans are disadvantageously placed: they are far removed from that mass of floating intelligence which pervades Europe, but more especially England; and in addition to this, as a people, and in their political capacity, they have nothing to contend for — nothing to call forth their energies, and but little of external excitement beyond the pursuits of gain, and merely animal gratification. In their civil condition, all obtain a living with ease: For religion, their priests think for them; they have neither persecution to excite zeal, opposition or controversy to awaken them to enquiry, nor yet virtue or knowledge sufficient to show them its advantages; whilst, in their political capacity, they have the cheapest, the easiest, and the most *reasonable* form of government in the world. To illustrate nations by individuals is an old, and by no means inappropriate mode of estimating political character; and, for myself, I never knew an individual who was freed from strong external excitement, or who possessed every thing which he desired without personal exertion, that did not sink into indolence, indifference, selfishness, and actual vice. This seems to be made, and wisely so, one of the terms and conditions of our nature — "Whom the Lord "loveth he chastiseth," is a sacred maxim; that chastisement is, I believe, as valuable as it is necessary. I have not indeed seen the character whom I could call excellent, that had not undergone trials, privations, and sufferings. To become intellectual, energetic, and virtuous, in the present state of our existence, seems to require that we should first know sorrow, and have been acquainted with grief; not that I am the advocate for political oppression in order to produce those consequences, or that I wish to see transplanted into this free and hitherto unoppressed country, enormous taxation — iniquity in high places — civil disabilities — religious exclusions — standing armies — and hired spies and informers; but that a something *must* occur, before this people can be roused from their present lethargy,—made, even in a limited degree, deserving of their unparalleled natural and political advantages—that something of this nature, among the wise dispensations of Providence, *will* occur, I have no doubt; for I cannot allow myself to draw the melancholy conclusion of Moore, that what we now see of the character of the people, bad as it may appear, " represses every " sanguine hope of the future energy and great- " ness of America."

To understand America correctly, it is, in some measure, necessary to recur to the character and condition of its first civilized population. They were, in the first instance, emigrants from the several European nations, particularly England; the most respectable class of which were those who fled from religious persecution; no inconsiderable number of transports; the great body of the rest were as emigrants ever are — the most enterprising, the most needy, but by no means the most intelligent of their native country. It is such only, generally speaking, that can be induced to quit the land which gave them birth; even although the exchange should bring with it the most decided advantages. The word *home* contains a sacred spell, which rarely can be broken. We cling to the hovels, the rocks, and the sands of our birth-place, with a filial affection which seldom ceases but with our existence. These feelings the Deity seems to have implanted for wise purposes in the bosoms of all men. The emigrant to a wilderness will therefore rarely be a man even moderate in his worldly circumstances; and he will still more rarely be possessed of regular habits, or a cultivated mind. *Exceptions* will exist of persons who take distant views, and who can bring every feeling and thought under the guidance of reflection and principle; but such will ever be but *exceptions*, while our nature remains the same. Such then were the seeds of American society; let us look at the circumstances in which these men were placed; in a country where civilization had made no progress; where every man, both in mind and body, was fully occupied in obtaining the bare means of subsistence; and where their relative situation towards the natives of the soil was calculated to deaden every just, benevolent, and humane sentiment. As society advanced, indeed, the whole population no longer remained "hewers of wood

" and drawers of water." Classification commenced; but still those whose views, means, or habits could be mental, were extremely limited in number. They left Europe at a dark period, not themselves the finest specimens of the national picture; even those amongst them who had leisure for literary objects, met with obstacles at every step—the want of books, the want of society, and of communication with learned individuals or of scientific bodies. There was besides no history attached to their country; they lived *indeed* in a new world, " which was endeared to them by no recollec- " tions, and which could neither excite nor " gratify their curiosity, by the records of the " past." The first accessions of strength from the "*old country*," furnished little besides an increase of the manual labour. The colonial government introduced some men of information: public education was attended to; riches increased; the slave-trade was encouraged; negroes were introduced in every American colony; the extermination of Indians went on, the invaders gradually seizing on their country. Literature was now in some respects advancing, though the colonists depended for their mental as well as bodily clothing upon the mother-country; English, Dutch, Irish, Scotch, Germans, and their several descendants, were becoming to speak one language, and have one common interest. They were, as colonists ever and necessarily are, inferior to the parent country in the first class of its intelligence, but above its grosser ignorance. Society had at this time acquired stability. The *Revolution* now took place. The motives and causes which led to this most important event are deserving of marked attention: they were not, as had been the case with most other great national struggles, a dissatisfaction *generally* with their government, or a desire to be an *independent people*. Their resistance went to one specific claim of the English ministry, *taxation without representation;* this object defeated, their design was to return to their former political condition: that there was no original intention to establish an independent constitution, is admitted by Mr. Jefferson in his "*Notes on Virginia.*" In the April of 1776, three months before the declaration of independence, Paine's "*Common Sense*" appeared. Previous to the publication of this book, the leaders in the contest were made acquainted with its object and general purport. They were then alarmed — completely frightened at the bare idea of declaring themselves independent. *Six* individuals could not be found, who, at that time, would go the length of a separation from the mother-country, from which a small concession, with regard to the stamp-act, was hailed with the most enthusiastic delight — the wish of the whole people being to heal the existing differences, and return to their former dependent situation. These facts are necessary to be borne in mind, as they will account for much which exists in the people of the United States at the present day. The effect of "*Common Sense*" upon the public mind was electric. Men were alarmed indeed—but they read, and conviction flashed upon their minds. Three months after the appearance of this book, the "Declaration of Independence" was signed. The contest now assumed altogether an altered aspect; the struggle was no longer for a rescue from a peculiar mode of taxation, but for the maintaining of rights, political and national, for vital and fundamental principles, which, if once established, would build upon their shores a temple of freedom, and leave it there, a model for other nations and for after ages. The friends of human liberty in Europe crossed the Atlantic to fan their darling flame. Others also emigrated of a more dubious character: America became the receptacle for speculators and fortune-hunters, for adventurers and base and demoralized characters of every shade and description. The peaceful pursuits of agriculture were exchanged for those of the sword; society was shifted from its base, and every thing became disorganized. Peace was at length proclaimed, but it failed to bring with it those halcyon days, of which the olive-branch is generally considered the precursor. America was now a chaos, bankrupt alike, it was feared, in morals and in finances. Their warmest patriots doubted whether their independence were not in fact a curse to them. The administration of Washington, which succeeded, was marked by policy, by sound views, and by political wisdom; but, in drawing up the constitution, the desire to guard against the *possibility* of corruption, nearly produced the effect of destroying all government — a jealousy of power, carried to an imprudent excess, had too much weakened the pillars which should support the political fabric. A revision of the principles of the federal union became necessary to the salvation of the republic. This question gave rise to two great political parties *, *practically* though not *theoretically* possessed of opposite principles of government, and fostering in their breasts, even unto this day, the most implacable hatred. The friend of domestic peace and of public morals, feeling, perhaps too acutely, present evils, without calculating that a time for their correction must arrive, fondly dwelt upon a remembrance of those days when

* Those who advocated the measure of a revision of the Constitution, for the purpose of increasing the powers of the general government, took the name of Federalists, and their opponents that of Democrats.

hey were children of the English family; forgetting, as men too frequently do when reviewing the past, all that was painful and unpleasant, and only cherishing the recollection and sighing after advantages of which they had been deprived. European politics became now the subject of general attention. The French revolution naturally produced unusual excitement: a large majority were its advocates. They considered the event as only a continuation of the struggle which they had commenced, for the emancipation of the world. Others, sickened with the effects of their own change, viewed it with jaundiced eyes. Great Britain, joining in the confederacy against the new Republic, and the excesses committed by the French, afforded fresh food for the nourishment of political parties on this continent. The *federalists* now obtained the additional title of English tories, and the *democrats*, that of French jacobins. Revolutionists upon the wildest principles flocked to America. The French party became so numerous and so strong, that those who differed from them were in fact exposed to a system of practical proscription throughout the Union. A head, less deliberate and cool than Washington's, would have been driven into an open alliance with republican France; as it was, the Gallic ambassador (Genet) nearly set the administration at defiance. So triumphant indeed were these advocates of desperate measures, that at one period an expression of difference of opinion endangered personal safety, and even a list of proscribed Americans (among which was Mr. John Quincy Adams) was suspended from the mast-head of a French frigate in Boston harbour. This danger, however, was by prudence ultimately avoided, and peril from the contrary side would seem next to have followed. The presidency of Mr. Adams (a federalist) succeeded that of Washington. Some of his measures were perhaps compelled by the circumstances of the times; but no friend of liberty can advocate his fourteen years' naturalization law; his frequent public prosecutions for libel; his plans for a standing army, and his aim to obtain the state and style of royalty. The effect of his administration was to re-excite all the violent and turbulent feelings of the democratic party, which Washington's policy had allayed. At the termination of the first period of his presidency, a desperate conflict ensued: the federal party were defeated in his person for the Presidentship by a majority of one. Mr. Jefferson rose upon his ruins, and from that time to the present, the democratic party have sat at the helm of state. The unsuccessful attempt at revolution in Ireland, threw into America a considerable number of well-intentioned perhaps, but certainly very diseased members of the body politic; while the accession of multitudes of the most ignorant classes of society from Holland and Germany, together with the vast increase of black population, rapidly added to the numerical population, extending the range and increasing the produce of manual labour without adding any thing that was valuable to, if I may so express myself, the stock of national mind. America, in the meantime, in her political capacity, was making rapid advances towards taking her standing as a first-rate power. Her internal resources were boundless; her geographical situation secured her from attack during the weakness, as it were, of infancy; her population went on increasing in a ratio not paralleled in modern times, but easily to be accounted for upon well-known principles of political economy. At this time it was that the disturbed state of Europe threw into her hands the carrying trade of the world, and enabled her to erect a mercantile marine, only second to that of Great Britain. This unexpected, and *unprepared-for* influx of wealth, demoralized, while it enriched; with the people, there was no preparation, no pupillage, no gradation, no step from the primitive log-house to the splendour of the palace. European luxury and vice, unadorned by European knowledge, and not ameliorated by European habits of refinement, rapidly overspread the land, and produced their natural and unavoidable consequences. The pursuits of the whole people assumed also a hazardous and *speculative* cast; opportunities for indulging which were constantly presented by the disturbed state of European commerce, and by their own vast unpeopled continent. The means of living were in the hands of every man, with the occupation of but one-fourth part of his time. They were in possession of political and domestic ease, the sources, or the value of which, their want of reflection prevented them from estimating; and having at once the means, the time, and the opportunity of gratifying their passions, or indulging their indolence, they have not pursued learning beyond their school-books. Thus, neglecting to encourage any pursuits, either individually or collectively, which may be called *mental*, they appear, as a nation, to have sunk into habits of indolence and indifference; they are neither lively in their tempers, nor generous in their dispositions: though a great political nation, they have little science and no literature; and, as individuals, while they are theoretically possessed of freedom and independence, they are too frequently but mere machines in the hands of interested and unprincipled men.

The war of 1812 forms an important epoch in their history; it not only called into action all their latent animosities, but it produced an effect which had not been anticipated. It was found that their resources, though vast, and even boundless, were as yet unorganized, and not of a kind of which they could immediately avail themselves. Party violence was extreme — loans could not be negotiated — government securities sold at $33\frac{3}{4}$ per cent. discount — specie had disappeared, and penny and two-penny notes were a common circulating medium. A convention was held of the New England States, which, had not peace intervened to prevent their views being carried into execution, would probably have terminated in a division of the States. Loans, contracts, jobs, smuggling, peculation, and fraud infected every part of the Union. The nation suffered, — but, as their sufferings were of short duration, they have now almost forgotten their existence.

Looking fairly therefore at all these circumstances, we ought not to be surprised to find that *American theory is at least two centuries in advance of American practice.* We have usually connected with our ideas of republicanism and unpolished manners, a simplicity and honesty of mind which more than compensate for all minor defects. That we should not meet with even an approach to these characteristics in America is by no means extraordinary, when we reflect upon their origin and the materials from which their present character is derived. They were not originally a new people, who have gradually advanced from barbarism to a knowledge of enlightened political principles; on the contrary, they formed not even the best portion of an old stock, and they have been placed in novel circumstances, and occupied in pursuits little calculated to increase political virtue, or advance mental acquirements. Their constitution itself is not an original production; it is modelled, in fact, upon that of England, partaking of most of its forms, intermixed with many peculiarities of the colonial *régime*. In the instance of Rhode Island, the original charter of Charles the Second is its present form of government. The laws of England are at this moment, almost without even an attempt at improvement, the laws of America. Old Bailey, Hicks's Hall, and Westminster Causes, with the acts of George the Third, &c. &c. &c. are now cited in the most distant courts of law — in the wilderness as well as in *old* America: even the French lawyers in Louisiana are compelled to substitute Coke's Institutes, Blackstone's Commentaries, and East's Reports, in the stead of the laws of the *ancien régime*, or the modern assistance which could have been derived from the *Code Napoleon!*

The theory of *education* is British, at least so far as that name can be given to mere externals; the plans of public schools, mode of study, and the authors used, being taken from English practice, but without the solidity of enquiry, and variety of assistance derived both from writers and professors, which characterize our present establishments.

The *reading* of Americans (for I have not seen in society an approach to what can be called *study*) is English; there being few native writers, and but a small number of these who possess the respect of even their own countrymen. Our novels and poetry, not excepting those which proceed from the Minerva press, meet with an immediate reprint, and constitute *practically* the entire American library.

There are *theatres*, either stationary or occasional, in most towns of which the population is two thousand and upwards; yet I know of but one native play (Bunker's Hill): the performers too are English, at least in the proportion to Americans of eight out of every ten; so that the stage of this country may justly be denominated British. Many of the vulgar sayings, and still more vulgar prejudices, of our little island are transported hither. Frenchmen and frogs, Irishmen and bulls, are even the subjects of American ridicule, and in the uncontaminated style of Spitalfields and Shoreditch. * — Another

* In Washington, on last St. Patrick's day, according to custom, a figure was stuffed similar to our Guy Faux, and called Paddy; he was placed within the gate of the Navy-yard, with pipes, tobacco, and whiskey. — In Philadelphia

source of intimate communication with England exists in the articles of clothing, and nearly every domestic utensil, being also the manufacture of our island. Yet, in spite of all these various ties of connection with England, and with Englishmen, they appear generally to regard both with jealousy and hatred. Did this dislike proceed from correct principles, I should think it honourable to their national character; for we, or at least our government, have certainly left no means untried to prevent them, in the first instance, from obtaining the natural rights of men, and — when that was found to be impossible, then to blast all the advantages they had gained, and crush their rising prosperity. But the American hatred of our country is not bottomed upon causes which *reason* would have dictated: its component parts cannot be denominated to be either rational or reflective: — it is, in source, and in mode of expression, an exact parallel to that of our most uneducated classes concerning the French people, who always dislike Frenchmen, and the only reason they can give for such feelings is, because they *are*

---

a gentleman informed me that there were numerous Paddies exhibited in the same style; some were carried by boys, begging to "remember poor Paddy." This offensive practice was carried to such an extent in New York a few years back, that serious riots were produced by it. There is now a law of that corporation prohibiting "Paddies" being exhibited on the 17th of March.

Frenchmen — and because the newspapers say Frenchmen ought to be hated.

To copy from a nation like England, which is so pre-eminently distinguished by knowledge, as varied as it is profound, can reflect disgrace on no country; but in the act of imitation there should be judicious selection, and not an indiscriminate application of institutions and practices, which, though perhaps suited to a peculiar country, and a very mixed state of society, cannot be expected to harmonize with the wants or the character of another people, under circumstances and in civil condition essentially different. The Americans seem to have forgotten this, and, like most imitators, very peculiarly excel in the *defects* of the original. This conduct, on their part, is attended with serious disadvantages to themselves, and prevents their possession of a solid base upon which to erect a purely American superstructure. At present their mental streams are derived from two sources, (those of the old and of the new world,) of opposite qualities, either of which used separately, or by a limited and judicious admixture, would be beneficial; but as they are suffered to flow on to the point of their junction without interruption or purification, they only produce muddy and infectious waters. Converse with an American upon the condition of the world at large, its political situation and true interests, he is rarely clear-headed;

not from want of capacity, but the sources of his knowledge have been so jumbled, and his information in general is so ill-arranged, that he is often, in the same breath, an advocate for the extremes of liberty and of slavery. The nation at large dislike England, and yet, both individually and collectively, would be offended should a hint be expressed that they were of Irish or of Dutch, and not of English, descent. They contend for the superiority of their genius in taste, mechanical arts, and literature, and yet they disregard fashions or books which are not imported from Great Britain. Notwithstanding this voluntary national dependence, there are, perhaps, no people, not even excepting the French, who are so vain as the Americans; their self-estimation, and cool-headed bombast, when speaking of themselves or their country, are quite ludicrous. An anecdote is told of General Moreau, who, at the commencement of the late war with England, was in America: a friend, addressing him, observed that his military talents would be of essential service to the Republic. He replied in the negative; adding, that there was not a drummer in the American army who did not think himself equal to General Moreau. This fact will apply to all occupations with an equal degree of faithfulness. Every man here thinks he has arrived at the acmé of perfection: the mechanics themselves possess the same feeling. When at

Newark, I was informed that some choice designs in chair-japanning and coach-plating were lately produced by two emigrants; the natives turned upon their heels, "Ay, they guessed them 'ere "were fashions they had left off." Every American considers that it is impossible for a foreigner to teach him any thing, and that his head contains a perfect encyclopædia. This excessive inflation of mind must be attended with many disadvantages; though when I look at the various causes which have combined to produce it, I am not much surprised at its existence. As a people, they feel that they have got to gain a character, and, like individuals under similar circumstances, are captious and conceited in proportion to their defects. They appear to aim at a standard of high reputation, without the laborious task of deserving it, and practise upon themselves the self-deception of believing that they really are that which they only wish to be. This feeling has not been lessened by their successes in the late contest with Great Britain; for, although in several engagements on our favourite element they had an overwhelming superiority, yet there were instances when that was not the case; and the defeat of English frigates, with even any disparity of force, was too great an honour to be estimated exactly as it merited. The boasting upon this subject is so extravagant that it burlesques the object of its praise. "America "is now the ruler of the waves;" and every song and joke, fact and falsehood that we have bestowed upon our tars, are transferred to the "Star-spangled banner, and the brave sons of "Columbia," with the characteristic fidelity of a national intellect, rendered barren from want of culture; and even on *such* an occasion has hardly produced an attempt at originality. *

* The following naval songs are in high repute. The servility of imitation which they exhibit (it is not even pretended that they are parodies) is a just characteristic of not merely American song-making, but of almost every pursuit in this country.

SONG.

" Tune — *Battle of the Nile.*

" Arise! arise! Columbia's sons arise!
" And shake off the torpor of sloth and inactivity;
" And while the loud cannon reverb'rates to the skies,
" United swear to perish or be free! —
" For mark where her Genius, on her mountains standing,
" Cries with a voice impressive and commanding,
" When heart and hand unites
" To guard our country's rights,
" Then death or independence still the watch-word shall be.
" Huzza! Huzza! Huzza! Huzza! Huzza! Boys!
" Rally round the standard which Liberty first
" planted here;
" Huzza! Huzza! Huzza! Huzza! Huzza! Boys!
" Columbia's sons will perish or live free!"

SONG.

" Tune — *Pull away, yeo ho, boys.*

" Yankee sailors have a knack,
" Haul away! yeo ho, boys!
" Pulling down a British Jack,
" 'Gainst any odds you know, boys.

My knowledge of the details of the late war was extremely limited when I first landed in this country. A short residence here, however, will force upon the attention of all persons an acquaintance with naval history. Every man, woman, and child in America talk about the Guerrière, the Java, the Macedonia, the Frolic, Lake Erie, Lake Champlain, and the "vast "inferiority of British sailors and soldiers to "the true-blooded Yankees." A non-intercourse act seems to have passed against the sciences, morals, and literature in American society; even the ladies are content to be silent, or, when they do express an idea, it is sure to contain the *refined* and *intellectual* names of Commodore Hull, Captain Laurence, and General Jackson. A knowledge of such events is certainly desirable; but to cause them, as they are here, to be the never-ending theme of conversation, the circle round which every thing revolves, is to make the going into society a punishment instead of a pleasure. This tendency is stated to have been finely ridiculed by Mr. Jeffrey, of the Edinburgh Review, who visited this country soon after the war. To a question

---

"Come three to one, right sure am I,
"If we can't beat them, still we'll try,
"To make Columbia's colours fly,
"Haul away! yeo ho, boys!"

said to have been put to him by Mr. Madison, "What did you think of the war, Mr. Jeffrey?" he coolly replied, "Upon my word, Sir, I did "not hear of it."

Naval affairs being so frequently the subject of remark, I took some trouble to investigate the real facts relating to them; and found that a large body of the American seamen were British subjects; and that, more particularly, the forces of their vessels almost ensured success. In the first victory, that of the "Constitution" over the "Guerrière," Mr. James, author of "The Naval Occurrences of the late War," states the broad-side metal in pounds of the American was 768; of the British, 517: the American complement of men, 468; of British, 263: of size in tons of the American, 1533; of British, 1084. In the affair of the "United States" and "Constitution," which defeated the "Macedonian" and "Java," a similar disparity existed; and in the Lake Erie fleet, the American amount of broad-side metal in pounds was 928; of British, 459: the size in tons, 1530; of British, 865: in complement of men, 580; of British, 345. These are matters about which I should have known little, and cared less, had they not been in American society the eternal source of conversation, to the exclusion of every subject of taste, morals, or literature, — indeed of every other, except the price of cotton, flour, and *niggars*.

The tyrannical conduct of our government in naval affairs, their system of impressment and of flogging, and the absurd and insolent claim of the right of search, might well, particularly the last, have exasperated the American nation, and more especially her seamen; still the Americans are deserving of great honour for what they really achieved. School-boys in the art of war, they were yet better prepared for it, and evinced more practical dexterity, than our hoary-headed practitioners. But with this limited degree of praise, they are not content; they are, forsooth, "the Lords of the ocean!" "Neptune's choicest sons!" "Victorious, "though the English had great superiority of "force!" "The star-spangled banner is the "astonishment, the admiration, and the glory "of the world!" — with volumes more of such frothy, senseless bombast.

Other causes of their great national pride and vanity suggest themselves to the mind. One may consist in their being so far removed from the seat of the arts and sciences, that their acquirements are not tried by the only effectual standard — comparison. They are left in undisputed possession of the belief that infancy is manhood; that puerility is superiority; and that mediocrity is first-rate talent. They have a political republic within themselves; but they send scarcely one representative to the general republic of letters. European writers too, who have never actually visited America, taking their ideas of the inhabitants, their manners and institutions, from the laws and political constitution of the country, have frequently been profuse in their eulogies. Speculating emigrants, from interested motives, have followed in the same track. American authors, in the sincerity of their hearts, have re-echoed these praises, while politicians, among whom I regret to see Mr. Munroe occupying a prominent part, have told them that they are "*the most enlightened nation* "*in the world!!*" Americans would be more than human, were they not injured by this powerful combination against their national improvement. Man's vanity is of all points the most tender; and there are few, I believe, willing to reject flattery, even from any source or to any extent. So far indeed is this carried in the United States, that if a traveller should point out the smallest defect or error, no inquiry is ever made by the Americans into the *truth* of the charge; the writer is immediately viewed as a foul calumniator, or guilty of premeditated falsehood and intentional insult; and is not unlikely to be denominated a hireling, in the pay of some foreign government. Should this tone of thinking remain uncorrected, it cannot but produce the most pernicious effects. By such a course, improvement must be checked and error perpetuated. The vanity of this people may thus be gratified; but they must be content to remain children in knowledge and improvemement of every kind, and submit to be rocked for ages in the cradle of European intellect.

There are additional considerations worthy of our attention in forming a correct estimate of the American people. One which suggests itself is, the want of *social subordination* which exists among them. Servants feel themselves independent of their employers, and children of their parents. This may be attended with some advantages: it may please when contrasted with the degrading slavery of the European world; but it is not free from serious and peculiar evils. It increases selfish feelings and pursuits; it individualizes society, and prevents a developement of those social qualities which are of important benefit to, as well as the greatest ornament of our nature. EARLY MARRIAGES partly proceed perhaps from this state of things, though the great source of their frequency is certainly, in conformity with a well-known theory — the ease with which the necessaries of life can be obtained. Arguments are not wanting in favour of youthful matrimonial engagements; and, without considering the matter in an individual point of view, it certainly contributes to the more rapid advancement of a country requiring population. Yet, strong as such reasons may be, I should, if morally considered, hesitate in bearing my testimony to their solidity. The youth of twenty, and the female of fourteen, are ill fitted for the cares, anxieties, and education of a family — neither their bodily nor mental strength has attained maturity. Those days also which ought to be devoted to the acquirement of solid information, and to the improving, perhaps it may be said, to the creating the character, are necessarily devoted to other objects. The cares of life, under such circumstances, begin to press upon individuals who have not previously had time or opportunity to learn its duties. No provision has been made for the support of a rising family — to *this* therefore every other object will generally be sacrificed : by these means a sordid and calculating spirit is engendered — the more generous feelings of our nature acquire neither strength nor stability ; and every mental and ennobling pursuit is abandoned with a view to the getting on in life.

The American female character requires our attention : in mental pursuits it would appear to be at present but little advanced. This proceeds no doubt from a variety of causes ; all that has been said of the male population, by a natural re-action affecting the female also. The demand, too, (if I may be excused a mercantile phrase upon such a subject,) exceeding the supply, together with the comparatively less value set upon domestic comfort, may, perhaps, have tended to produce the extreme attention to mere personal ornament, and the universal neglect of either mental or domestic knowledge, which appears to exist among the females here, as compared with those of England.

The reflections generated by these considerations are, what my personal observation has confirmed — that a great part of the nation are content to be employed in procuring the first necessaries of life, and in mere animal enjoyment. These several causes may have assisted in the production of a general fact, that here all knowledge, beyond that of immediate pecuniary interest, is superficial.

The *statesman* of America has heretofore been altogether of a different, and, perhaps, a superior race to those of Europe. There has been in this country nothing of the *regularly-trained* and *family-born great man*. A senator, a secretary of state, or a president, is commonly a lawyer, who has risen by his talents or perseverance; and, in addition, he is not unfrequently a farmer: and when his official duties have terminated, he returns from Washington to his home, and resumes his former occupations. From this domestic and sound mode of conducting the public weal, there has of late years been a partial deviation. Certain families have edged themselves into government-offices, and have proved to be, in practice at least, adherents of the doctrine of *hereditary* descent; yet the general features remain as described: and, however discordant the fact may appear with the principles of legitimacy, I believe none will be found hardy enough to assert, that these men display any want of the knowledge or ability required by their station; or that they do not play their parts with as much vigour, effect, and integrity, as if they had been the descendants of an ancient and titled aristocracy. *

The existence of slavery in the United States has a most visible effect upon the national character. It necessarily brutalizes the minds of the southern and western inhabitants; it lowers, indeed, the tone of humane and correct

* To judge indeed by the amount of *salaries*, there must be a lamentable deficiency of intellect on the part of the Republican statesmen: —

The President of the United States receives an annual salary of only 5625l. and this is found to procure able men, *who have really talent and mind at their own disposal.* The Vice-President, Secretary of State, and Chief Justice, each are paid 1125l. per annum; other Judges, 900l.; the Secretaries of the Treasury, War and Navy departments, each 900l. per annum; the Governor of the State of New York, 1687l. 10s.; ditto of Vermont, 135l.!!

feeling throughout the Union; and imperceptibly contributes to the existence of that great difference which here exists between theory and practice. The treatment of the Indian nations is but ill calculated to excite liberal or humane feelings; for, however Mr. Munroe and others may attempt to philosophize upon the benefits which arise from uncivilized man's making way before a more "*dense population*," the admitted fact is, that Americans are making continued encroachments upon the aboriginal inhabitants, either under the semblance of treaties, or by direct warfare, produced, as the present one is said to have been, by designed aggressions, and aggravating insults on the part of the people of the United States.

The diversity of laws in separate States, by which acts considered as a crime in one part are not punishable in another, and also many confused impressions of right and wrong, generate much evil, while the state of the bankrupt laws, and an immense and complicated paper currency *, are universal and increasing evils; each of these having opened an extensive field to the calculations of avidity and the specu-

* The New York brokers publish a weekly list of the price of the notes of all parts of the Union, in the money-market of that city. There are notes of all the banks to be had at every variety of price, from $\frac{1}{4}$ per cent. to 40 per cent. discount.

lations of the dishonest. The list of insolvencies in the State from which I now write is enormous. Failure in trade, so far from being a cause of loss, or a subject of shame, is generally the means of securing a fortune; and so callous upon this subject has the public mind become, that no kind of disadvantage or disgrace attaches to the individual, who takes, therefore, little pains to disguise the source of his wealth.

Although *pauperism* has not arrived at English maturity, nor does it often attract the public eye (for myself, I have seen but three beggars, one of whom accosted me in the gallery of the House of Representatives in Washington); yet it does exist, and that to an extent which I had not imagined until the perusal of Governor Clinton's most able address to the New York legislature. He there remarks—" Our statutes relating to the poor are " borrowed from the English system. And the " experience of that country as well as our own, " shows that pauperism increases with the aug- " mentation of the funds applied to its relief. " This evil has proceeded to such an alarming " extent in the city of New York, that the " burdens of heavy taxation which it has im- " posed, menace a diminution of the popula- " tion of that city, and a depreciation of its real " property. The consequences will be very " injurious to the whole State; for the decay

" of our great market will be felt in every de-" partment of productive labour. Under the " present system the fruits of industry are ap-" propriated to the wants of idleness; a labo-" rious poor man is taxed for the support of an " idle beggar; and the voice of mendicity, no " longer considered degrading, infects a con-" siderable portion of our population in large " towns. I am persuaded that the sooner a ra-" dical reform takes place, the better. The evil " is contagious, and a prompt extirpation can " alone prevent its pernicious extension."

To pauperism may be added LOTTERIES, which are numerous in all the States; and in many the English exploded iniquity of *insurance*, and "*little goes*," exist in full operation.

The *commerce* of the United States has experienced a great revival since 1815. During the calamitous period of war, the merchant-ships were rotting, and their owners became bankrupt. The following statement, the amounts of which are in dollars, copied from official reports, presents a most interesting detail of the trade of America at this time: —

Exports for the Year ending Sept. 30. 1817:

The *domestic* products or manufactures exported, amounted to -	Dollars 68,313,500
The *foreign* products or manufactures -	19,358,069
Total -	Dollars 87,671,569

The exports were,

		Domestic.	Foreign.
To the northern countries of Europe		3,828,563	2,790,408
Dominions of the Netherlands		3,397,775	2,387,553
Ditto	of Great Britain	41,431,168	2,037,074
Ditto	of France -	9,717,423	2,717,395
Ditto	of Spain -	4,530,156	3,893,780
Ditto	of Portugal -	1,501,237	333,586
All other dominions -		3,907,178	5,198,283
	Dollars	68,313,500	19,358,069

The exports were,

	Domestic.	Foreign.	Total.
From NewHampshire	170,599	26,825	197,424
Vermont -	913,201	——	913,201
Massachusetts -	5,908,416	6,019,581	11,927,997
Rhode Island -	577,911	372,556	950,467
Connecticut -	574,290	29,849	604,139
New York -	13,660,733	5,046,700	18,707,433
New Jersey -	5,849	——	5,849
Pennsylvania	5,538,003	3,197,589	8,735,592
Delaware -	38,771	6,083	44,854
Maryland -	5,887,884	3,046,046	8,933,930
Dist. of Columbia	1,689,102	79,556	1,768,658
Virginia -	5,561,238	60,204	5,621,442
North Carolina	955,211	1,369	956,580
South Carolina	9,944,443	428,270	10,372,613
Georgia -	8,530,831	259,883	8,790,714
Ohio - -	7,749	——	7,749
Louisiana -	8,241,254	783,558	9,024,812
Michigan territory	64,228	——	64,228
Mississippi do. -	43,887	——	43,887
Dollars	68,313,500	19,358,069	87,671,956

Of these exports there were —

1.	Derived from the sea - -	Dollars 1,671,000
2.	from the forest - -	6,484,000
3.	from agriculture - -	57,222,000
4.	from manufactures - -	2,202,000
Uncertain	- - - -	734,000

The duties collected on the importation of articles, which were afterwards re-exported, without being entitled to drawback, amounted to 627,206 dollars, 37 cents.

The *flour* exported from October 1. 1816, to September 30. 1817, amounted to -	Dollars 17,751,376
The *Sea Island Cotton* exported within the same time - - - - - -	3,240,752
Other Cotton exported, amounted to -	19,386,862
Tobacco, amounted to - - -	9,230,020
Rice - - - - - -	2,378,880
Fish - - - - - -	1,328,050
Timber and *Lumber*, of all descriptions -	3,381,349
Pot and *Pearl Ashes* - - -	1,967,243

These form the principal exports of domestic product: the *iron*, in all shapes, exported, amounted to 138,579 dollars. Amongst the most curious exports may be ranked *maple sugar*, which amounted to 4,374 dollars. The gun-powder exported, amounted to 356,522 dollars.

Although this does not equal in amount the business done previous to the issuing of the English Orders in Council, it is still very large in extent; and the articles of export being all bulky, they operate as an important nursery for seamen. *

The FINANCES of the United States are derived from sale of lands, and duties on imports.

* Among the articles of *import* to the ports of New York, Philadelphia, and Baltimore, it is a curious fact, that English coal, cheese, potatoes, and porter are frequent: in the more southern States, including even New Orleans (the depot for western country produce), Irish provisions, and English cheese and hams are imported!

The latter, in an especial degree, are found very productive. Still this is *in fact,* though it may not be *in name, internal* taxation. It may be well to remember, that one-half of the amount collected is upon British goods, most of which are articles, *not of luxury,* but of *necessity ;* so that the population of America perform the double duty of defraying their own taxes, and contributing towards the payment of ours.

The *Liberty of the Press* exists here to an almost unlimited extent: and yet it is not used as an organ for putting the people in possession of even domestic information. The newspapers are miserably edited, seldom containing any thing but advertisements, shipping intelligence, and English extracts. The proceedings of Congress are not systematically reported. Sometimes the substance of a debate will be given three weeks after its occurrence. The business of the State-legislatures rarely appears at all in the public journals, except in the shape of bare lists of bills passed or rejected. The transactions in courts of law, and all minor home proceedings, rarely appear upon record. These sins of *omission* are certainly to be lamented, as, by their existence, an interest fails to be excited in the public mind on those occurrences, and those subjects, which are, unquestionably, of first-rate importance. During the late war, it is stated, a military scheme, modelled upon the

French law of conscription, was in the contemplation of the then Secretary, but now President, Munroe; the chief of the naval department also recommended to Congress, a plan for the *impressment* of seamen, to man their infant navy: but such is the habitual indolence of the people, and their indifference with regard to public affairs, that these events are known but by few individuals.

The *Government*, it will be seen, are not free from charges of mal-administration; but when compared with England, America can *afford* an annual increase of corruption for, at least, a few centuries to come; and although the people are unworthy of, and not alive to their unequalled advantages, they still *are* their *own governors*, and they are vain of the distinction. This *one fact*, assisted by the jealousy of rival parties, must preserve the United States for many years, from any lengthened series of obnoxious measures, and protect the people from gross inroads upon their liberties or their constitution.

The state of *mechanic arts* varies, of course, according to the profession. Those which have been encouraged by not being exposed to European competition, and which have had the combined benefit of emigrant and native ingenuity have excelled. Among these I would class shoe, coach, and cabinet making, together with steam-boat and ship-building: I was going to say bank-note engraving, but that would not, perhaps, be correct as a general statement of the art in America, though the house of Murray, Draper, and Fairman, of Philadelphia, probably surpass in the excellence of their art any others in the world: their notes, executed for the United States' Bank, exhibit such eminent talent, that forgery may safely be said to be impossible. Why does not your Bank of England employ this house? or, if that would be too humiliating to their pride, why not engage a first-rate English Artist, instead of issuing premiums upon forgery, in their disgracefully executed national notes? Piano-forte making may be similarly classed: generally, it has not arrived at much perfection, although an individual, (Mr. Stuart, an English gentleman,) who lives at Baltimore, manufactures pianos which I should have little fear of comparing with those of Clementi or Broadwood.

Of the LITERATURE of the United States I can say but little. Having examined booksellers' collections, private and public libraries, I find that, like dry goods stores, their stock consists only of British manufactures. Three American works have lately appeared: the first, a novel, called "Keep Cool," I have met with in most of the western and southern States. Upon its merits I cannot pretend to give an opinion. I took it up several times, with a previous resolution to read at least six pages, but at no one time could I force myself through a third. With Mr. Wirt's "Life of Patrick Henry" I have been much interested: it evinces a mind familiar with polite literature; and if the title were altered from the "Life of Patrick Henry," to that of "Sundry "Essays, designed to prove the elegance of the "English Language, the extent of the author's "powers of imagination and talent of descrip-"tion, with occasional hints concerning the Life "of Patrick Henry," it would be more descriptive of the book: for any reader who takes up this work with the design of becoming acquainted with the late Virginian patriot, will find frequent disappointment, on the introduction of each incident of Mr. Henry's life, by the extravagant bombast of the biographer. The work, in short, though bearing evidence of considerable talent, evinces, from the commencement to the termination, a disregard of the requisites for the task which is undertaken, and this by allotting to Patrick Henry a station in the drama inferior to that of the author, Mr. Wirt.

Mr. Bristed's "Resources of the United "States" has just been published. The author, I am informed, is an Englishman by birth. His work evinces that he is an American Federalist by adoption. It contains many important statements, and the usual political admixture which distinguishes the American writers (particularly those of this gentleman's party) upon Government. The following maxims are laid down, *in connection with the broadest principles of liberty*, the whole presenting a code of political economy for which it is difficult to invent a name. " *It is the duty of every* FREE " *Government to train its people gradually to bear* " *a due weight of internal taxation.*"—" It is " worse than childish, it is insane policy" (a compliment to the President) " to trust for the " public revenue to the duties upon imported " goods."—" The reduction of the direct tax " from six to three millions of dollars, and the " limitation of those three millions to only one " year, *are fearful omens of the entire extinction* " *of that tax!*"—" The liberties of Britain are " *not about to expire under the pressure of her* " *military, or the encroachments of her govern-* " *ment. If they are to perish, they will perish* " *under the daggers of her Democracy. If she* " *is to be blotted out of the list of independent* " *and powerful nations, it will be by the parri-* " *cidical hand of her own rabble, led on to their* " *own and their country's ruin, by anarchical re-* " *formers, alike bankrupt in fortune, reputation,* " *character, and principle!*"—Yet, it is said, " *to* " *crown all, the* POLITICAL SOVEREIGNTY *of the* " *nation residing in the people gives the American* " *people* an elevation *unknown and unattainable in*

" *any other country*."—" Liberty has struck deep " root in this country. It is entwined with the " first affections of the heart: it is spun into " the primitive staple of the mental frame of " the Americans. It thoroughly pervades, and " perceptively modifies even their domestic life. " It has, in fine, become the common reason, " and the want of the whole American people." —" The prosperity and happiness of the Ame- " rican citizens seem too great a price to pay " for the privilege of manufacturing a few yards " of broad cloth, or a few pieces of muslin. " England herself is a portentous illustration of " this truth: now at this time, and for the last " five and twenty years, her manufacturing dis- " tricts have sent forth, and are issuing out, full " bands of Luddites and Spenceans, and Jaco- " bins and anarchists, and rebels and assassins, " that continually put to the strength, and " strain the nerves of her Government."— I send these extracts for the purpose of presenting you at one view the *mind* of the whole Federal party, *and indeed that of the entire American people*, concerning English reformers and United States' liberty.

Salmagundi *, a work written after the man-

* Of this work I perceive an English edition has been published, with notes and a preface by the editor, illustrative of the character of the Americans; but upon the merits of those, not having read them, I can give no opinion.

ner of the Citizen of the World, is a most able native production: for amusement, wit, talent, and satire I should conceive it can have few equals. Mr. Erving, the present ambassador at the court of Madrid, is said to be one of the authors. Mr. Quincy Adams has published *Lectures delivered at Cambridge College*, in two volumes. You have, I believe, Joel Barlow's national epic, "*The Columbiad.*" There are several other American works; but, upon the whole, the *native* library is extremely circumscribed.

In the *Fine Arts* much advancement has not been made. Individuals have excelled, as in the cases of Mr. Alston and Mr. West, both natives of America. The proofs of their talent, but particularly those of the latter, must descend to future ages. Still, the mind of the American nation is scarcely alive to an enjoyment of the more noble productions of art, or the higher walks of mental cultivation.

I have thus endeavoured to lay before you a true representation of the American character, with the sources from which it may have been formed, and the causes which have conduced to its production. Although I believe it must improve, yet I am by no means sanguine in my anticipations that improvement will be immediate, or even rapid in its progress. Many of the causes, external and internal, which have already operated, will continue to exist; and, as I have before said, there would appear to be placed in the very stamina of the character of this people, a coldness, a selfishness, and a spirit of conceit, which form strong barriers against improvement. Let us, however, still hope for the best. In opposition to these obstacles, there are strong and living truths abroad. The *principles* at least of liberty are acknowledged, and the *fact* of a free government exists as an example to the world. As rational men, these things are worthy of our respect; and, in the hand of Heaven, we may be assured that all the rest, however dark and unintelligible to us it may appear, will still finally and effectually "work together for good."

27th April, 1818. — A packet of your letters is just arrived, bearing date March 3d. You can scarcely conceive, my dear friends, the delight which their perusal has afforded me. I could fain have launched out into praises of the inventor of writing and the establishment of post-offices: but these are stale topics. Your statement of the non-arrival of my Philadelphia and Illinois Reports give me some uneasiness, though I can have little doubt but that they are now in your possession; as I perceive, by the recent ship news, that the vessels which conveyed them had arrived in England. You state that Mr. Birkbeck has published a book in London, "Notes on a

"Journey to Illinois," and that it has produced an extraordinary sensation. This intelligence does not at all surprise me, and my ideas, upon the perusal of that work, as published in this country, were, that in several of its occasional admissions it confirms my sentiments. I have this day re-read it with minute attention, and feel so confirmed in my first impressions, that I experience an increased dependence upon my views of this nation, from having the support of Mr. Birkbeck's high authority.

As Captain —— will not sail until the 29th, I have nearly two days of leisure, and I do not know that they can be better occupied than in making some remarks upon Mr. Birkbeck's "Notes," which may tend to illustrate at once that gentleman's views of America and my own. My references are to the American edition: this will occasion you some trouble, but that, under my present circumstances, I cannot prevent.

Mr. Birkbeck's entrance into this republic was not, with regard to local circumstances, quite so favourable as mine. The State in which he landed is one of the TWELVE *in which absolute slavery exists*, whilst, on the contrary, in that I first visited, actual slavery had been abolished by law, and it only continues to linger among the *practical* institutions of the people.

Mr. B. says, (at page 22.) "I could hardly

" bear to see negroes handled like cattle; in
" selling these unhappy beings, little regard is
" had to the parting of the nearest relations."

While waiting at a tavern, Mr. B. is furnished with evidence of the intellectual character of the Virginians, of which, by the way, I cannot but think his estimation is far beyond their deserts: —

" As it rained heavily, every body was con-
" fined the whole day to the tavern, after the
" race which took place in the forenoon. The
" conversation which this afforded me an oppor-
" tunity of hearing, gave me a high opinion
" of the intellectual cultivation of these Vir-
" ginian farmers." (Page 16.)

I have frequently partaken in the conversation of the same class of individuals, and in no instance could I conscientiously draw the same conclusion with Mr. Birkbeck. Mr. B. however, in the succeeding paragraph, furnishes his readers with the evidence upon which his judgment is formed.

" Negro slavery was the prevailing topic,
" the beginning, the middle, and the end,—an
" evil uppermost in every man's thoughts, which
" all deplored, many were anxious to fly from,
" but for which no man can devise a remedy.
" One gentleman, in a poor state of health,
" dared not encounter the rain, but was wretch-
" ed at the thought of his family being for one

"night without his protection *from his own* "*slaves.*" (Page 17.)

Yet at the same time it is said, "Virginia "prides itself on the comparative mildness of "its treatment of slaves!" (Page 22.)

Mr. Birkbeck's gratitude for the liberal reception which he experienced from "the high-"spirited independence of the Virginians," must surely have biassed his judgment, when he concluded, "that slavery was an evil uppermost "in every man's thoughts, *and which all de-*"*plored.*" That indeed many feel they cannot defend this system by a reference to abstract principles, or the rights of man; that they dread the terrible though rarely inflicted vengeance of their victims, is probable enough; and that when they are engaged in argument with an able and enlightened opponent, and cannot defend the strange inconsistency existing between their *professed* love of political freedom and their actual domestic tyranny; that they should *then*, I say, and under such circumstances, deplore the evils of slavery, is natural enough; but that they are *sincere* advocates for its abolition, or even for a *mitigation* of its horrors, is what I have not seen the shadow of an evidence to induce me to believe; neither could I have supposed that Mr. Birkbeck would have been so unphilosophical as to conclude, that the mere assent to an abstract proposition when the mind is not at the moment *interested* in its denial, is to be fairly taken as a just criterion, by which to judge of the *true* feelings and character of a people. Let them be judged by their actions; — it is these only that speak the man.

Mr. Birkbeck says, " A Virginian planter is " a republican in politics, and exhibits the high- " spirited independence of that character." (Page 16.)

Feeling a sincere respect for a character really deserving of this high commendation, I cannot willingly award it to slave-holders. The following advertisements I take from a newspaper, as affording some evidence upon the *consistency* of the " Virginian character:" they were printed as they stand, adjoining each other. They speak a language too plain to require comment; I therefore leave them to their naked merit.

" The Synod of Virginia having, at their last meeting, ap-
" pointed the first Thursday in December to be observed, by
" all the churches under their care, as a day of thanksgiving
" to God for the bounties of his providence and the blessings
" of his grace, to be accompanied with humble supplication
" for the continuance of the former and the increase of the
" latter; I propose, in cheerful compliance with the resolu-
" tion of Synod, to preach on the occasion to-morrow at
" eleven o'clock in the forenoon, in the new methodist
" church on Shockhoe-Hill; leave having been given.

" JOHN D. BLAIR."

" NEGROES AT AUCTION.

" This morning, in front of our office, at 11 o'clock,
" will be sold for cash, 4 Likely Negroes.

" J. BROWN, JR. and W. FINNEY, *Auctioneers.*

Mr. Birkbeck's departure from this State is in a tone of liberal feeling. He observes (page 30.), "On taking leave of Virginia, I must observe "that I found more misery in the condition of "the negroes and *a much higher tone of moral* "*feeling* in their owners than I had anticipated, "and I depart confirmed in my detestation of "slavery in principle and practice, *but with* "*esteem for the general character of the Vir-* "*ginians!!*"

The precise nature of Mr. Birkbeck's expectations as to the "*tone of moral feeling*" which he should find existing among the Virginian planters, it is scarcely perhaps possible to ascertain, or, consequently, to canvass. I can only hope that the use of such an expression at all may not, however unintentionally, have the effect of misleading; for I must own I can have no conception of the existence of a "*tone of* "*moral feeling*" among men who falsify, and that not by *occasional* misdeeds, but by the whole tenor of their conduct, and every habit of their character, even the possibility of its existence. Indeed I would put it to any advocate of liberal and of enlightened political principles, how far it is really possible for us, on cool reflection, to entertain "esteem for the *general* "character of the Virginians," or whether it be possible to respect men who *profess* the most enlightened opinions, and yet are, in Mr. Birkbeck's language, "*slave-masters, irascible, and* "*too often lax in morals!*" and of whom "*a dirk* "*is said to be the common appendage to their* "*dress.*"

The character of the Americans generally is a subject of great interest to all who contemplate becoming their fellow-citizens. Mr. Birkbeck is diffuse upon this subject; he remarks (page 40.) "that in every department of common life we here see employed persons *superior in habits* and education to the same class "in England;" and further (page 72.), the "inhabitants are friendly and homely, not to "say coarse, but well-informed; surprisingly "more so than the English peasantry;" and that, during his journey from Norfolk to the heart of the Allegany mountains, "he had not "lost sight for a moment of the manners of "polished life." (Page 40.) These are certainly captivating descriptions, and such as I had anticipated, before I left England, to be the character of the Americans. Some explanation, however, I conceive to be necessary: the difference between American character and society and those of England is so great, that I almost despair of conveying to your minds a faithful impression on the subject. The agricultural labourer here is certainly better educated than one of the same class in England; he is not born nor does he continue to vegetate on the spot which gave birth to his father and grandfather; he not only frequently changes his station, but also his occupation; this necessarily communicates a range of ideas more extensive than that possessed by the English labourer; but when the *whole character* is looked at, and not the mere freedom from rusticity of manners, and an extension of geographical knowledge, a different conclusion would, perhaps, present itself; and I much doubt, could I now converse with Mr. Birkbeck, with his present improved knowledge of the American people, whether he would at this moment award to them the meed of superiority of character, more especially in connection with their "*habits,*"—and with regard to the "manners of polished life," and their being carried "*even to the heart of the* "*Allegany mountains.*"—I am surprised at the assertion; but wishing to speak with proper deference of Mr. Birkbeck, and in looking back to what I myself saw of the inhabitants of those mountains, I really cannot see how we can talk of the "manners of polished life" in a tract of country which presents an absence of all regard to manners, together with an absolute indifference to every person, and a cold disregard of all objects except as they may promote the merely mercenary and selfish pursuits of each individual. Indeed, without calling upon you to trust to my impressions, I can scarcely see how the existence of these "manners of polished life" is reconcileable with what Mr. Birkbeck himself acknowledges, — and that unwillingly too; but that feeling by no means weakens the force of his testimony on the subject; he says then, "that he has seen a "deformity so *general, that he cannot help esteem-* "*ing it national,*" which is, "that cleanliness in "houses, and too often in person, is neglected "to a degree which is very revolting to an Eng- "lishman." In comparing the two countries, and previous to awarding the palm of excellence in morals and manners to the inhabitants of the New World, let us remember also the strong but too-well founded assertion of Mr. Birkbeck (page 105.), that "intellectual culture has *not* "yet made much progress among the generality "of either sex;" and more than this, and worse than this, that "ALL AMERICA *is now suffering* "*in morals through the baleful influence of negro* "*slavery, partially tolerated, corrupting justice* "*at the very source*" (page 25.); and if, turning from general representations, we look to the more newly settled part of the country, we shall find Mr. B. declaring that "an unsettled coun- "try, lying contiguous to one that is settled," (which must be more or less the case with most parts of the western country, and in an especial degree with Illinois,) "is always the place of "retreat for rude and even abandoned charac- "ters, who find the regulations of society in- "tolerable." (Page 109.)

If it be therefore from Mr. Birkbeck's work that you would form your estimate of this country, you ought to do so, not by individual parts, but by a candid consideration of the whole; and should inconsistencies appear, to which, from various causes, any writer on a new country may be exposed, then of course you will take into your consideration all the circumstances of the case, and form your judgment accordingly. The fact, with regard to the state of knowledge in this country, to me appears to be, that men are, in point of information, almost upon a dead level; that *gradation* of intellect which exists in England being here unknown; so that, in conceding the point of greater intelligence to the American labourer, it by no means implies a *general* superiority. Let us go a little higher in the scale of society than our "hewers of wood and "drawers of water;" suppose, for an illustration, we take the English country gentleman in the person of Mr. Birkbeck, and compare him with the American land-owner, then indeed the contrast becomes striking. His agricultural pursuits will doubtless be conducted with vigour and activity, and with that application of scientific knowledge to practical pursuits, so common in the country he has quitted; while literature, experimental philosophy, or other departments of mental culture, will occupy his leisure hours. On the other hand, to use his own language,

" *they* cultivate indolence as a privilege, exist " in yawning indifference, surrounded with nui- " sances and petty wants, the first to be re- " moved and the latter supplied with a tenth of " the time loitered away in their innumerable " idle days." (Page 143.)

The American character is, in one passage, (p. 74.) represented to us as arrived at so high a state of perfection, that even national antipathies are annihilated. " National antipathies are " the result of bad political institutions, and " not of human nature. Here, whatever their " original, whether English, Scotch, Irish, " German, French, all are Americans; and " of all the unfavourable imputations on the " American character, *jealousy of strangers* " *is surely the most absurd and groundless.* " The Americans are sufficiently alive to their " own interest, but they wish well to strangers, " and are not always satisfied with wishing, " if they can promote their interest by active " services."

My judgment faltered upon the first perusal of this passage; — it so entirely contradicts every conclusion which I had come to upon the subject, that it caused me to hesitate as to the correctness of my own impressions: but surely Mr. Birkbeck here claims for the Americans a perfection, which is not only contrary to what they practise, but perhaps is superior to human nature itself, or, at any rate, to that class of *earthly beings* with whom, in this age, we must be content to associate. That national antipathies, indeed, are weakened in infant colonies, similar to that in which Mr. Birkbeck himself is now engaged, is, no doubt, as consistent with fact as it is with the laws of our being; for in such cases each individual is so dependent upon his neighbour, that self-interest breaks down minor feelings: but from what I have seen of this country, I have no hesitation in saying, that any Englishman who had candidly surveyed it *as a whole*, and observed the feelings of its inhabitants, particularly in the old settled parts, and where the population is dense, would declare that national antipathies exist here to an extent exceeding any thing which he had ever seen, or could have conceived, when in England. I have already stated many facts which will tend to support this assertion. Let me now observe, that the State of Pennsylvania presents a further illustration of this subject. Between the Americans of Irish and of German extraction, there exists the most deadly animosity, "even unto the third "and fourth generation." In the mind of a German American, the term "Irishman" is one of the most foul reproaches with which his range of ideas supplies him. Throughout America, (the parts at least which are populated,) Irishmen are despised, and Englishmen are viewed with cool malignant jealousy and hatred. Instead, indeed, of Americans "wishing well to "strangers and promoting their interest by active "services," they appear to me to possess in a large degree, and from similar motives too, the feelings which Mr. Birkbeck ascribes to some classes of the back woods' men — "a dislike to and jea-"lousy of all strangers." Mr. B. in this case, I presume, judges from his own individual experience; but it should be remembered that he is himself a man of property; that such persons generally meet with a liberal reception — *nowhere more so than in America;* and also, that as his residence has been in the heart of a wilderness, he may be expected to know but little of the manners, feelings, or state of society of the whole United States, the greater portion of the most populous parts of which he has not even visited. There are some minor points that it may be well just to glance at. Mr. B. says, (p. 46.) "The journeymen of "Pittsburgh, in various branches—shoemakers, "tailors, &c. earn two dollars a day," (54s. per week,) and that those among them who are improvident, do not expend their money "in ab-"solute intemperance and profligacy; they in "general waste their surplus earnings in ex-"cursions or entertainments."—I have only to remark on this, that in October 1817, when I was at the place in question, the earnings per week were, according to the statements given me by the mechanics themselves, — tailors, 31s. 6d. to 45s.; shoemakers, 31s. 6d. to 36s.: and all the mechanics with whom I conversed complained of the difficulty which they experienced in getting *paid* for their labour, much of what they did receive being given them in orders upon shops for necessaries and clothing; the extra price charged by the storekeeper, under these circumstances, causing, in their judgment, a clear loss to them of *three quarters of a dollar per week.* As to the pursuits of this class of men, *in Pittsburgh particularly,* it will, I believe, be found upon enquiry, that their "surplus earnings" *are* expended in "absolute intemperance and profligacy."

It is perhaps from a passage like the following that you may have been induced to form some conclusions on the state of this country; — "Vessels," says Mr. B., (page 48.) "of all sorts and sizes, from 500 tons downwards, continually passing, and steam-boats crowded with passengers (on James River); *the same on the Potowmac;* and in the winter, when the navigation is interrupted by frost, stages twelve or fourteen in file are seen posting along to supply the want of that luxurious accommodation." — This description, I fear, would give you too flattering an idea of the state of things here. The commerce of the *Potowmac* will be seen, by a reference to American imports and exports, to be extremely limited. At George-town, there may be an average, at any one time, of ten sloops; at Alexandria, an average of twelve square-rigged vessels, and perhaps 20 sloops. As to " stages travelling twelve or fourteen in file," I have frequented the *best roads* when steam-boat navigation has been interrupted by ice, and have never seen a number exceeding four, and not commonly more than one stage, during a route of several days.

Upon the principles of *taxation*, this government appear to be considered by Mr. Birkbeck as complete novices; — *so new* (page 75.) *is " the government of this country in the art and " mystery of finance,* that the revenue derived " from all this wealth hardly exceeds 40s. sterling per square mile."

A reference to the articles taxed during the late war will be, perhaps, the best mode of ascertaining in this particular the talents of the American government. In the session of congress in 1813, duties were laid on stills; on brandies; on carriages of every description; licences for retailing *all goods* of foreign manufacture; the same for selling spirits; the same on auction sales; on sugar; and on paper. In 1814, further duties were laid on these several articles, and also on various goods manufactured within the United States; among which were household furniture, leather, tobacco, beer, shoes, boots, saddles, bridles, cards, umbrellas, paper, caps, hats, candles, and iron ware; and to illustrate the subject of taxation, I subjoin a list of stamps as sold in the city of Philadelphia.

" *Stamps for Sale by John Bioren, Printer and Bookseller, No. 88, Chesnut Street.*

" INTERNAL DUTIES, payable by law, after December 31st, 1813.

" *On Carriages.*

	Dolls.	Cts.
" Upon every coach, the yearly sum of -	20	00
Upon every chariot and post-chaise - -	17	00
Upon every phaeton and every coachee, having pannel work in the upper division - -	10	00
Upon every other four wheel carriage hanging on steel or iron springs - - -	7	00
Upon every four wheel carriage hanging upon wooden springs, and every two wheel carriage hanging on steel or iron springs - - -	4	00
Upon every other four or two wheel carriage -	2	00

" *On licences to distillers of spirituous liquors.*

" For a still or stills employed in distilling spirits from domestic materials, for each gallon including the head thereof;

For 2 weeks (per gallon) - - -		9
For 1 month - - - -		18
For 2 months - - - -		32
For 3 months - - - -		42
For 4 months - - -		52
For 6 months - - - -		70
For 1 year - - - -	1	08

	Dolls. Cts.
For stills employed in distilling from foreign materials	
For 1 month (per gallon) - - -	25
For 3 months - - - -	60
For 6 months - - - -	1 05
For 1 year - - - -	1 35

" *On sales by auction.*

" On goods, wares, and merchandize, for every 100 dollars - - - -	1 00
On ships or vessels, for every 100 dollars -	25

" *On refined sugar.*

" On every pound - - -	4

" *On licences to retailers of wine, spirituous liquors, and foreign merchandize.*

" On retailers of merchandize, including wines and spirits - - - -	25 00
On wines alone - - - -	20 00
On spirits alone - - - -	20 00
On domestic spirits alone - - -	15 00
On merchandize other than wines and spirits -	15 00

" Where the population is not more than 100 families to a square mile.

" On retailers of merchandize, including wines and spirits - - - -	15 00
On wines and spirits - - -	15 00
On spirits alone - - - -	12 00
On domestic spirits - - -	10 00
On merchandize other than wines and spirits -	10 00

" *On notes of banks, bankers, notes, bonds, &c. discounted by banks, &c. and on bills of exchange.*

" On any promissory note or notes, payable either to bearer or order, issued by any of the banks or companies, who issue and discount notes, bonds or obligations, either incorporated or not incorporated, which now are, or here-

Dolls. Cts.

after may be established in the United States, or by any banker or bankers, according to the following scale: viz.

" If not exceeding 1 dollar			1
If above 1 and not exceeding		2	2
2	- -	3	3
3	- -	5	5
5	- -	10	10
10	- -	20	20
20	- -	50	50
50	- -	100	1 00
100	- -	500	5 00
500	- -	1000	10 00
1000	- -	-	50 00

" On any bond, obligation, or promissory note or notes, not issued by any bank, companies, or bankers aforesaid, discounted by any such bank, companies or banker, and on any foreign or inland bill or bills of exchange above fifty dollars, and having one or more endorsers, according to the following scale: viz.

" If not exceeding 100 dollars			5
If above 100 and not exceeding		200	10
200	- -	500	25
500	- -	1000	50
1000	- -	1500	75
1500	- -	2000	1 00
2000	- -	3000	1 50
3000	- -	4000	2 00
4000	- -	5000	2 50
5000	- -	7000	3 50
7000	- -	8000	4 00
8000	- -		5 00

" 'The secretary of the treasury may agree to an annual composition with any bank, in lieu of stamp duty, or one and a half per centum, on the amount of the annual dividend made by such bank.'

On the grand subject — that of emigration, notwithstanding all the captivating circumstances stated as attendant upon it, a few facts are *admitted* by Mr. B. himself which require your most deliberate and serious consideration. — First, then, that gentleman informs us, that "every service performed by one man for "another must be purchased at a high rate, "*much higher than in England;* therefore, as "long as the English emigrant is obliged to "purchase more than he sells of this service, or "labour, *he is worse off than at home.*" (Page 48.) Second, "After you have used yourself "to repose on your own pallets, either on the "floor of a cabin, or under the canopy of the "woods, with an umbrella over your head and "a noble fire at your feet, you will then escape "the only serious nuisance of American tra-"velling, viz. hot rooms and swarming beds." (P. 126.) Third, "A traveller should always "carry flint, steel, and a large knife, or toma-"hawk, &c. &c." (Page 108.)

The instances of great success, of which Mr. Birkbeck states several, are no doubt correct: but he certainly might have enlarged the view he has taken; and perhaps rendered it more correct by the enumeration of many failures. At least, I am myself in possession of several cases, on *both* sides of this question; but thinking the criterion to be altogether an uncertain one, I wave their enumeration. Such individual instances exist in every nation, and in every state of society; and are very frequently caused, not by peculiarity of country, but of *individual character*. I notice this, because I know that a reader, whose situation is similar to that in which the persons described were originally placed, might naturally be disposed to imagine, that if *he* were in America, he would be equally successful; when probably, he may be altogether unfitted for such circumstances. A writer, adverse to this country, could find no difficulty in selecting instances of failure. Indeed, Mr. B. has himself, upon another subject, said, that "hundreds of these speculations," (making settlements,) "have failed;" so that if the criterion be a correct one, the argument might be turned against himself, for these instances of failure would prove that success is not attainable in the United States. A subject, however, of this magnitude, must be viewed in the general and not in the detail. A man that can "turn his hand to any thing," be active, industrious, sober, economical, and set privations at defiance, will I believe be more successful in America than in any other country on the globe.

CAUSES OF LEAVING ENGLAND.

The soundness of Mr. Birkbeck's political reasons for emigrating must be left for every man to judge of in his own mind. By us they will be viewed favourably, because they are precisely our own. His *moral* reasons require some remark: his objects he states to be, "to procure for his children a career of enterprise "and wholesome family connexions, in a society "whose institutions are favourable to virtue." (Page 8.)

"That institutions favourable to virtue shall "produce effects correspondent to their character upon the society blessed with them, is "a conclusion so natural, that we should be inclined to suspect an error in the estimate of the "institutions themselves, if we found a vicious "people under a good government." Page 9.)

These are conclusions, I conceive, exactly such as a man versed in theoretic speculations upon the nature of society would arrive at, when contemplating a country like this, previous to his leaving Great Britain. But I am sorry to say, that a very brief residence in America will most effectually dispel the charm; and I am much concerned, that Mr. Birkbeck, when writing his book in this country, should have, I think, so unnecessarily and gratuitously placed in the hands of those, who always oppose correct principles, a weapon with which, *from his own admissions,* they can so effectually cut down himself, and, what is of infinitely more importance, the principles which he advocates. When he asserts that the constitution of the American government is good, he takes a position so strong, that he cannot by any combination of talents be dislodged from it; but when he extends his ground by concluding "*that we should* "*be inclined to suspect an error in the estimation* "*of the institutions themselves, if we find a vicious* "*people under a good government,*" his line is most effectually weakened. The American people "are like their fellow men, have," as he himself expresses it, "their irregular and rude "passions; their gross propensities, and their "follies; so that after all this is the real world, "and no poetical Arcadia." (Page 131.)

Could we begin society anew—transported from our present abodes, could we be placed in another Eden, possessing there the aid of all the knowledge and virtue, and freed from all the error and vice of the present day, then we should have *rational* grounds to anticipate, that, under a good government, there would necessarily be found a virtuous people. But as this is not the case, we must, in forming our judgment on such a subject, look at man as he is, and speculate on society as we find it; and I think we shall discover, that the materials which go to the formation of individual and of national character, spring up from a thousand other sources besides that afforded by political institutions. This view of the subject may assist us in solving an otherwise difficult question, namely, why it is, that the people of England are so much in advance of their government; and why, on the other hand, the people of America remain so very far behind the principles upon which *their* political system is founded.

I have met with but one American *Review* of Mr. Birkbeck's work; it is contained in No. 207. of "*The Port Folio,*" a respectable and long established literary publication, edited by Mr. Hall, of Philadelphia. As this article contains a fair specimen of American writing, and also admits some *awkward* political facts, which under other circumstances might perhaps have been concealed, I copy it for your information: —

"Mr. Birkbeck landed at Norfolk, with which town he "is not much pleased. A Virginian tavern he describes "as resembling 'a French one with its table d'hôte, "though not in the excellence of the cookery; but,' he "adds, that it 'somewhat exceeds it in filth, as it does an "English one in charges.' The gentlemen, he thinks, "are republican in politics, but irascible, and often lax in "morals. On his approach to Richmond, he found himself "at once in the society of persons 'who appeared to be as "polite, well dressed, and well instructed, as if they had "been repairing to the capital of Great Britain,' — whereat, "no doubt, he marvelled mightily. In the city he finds a "population of 13,000 inhabitants, of which nearly one half "is stated to be, we hope erroneously, *negroes*. Provisions

" are scarce, dear and bad, in that city. The author was " *horrified*, he says, and well he might be, at the sale of " negroes, in open market. This is a foul blot in an escut- " cheon which is blazoned with high honour, with intelli- " gence, beauty, and taste. The good folks of Richmond, " he says, are making ' a *grand stir* about a monument to " the memory of Gen. Washington;' and he takes occa- " sion to point out ' the mutilated bust of La Fayette in " their capitol, which now stands an object of horror, or " derision,' — as worthy of attention. The project of a " monument was settled long ago, as may be seen by refer- " ence to the debates in our congress (particularly in the " senate) soon after the accession of Mr. Jefferson. Our " traveller bears testimony to the ' urbanity and real polite- " ness' of the citizens of Richmond; and is pleased to " declare, that he saw ' as good husbandry as would be " expected in some well-managed districts of Great Britain.' " We were about to make some remarks upon our author's " practice of making comparisons, but an intimation at the " end of the volume, which just presents itself, renders all " observation unnecessary. We find that the volume is " intended to contain ' just the particulars' which the author " wished to communicate to his friends, and therefore it may " not be improper to take England as the standard of " excellence, in order to disabuse honest John Bull of the " impositions which have been palmed upon his voracious " credulity. When we find such gross ignorance respecting " this country, as was displayed in debate by one of the " hereditary counsellors of the crown (Lord Stanhope — vid. " Port Folio, 1816, page 341.) — it seems to be absolutely " necessary to permit writers so say at once, that what they " wish to describe is ' exactly like what we have here in " Lunnun.' It may then be believed that we are white, " can speak the English tongue, and do not carry our heads " under our shoulders: and when Lord Stanhope, or any " other expounder of the laws, undertakes to state, that an " action against a clergyman, on a bond, cannot be enter- " tained in Connecticut, he must be informed, that in matters " of this sort, the courts of Connecticut and Westminster

" Hall are governed by the same principles. If the earl " has inferred the fact from the rule *de non apparentibus*, it " is very probable that a New England docket would bear " him out; at least we should be certain of finding, for one " of our clergymen in this predicament, at least a hundred " in England scampering at a fox chase.

" But to return to Mr. Birkbeck. In travelling and " travelling along, he came to some paths, ' which, for the " most part, were only distinguishable from the rugged " waste by a slight trace, like that of a new-formed road, " or, in some instances, by rows of Lombardy poplars.' " Here he looked up, and he saw *a splendid palace;* but he " ' could liken it to nothing in America, except the painted " face and gaudy head-dress of a half-naked Indian.' The " reader will be mortified to learn, that these paths are the " '*intended* streets radiating from the capitol,' and the " palace, the very capitol of the far-famed City of Washing-" ton. Year after year, the most excellent schemes for " improving our moral and political situation are submitted " to congress, and the veterans of the revolution are borne " on ' trembling limbs' to the seat of government, to implore " for *a settlement of their accounts;* but neither our ancestors, " nor those who are to follow us, can be heard, until this " morass shall be drained, and the ' rugged waste' be filled " with houses. If Great Britain is cursed with a national " debt, we have our national city, from which it is to be " feared, that nothing short of Aladdin's Lamp will ever " relieve us. ' What is the matter?' said a gentleman at " the head of his table, addressing a guest who arose almost " immediately after the removal of the last dish, at an enter-" tainment given in this splendid city — ' I beg you to " excuse me — I have promised to take tea with your " *neighbour*.' — ' Well, well, — there's time enough for " that — pray sit down. — It is only six o'clock.' ' True, " my good sir,' said the guest — ' but you forget that I have " seven miles to ride, and your roads are very deep!' If " the money which has been exchanged for the costly " columns that have recently arrived from Italy, had been " expended in the construction of ' good roads, substantial "bridges,' and a few lamps, our traveller would have found "less reason for ridicule and complaint.

"Mr. Birkbeck commences his journal in April, 1817, "'*five hundred* miles east of Cape Henry.' He informs us "that he has quitted England for the purpose of becoming "a citizen of the United States. Of his situation as an "English farmer, he draws a picture which appears to him "very gloomy. He had no voice in the appointment of the "legislature — he had no concern in public affairs — he "could not appear at county meetings, &c. It is impossible "to reconcile the reports concerning the state of Great "Britain, which are made by travellers and emigrants. "Within a few days past, we were assured, by an intelligent "gentleman, who had recently visited Europe, most cer-"tainly with no favourable prepossessions in favour of "England, that he had not seen so much contentment and "cheerfulness in any other country. *We hope Mr. Birk-"beck has too much good sense to rate his share of felicity by "the considerations which he mentions. If he does, his new "settlements will make but slow progress. We understand "the trade of politics here quite as well as they do in foreign "parts; and it is just as difficult for modest merit to rise "from obscurity, when opposed by the intrigues of a caucus, "or the glare of wealth. We have no rotten boroughs to "sell; but when a voter is to be seduced or supplanted, we "have powerful engines in the shape of an enviable appoint-"ment abroad, or a profitable contract at home.* Man is the "same in all countries. These inestimable privileges, for "which our author sighed in vain, may easily be purchased "in any of our States, unless we except Massachusetts, "where a vote may sell high, because an office there makes "a man *honourable* during life." *

---

* In confirmation of this assertion of the reviewers, I would remark that *Honourable*, and other titles, are much sought after in America. The following extract from the "Boston Sentinel," of August 27th, will illustrate this idea: —

"*Dinner to Mr. Adams.* — Yesterday a public dinner was "given to the *Hon.* John Q. Adams, in the Exchange

You will perhaps censure me for occupying your attention with selections from Mr. Birkbeck's publication, when you are in possession of the original: my reasons for so doing, are derived from a fear, and indeed, from what you say, a belief that, because Mr. B. sets at defiance every difficulty, treating the most serious privations as a mere jest, you might possibly feel disposed to join in the opinion. The fact is, that by his style and manner he has so captivated many of his readers (Americans excepted), that they begin to feel the conveniences and establishments of civilized life a source of misery, instead of an advantage. There is, moreover, something very imposing in the circumstance, that a man of his talents and property should be perfectly satisfied with the change, notwithstanding all its attendant privations. This certainly has its weight, but having once taken the step he has done, I would merely suggest (without pretending to enter very deeply into the recesses of *the human mind*) a few considerations, why

---

" Coffee-House, by his fellow-citizens of Boston. The *Hon.* " Wm. Gray presided, assisted by the *Hon.* Harrison Gray " Otis, George Blake, Esq. and the *Hon.* Jonathan Mason, " vice-presidents. Of the guests were, the *Hon.* Mr. Adams, " late president of the United States, his *Excellency* Go- " vernor Brooks, his *Honor* Lt. Gov. Phillips, Chief Justice " Parker, Judge Story, President Kirkland, Gen. Dearborn, " Com. Hull, Gen. Miller, several of the reverend clergy, " and many public officers, and strangers of eminence."

any man, under his circumstances, would naturally look with a very lenient eye upon all defects, and where even a mole-hill in the way of excellence existed, feel inclined to magnify it into a mountain. In leaving England he evidently turned his back upon it for ever. He was disgusted with the government, and hardly any extent of disappointment would probably induce him to place himself in the humiliating situation of returning. He has gone into the wilderness—purchased a large quantity of land—has made his final election—has reasonable hopes of the speculation proving profitable—would not be disappointed with having neighbours *natives of his own country*, and similar to himself in property and in information—must desire that the value of his lands should advance as largely and as rapidly as possible; which can only be effected by emigration being directed to that point, and he having no claim to the character of a superhuman being, would not feel his sense of importance lessened, by being the founder of a large English colony. Taking these considerations into our calculation, and reflecting upon their *necessary* effect on the mind of any man so circumstanced, we may be supplied with an explanation of much that is contained in the "Notes on a Journey to Illinois."

Upon the subject of our emigration, I confess I cannot make up my mind; and that, among other reasons, causes me to desire to return to England as expeditiously as possible, that I may personally consult with you all. But with regard to the " very favourable" effect of Mr. Birkbeck's book, if you will carefully go through it again, detaching his statements from his individual feelings, you will, I think, find that if my " Reports" have reached you, they will receive no ordinary support from Mr. Birkbeck's *admissions*.

As to America generally — it possesses some most important advantages, among which are to be enumerated, an extensive and, in parts, a very fertile country — a population not filled up — and, above all, a *reasonable* and a *cheap* government. These give to the poor man a recompense for his labour proportionate to his deserts: they also open numerous sources for the valuable employment of capital; and they give a solid satisfaction, *as to the future*, in the mind of a man of family or of property, which it is impossible to derive from a contemplation of the present condition, and the present policy of any of the old governments.

In your commission to Mr. Flower for the purchase of Illinois land, you have, I doubt not, exercised all the caution which such an important procedure requires; for myself, I feel anxious for the full discussion of the subject;

but I shall defer stating my ideas further, until I have the pleasure of doing so in person. In conclusion, let me express my anxious hopes that you are all in perfect health; and as this Report will close my communications to you upon the subject of America, I assure you, it is the warmest wish of my heart, that my conduct and exertions, during the course of this short but important mission, may have deserved and may receive your full approval. Should my statements have received credit, and should they have made a similar impression upon your minds which the *reality* has produced upon my own, you must have found, like myself, frequent cause of surprise and astonishment. I perfectly remember, indeed, the impressions with which I first visited America — impressions which you all possessed in common with myself. America, we believed to be (and I am sure I *wished* to find it so) the abode of freedom and toleration, in *practice* no less than in theory. We fondly regarded it indeed, as,

" That land where '*self-government*' calls forth the mind.
" And the rights and the virtues of man are combined;
" *Where the thought, unrestrained, 'mid truth's regions may fly*
" Uncaged from the earth, may aspire to the sky;
" *What the bosom conceives*, that *the tongue may express*:
" Not bounded by *bigots* the power to bless;
" That land where *Religion*'s sweet voice may arise,
" *Where, with Liberty, Virtue may walk 'neath the skies*:

"Where, safe from each danger, secure from each storm,
"*Lovely Freedom may nurse youthful Piety's form;*
"*Where man, feeling his value, the impulse once given,*
"*May* dare *to deserve the rich blessings of heaven!*"

How far the country may have answered these our sanguine expectations — at least, how far I have believed them answered, I must leave each of you to conclude from the facts I have forwarded, and the general tenor of my observations upon them.

EIGHTH REPORT.

Illinois Land. — *Commission to Mr. Flower.* — *Mr. Birkbeck's Mode of extolling Illinois.* — *Climate of Eastern Cities.* — *Ohio Land.* — *Profits on Capital.* — *Society in the Western Country.* — *Emigration.* — *Letter from Cincinnati.* — *Spanish Patriots.* — *What Classes of Emigrants may succeed and what not.* — *Plan of Mr. Birkbeck's Settlement.*

Plaistow, Essex, England, Sept. 1st. 1818.

AGREEING with the suggestion of our friend L———, that my Reports require some general observations, as a sort of *wind-up* on the subject of America, I sit down for the purpose of endeavouring to give such accordingly; which, when effected, may remove the necessity of my frequently communicating with our more distant friends in Leicestershire and Yorkshire. I propose also, at the same time, to adopt the hint of Mr. A———, relative to our supposed property in the Illinois; and shall further give my opinion of Mr. Birkbeck's "Letters" from that State.

In regard to the first, we should, I think, be particular in correcting an idea which many entertain, that we are *actual* land-owners in the Illinois; when the fact of the case is, that Mr. George Flower, (the associate of Mr. Birkbeck,) who sailed in the "Anne Maria" from Liverpool some weeks before my arrival in England, was commissioned to purchase for us nine thousand acres, adjoining his and Mr. Birkbeck's settlement; and as we have since received but one letter from him, and that merely announcing his arrival in New York, after a fine passage of thirty days; we are not yet, at least to our knowledge, American land-proprietors.

With respect to Mr. Birkbeck's "Letters "from Illinois," several of our London friends (who had seen some of them in manuscript long before their publication) know my opinion; but to those in the country, who had not even heard of them, until their appearance before the public, I would offer a few brief remarks; though to make such must necessarily be extremely difficult, as the work consists of copies of private correspondence, in which the *details* necessary for the consideration of a proposed emigrant not being required, are therefore but very partially given. I shall, however, be relieved from a lengthened consideration of them, as much of what I have said in my communication from New York, concerning the "Notes," will be strictly applicable to the "Letters;" the latter giving but little additional information. One thing I would observe, and which is a subject of regret to those who wish well to Mr. Birkbeck's reputation, that the charge would seem but too well founded that his "*Letters* are less impartial, less philo-" sophic, and less *disinterested* than his *Notes*." In his exclusive recommendation of the Illinois, there would seem almost a fixed determination to be self-satisfied; indeed he admits, "that look-" ing at it now with a favourable eye, as I *wish* " *to do*, I see new advantages continually rising " before me." (P. 79.) And it must be lamented by Mr. Birkbeck's friends, that his eagerness to advance his own settlement is rather too apparent; for not only Great Britain, but also every other part of America must be pressed into the service of extolling Illinois. We are told, in regard to England, that "the soil is " worn out;" and in relation to *old* America, that the climate of the eastern cities presents " melting, oppressive sultry nights, succeeding " broiling days, and forbidding rest, which are " said to wear out the frames of the languid in-" habitants of the eastern cities, but which are " unknown here."

That the climate of the eastern cities is probably not so healthy as that of England, I believe; but much which causes this difference equally exists in the western States. For myself, I heard more of "sickness" (the term by which every kind of indisposition is designated) in the western than in the eastern States; and the appearance of the people entirely confirms the belief that, as yet, *old* is more healthy than *new* America; not, I should presume, from a *natural superiority* of climate, but the more extended cultivation of the country gives it, of course, an actual, although probably only a temporary superiority.

English emigrants are told in the "Notes," that "those who are not screwed up to the full "pitch of enterprise, had better remain in Old "England than attempt agriculture, or business "of any kind, (manual operations excepted,) in "the Atlantic States."—What does Mr. Cobbett say to this, as *from personal knowledge* he can recommend the Atlantic States only?—And in the "Letters," that even "land in Ohio cannot "be had at less than from 20 to 50 dollars per "acre;" that it is "technically called im-"proved," but it is in "fact deteriorated;" that it was "impossible to obtain a good posi-"tion in Ohio, at a price which common pru-"dence could justify, or indeed at any price." To fairly consider those statements would require a repetition of the information which I sent you from Kentucky and Illinois; to that, therefore, I wish to direct your attention; and I here merely insert an advertisement taken from the Philadelphia "Democratic Press," January 1818.

" OHIO LANDS.

" Eleven hundred and ninety acres of land, for sale for Cash,
" or Real Estate in Philadelphia, situated on the East Fork
" of Todd's Creek, a branch of the Little Miami, in the
" county of Clinton, about ten miles from the seat of justice,
" Wilmington; about 5 miles from Lebanon, the next county
" town; and about 3 miles from the great mail road to Cin-
" cinnati. For terms, apply at the office of the Democratic
" Press, or of William Lowry, Lebanon, Ohio.
" Jan. 21.—wfm3t."

The price asked for this land is *seven* dollars per acre.

The power of capital is depicted very strongly. Mr. B. states, " the fact is, however, that *the* " *profits of capital on every thing in this country* " *are marvellous.* In the case of live-stock, the " outgoings are so small, that the receipts are " nearly all clear." (P. 18.) Looking at this paragraph, and several others throughout the " Letters" of a similar tendency, I must observe that these " *marvellous profits*" *are matters of speculation*, and, like all such, are liable to afford great success, or equally exposed to great and ruinous failure: even in Mr. Birkbeck's own case, they are, as yet, in *anticipation*. These *miraculous* schemes belong more to the age of Sir Walter Raleigh, than to the sober character of the nineteenth century; but in Mr. Birkbeck's letter to his son, he remarks upon " *pro-* " *fits*," that " housekeeping and other expences " being paid, there remains a profit of 22 per "cent. on the capital; and you are improving "your own estate." (P. 49.)

From this, *which is a defined statement*, you may derive some satisfaction in calculating the profit and loss of a removal to the western country; and not be induced by general assertion to expect to find the territory of Illinois "paved "with gold," or to discover there the philosopher's stone.

Among other inducements held out to his friend to emigrate, Mr. B. represents *even the society* of the wilderness as desirable. He says, "In good faith, I think you would have nothing "to regret in exchanging such a circle as I "fancy yours to be, for any society that would "surround you in these wild woods." (P. 26.) What this latter society would prove, I might pourtray from the information which I have myself collected; but I shall prefer quoting Mr. Birkbeck's own excellent description from other parts of his work.

"Its elements" (those of society) "are rude "certainly, and heterogeneous. The first settlers, "unprotected and unassisted, amid dangers and "difficulties, have been accustomed, from early "youth, to rely on their own powers; and *they* "*surrender with reluctance, and only by halves,* "*their right of defence against every aggression,* "*even to the laws which themselves have con-* "*stituted!*" (P. 97.)

These laws, we are told, have been made, "anxiously studious of mildness;" but that in practice "they seem inefficient:" for that "deeds of savage and even ferocious violence" are committed, "too common to be viewed "with the abhorrence due to them." (P. 97.) This admission of such a difference between the *theory* of law and its *practical execution*, is of the first importance to every man who contemplates becoming a member of such a community: and this though we are told in the succeeding paragraph, that the innate feeling of justice is so strong, that "if a man, whom the public voice "has proclaimed a thief or a swindler, escapes "from justice for the *want of legal proof of his "guilt*, THOUGH THE LAW AND A JURY OF HIS "FELLOW-CITIZENS HAVE ACQUITTED HIM, *ten "to one but he is met with before he can quit the "neighbourhood, and, tied up to a sapling, re-"ceives a scourging that marks him for the rest "of his life!!!*" (P. 97, 98.)

This is certainly another most important *admission;* and although it may be passed off in half seriousness—half raillery—yet it is *no joke* to be told that a man, whom "*the laws and a "jury of his fellow-citizens have acquitted,*" should be liable "*to be tied up to a sapling, and "receive a scourging that may mark him for the "rest of his life.*" There are no doubt some instances where this barbarous procedure would be merited; but how often is the "public voice" mistaken in its "proclamations?" It is also to be presumed, that many of these *innate* lovers of justice were not in court, could not have heard the evidence, and yet they exercise, at the dictation of their own sovereign will, the power of inflicting a punishment more severe than would have attended convicted villainy. The judges too would seem to partake of this "free" order of things. "A notorious offender "had escaped from confinement, and, mounted "on a capital horse, paraded the town where "the judge resided with a brace of pistols, "calling at the stores and grog-shops, and de-"claring he would shoot any man who should "attempt to molest him. The judge hearing "of it, loaded a pistol, walked deliberately up "to the man to apprehend him, and on his "making a shew of resistance, shot him imme-"diately!" (P. 62.)

Of what benefit, I would ask, can civilization, of what advantage can "*mild laws*," or *any* laws be, to a people that have such judges, and who set their own legislature at defiance? who disregard the verdict of a jury, and who inflict upon an ACQUITTED fellow-citizen "deeds "of savage and even ferocious violence?" And these form part of that society concerning which Mr. Birkbeck writes to a friend in England, that he would "have nothing to "regret in making the exchange." But Mr. Birkbeck is satisfied, and "*liberty* is no subject "of dispute or speculation among us back "woods' men—it is the very atmosphere we "breathe." "In passing" also "from theory "to practice," Mr. B. "has experienced no "diminution of his love for freedom:" nor have I done so either; but I certainly *have* experienced a most sensible diminution in my love for the *possessors* of freedom; and so when I consider his language elsewhere, I must conclude has Mr. Birkbeck, when I find him declaring that he wants language to express "the "loathing" he feels for personal slavery; that when "PRACTISED BY FREE MEN IT IS MOST "DETESTABLE;" that "*it is the leprosy of the* "*United States, a foul blotch, which, more or* "*less, contaminates the* ENTIRE *system in public* "*and in private, from the* PRESIDENT'S CHAIR "TO THE CABIN OF THE HUNTER!" (P. 71.)

Previous to my offering some explanation relative to *the Kentucky resolutions in favour of the Spanish patriots*, I would remark, that the *American* emigration to the western country is certainly very great. Mr. Birkbeck says upon this subject, that he had "just read a statement of "500 emigrants per week passing through Al-"bany westward. This occurred on *one road*, "and that far to the north. If it were really "so unwise to migrate westward, out of the

" tens (I was going to say hundreds) of thou-" sands who move annually from the eastern " States into this western wilderness, we should " hear of some returning." (P. 10, 11.) With regard to the force of the remark, that so many pass on *one road, and that far to the north*, it is well to understand, that there are but *two* roads to the western country which are generally frequented by emigrants; and indeed but *one* which is travelled by stage waggons. Respecting none returning, I insert the following letter from the " Eastern Argus;" not because it conveys my ideas, for, in fact, I differ from the writer, but to shew that opposite opinions *are* entertained upon the subject of western emigration.

" EMIGRATION TO THE WEST.

" The following is an extract of a letter from a gentleman " who recently left this place in company with two others, " for the purpose of establishing themselves in business in the " western country. The letter speaks too plainly for itself " to stand in need of any comments of ours. We have never " had a doubt that a vast number of the emigrants, we be-" lieve a very great majority, have been sorely disappointed " in their calculation. Many have returned, and many " more, after spending a considerable part of their property " in a long and expensive journey, have found themselves " obliged, much against their will, to continue. Some we " have known who, after spending all their property in jour-" neying over the country to find a suitable place for settle-" ment, have returned as soon as they could save, with great " frugality, enough from their earning to pay their expences " home. We recommend this letter to those who are about " to seek for mines of wealth beyond the mountains; but at "all events, before embarking their fortune in such an en-"terprise, we would urge upon them to see and converse "with some judicious person who has had an opportunity "of seeing the country and judging from his own observ-"ation.

"*Cincinnati, Aug.* 13. 1817.

Dear Sir,

"I arrived here the first day of the present month, after "a tedious journey down the river of twelve days, and must "confess I am greatly disappointed in my expectations. "I received two letters to this place from the brother of "Ruggles Whiting, he being at Boston himself. After "showing my documents to the gentlemen to whom they "were directed, and receiving from them all the civilities "they could bestow, and opinions as to business, I am con-"vinced that it would be folly in the extreme for me to "attempt to do any thing in the grocery line. Business, "they say, is duller than it ever was before known. We "all, to tell the truth, are disappointed, and are determined "not to stop here longer than a week from this. We are "at present undetermined what route to take; there are "only two that we have in mind; one is, to wait here about "three weeks and then take passage to New Orleans, for "which we can receive fifty dollars a piece, and not much "labour, only to use the oars to keep the boat from striking "rocks. These boats are about 25 feet long and 15 wide, "and carry from 3 to 500 barrels salt, flour, &c.: the cur-"rent sets them, in good water, from 80 to 100 miles per day. "The other route is to tramp from here to Alexandria (Col.) "which is not far from 600 miles. I think we shall adopt "the former.

"I will state some of the disadvantages that present "themselves; the first is, my goods must come from New "Orleans, which is 1700 miles from this: I have to pay five "cents on the pound for transportation: their usual passage "from here to that place is about 30 days, from that to "this 100 days; and by the time I could get my goods "here, it would cost me all the cash I have for board, which

" is from three to seven dollars per week. Shop-rent is " higher here than in Boston. You cannot hire a store here " like one in Haymarket Row [Portland] under 1300 dollars " the year. As to health, I am told by a doctor whom I have " had to vaccinate me, that there are in this place *eighteen* of " his profession, and all of them getting rich ; and I should " think they would — he charged me two dollars for vaccin- " ating.

" Upon the whole I must say, that I wish myself in New " England, and probably shall be in about three months. I " should advise no friend to emigrate to this place, except " he be a farmer, and he ought to come (if at all) at *ten* " years of age, and by the time he is *forty*, if he is indus- " trious, may do.

" This probably will be the last you will hear of me until " about the 1st of October, when I expect to be in New " Orleans.

" Respectfully, &c.

W****** M**** "

At page 103. Mr. Birkbeck inserts the excellent *Resolutions passed in the State of Kentucky in favour of the Spanish Patriots.* The inference which the reader must naturally draw from thence is, that these rosolutions are expressive of the feelings of *Americans generally* upon that interesting subject. Mr. B. observes, in introducing them, that they " shew that the citizens " of Kentucky are sensible that to be in the " possession and exercise of the rights of self- " government is a blessing ;" — (*Kentucky is a slave State*) — " and that their hearts are enlarged " by it, and inflamed, not by jealousy of their " neighbours' welfare, but with zeal to promote " it." That " these resolutions are indicative "of a good spirit, and *thus are in accordance "with the general feeling, as far as I can gather, "of the citizens of all the States of the Union.*" Now what are the simple facts of this case?—Mr. Clay, the speaker of the House of Representatives, is a resident of, and member deputed from, Kentucky; he is well known to be straining every nerve to obtain the next Presidency; he is extremely mortified at Mr. Adams's having received an appointment to the office (Secretary of State) which is considered that of the "heir "apparent;" he is taking every *safe* means to thwart the proceedings of the general government; he sees that they are backward in the cause of the patriots; he knows that by being its advocate he will not endanger any acquired popularity, for the Americans *theoretically* cannot oppose the glorious cause of the Spanish colonies, and in the probable event of their success he will acquire the charater of a great statesman. He therefore set on foot, in the legislature of that State in which he had most influence (Kentucky), resolutions in favour of the patriots. When they were discussed in the senate of Kentucky, counter resolutions were proposed by Mr. Owens, as a substitute for those of Mr. Bledsoe; but upon the vote the latter passed. Let us next look at the assertion that these resolutions are in accordance with the general feelings of the "citizens "of *all the States in the Union.*" From what sources I would ask, and I ask it with regret, are we justified in drawing this inference? Is it from the law recently passed to prevent the shipment of warlike stores? is it from the seizure of Amelia Island? is it from the imprisonment and barbarous treatment of the British officers at Philadelphia, who were there on their route to join the patriots (and *because they were going to join the patriots*)? or is it from *the very remarkable fact, that, I believe, up to the day of my leaving America*, which was the 10th May, (although the resolutions are copied from the "Western "Citizen" of the 10th February,) *not one state, county, city, or borough throughout the whole Union, had followed the example of Kentucky!!!*

I have been thus free in my strictures upon Mr. Birkbeck's "*Letters*," because I have seen the effect which they have produced upon your minds, and I believe that effect to be an improper one. This has arisen, I apprehend, more from the *mode* in which the information is conveyed than from the information itself; for it appears to me that throughout the work there are those *admissions* which no colouring ought to prevent the mind of a reader from viewing as most serious considerations, connected with an Illinois settlement. Mr. Birkbeck, in fact, writes with such superior talent, throwing at the same time such a charm over every thing he describes, that it is difficult not to be captivated — and influenced, as he has naturally been, by his situation; giving little or no attention to the important consideration that the mass of those who read his book know nothing of the *objections* to the country concerning which he writes; that they *really can have no conception* of the entire change of life which is required — of the *extreme difference* which exists between an English residence, and one in the back woods of America; and that many of them may possess neither the enthusiasm nor the *accommodateableness* (as a correspondent of mine at Liverpool expressed it) of which Mr. Birkbeck and his family so evidently and so largely partake: — I say, not perhaps sufficiently attending to these circumstances, he appears to me to bring every thing which is pleasing in his new settlement forward upon the canvas, throwing every objection into the shade, insomuch that his two works, however contrary to his actual intention, have, I really fear, the effect, to general readers, of making "the worse appear the better reason." For myself, highly as I think of Mr. Birkbeck, (though I have not the honour of a personal acquaintance,) and anxious as I certainly am, that, in the event of our going to Illinois, we should be in his neighbourhood, yet we must all of us be ready to allow that every one in resolving upon a measure so important, not only to himself but to his posterity, as emigration certainly is, should examine and re-examine every statement; exercising the most deliberate caution, and, if possible, expelling altogether the mere suggestions of the imagination, remembering that, in the language of Mr. Birkbeck, the country he describes " is the real world, and no poetical " Arcadia."

In going to America then, I would say generally, the emigrant must expect to find—not an economical or cleanly people; not a social or generous people; not a people of enlarged ideas; not a people of liberal opinions, or towards whom you can express your thoughts " free as air;" not a people friendly to the advocates of liberty in Europe; not a people who understand liberty from investigation and from principle; not a people who comprehend the meaning of the words " honour" and " generosity." On the other hand he will find a country possessed of the most enlightened civil and political advantages; a people reaping the full reward of their own labours, a people not paying tythes, and not subjected to heavy taxation without representation; a people with a small national debt; a people without spies and informers; a people without an enormous standing army; a people in possession of an extent of territory capable of sustaining an increase of millions and tens of millions of population; and a people rapidly advancing towards national wealth and greatness.

The classes of British society who would be

benefited by an exchange of country, are, I conceive, first, that large and much injured body of men, who are here chained to the country and the political system, which oppresses and grinds them to the earth, — I mean *our extreme poor.* They would not be in America a week, before they would experience a rapid advance in the scale of being. Instead of depending for subsistence upon charity soup, occasional parochial relief, and bowing with slavish submission to the tyrant of the poor-house; they would, if industrious and willing to labour, earn 4s. 6d. to 6s. 9d. a day, have meat at least seven times in the week, and know "no one who "could make them afraid." The second class would be the mechanics, in branches of first necessity, with the general exclusion, however, of those acquainted with the British staple manufactures of cotton and woollen only; but for others, whose earnings here are under 30s. a week, or whose employment is of that precarious nature, that they cannot reasonably calculate, by the exercise of prudence and economy, on laying by any thing for what is called "a rainy day," or on making a provision for old age — for such persons as these, *particularly if they have, or anticipate the having a family,* emigration to America will certainly advance their pecuniary interests, though it may not enlarge their mental sphere of enjoyments. To these two classes, I would further add that of the small farmer who has a family, for whom he can now barely provide the necessaries of life, and concerning a provision for whom, when his own grey hairs are approaching to the grave, he can look forward with but little confidence or satisfaction; to such a man, if he should have one hundred pounds clear, that is, after paying all his expences of removal, &c., America decidedly offers inducements very superior to those afforded by this country. Such a father would there feel himself relieved from a load of anxiety, the weight of which upon his spirits, and its influence in repressing his exertions, he is perhaps himself scarcely aware of, till he feels the difference by comparison when he has shaken it off in the New World;—but still to every proposed emigrant, even of these classes, I would say, that he must not expect to find either the country full of gold, or its inhabitants as agreeable or as sociable as the perhaps unequalled people of England. He must prepare too for very many privations, and should previously have the *mind* of his family, particularly that of the mother of his children, so entirely in unison with his own, that they can all have the fortitude and good sense necessary to bear under the numerous privations they will certainly be subjected to, keeping in mind the substantial advantages they will enjoy, and setting off present evil against their future and increasing prosperity, which, in such a country, with a soil yet uncultivated, and in the infancy of its resources, may be considered as almost insured to them.

The man of small fortune, who cares little about politics, to whom the *comforts* of England are perhaps in some degree essential, but who wishes to curtail his expenditure, would not act wisely by emigrating to America. Indeed, should such a man make the attempt, he would return as expeditiously as did a family who arrived at New York in the Pacific, on the 25th March, with the intention of continuing, but who took a passage back in the same vessel the following week; —they went to America in the cabin, they departed from it in the steerage.

The artist *may* succeed, but the probability is, that he will not do so. I know instances on both sides, where, perhaps, equal talent has been possessed. A Mr. Shiels, a portrait-painter, who was a fellow-passenger of mine in the Washington, has been eminently successful in New York; Mr. ———, who arrived about the same time, has been unable to procure his boarding expences. Generally, I should not anticipate, judging from the character and habits of the people, that, at least, the superior artist would find it to his advantage to emigrate. The lawyer and the doctor, and, turning to another class, the clerk and the shopman, will find no opening in America.

The London linen and woollen draper, and haberdasher, who has large capital, good connections in this country, and who would adopt the most improved English modes of transacting retail business, would, I think, be very successful; — though, it should be understood, that shopkeeping is overdone throughout America; but their plan of doing business is so defective, that I conceive there may be a good opening for a person with the above qualifications.

A literary man will not meet with any encouragement, the American library being imported, and newspaper editors having no inducement to occupy their talents upon any topics beyond extracts from English papers, advertisements, and shipping intelligence.

The very superior mechanic, in a business of which the articles have heretofore been imported, might succeed; and if he did so at all, it would probably be in an eminent degree. Two cases of this sort came under my knowledge: Mr. ——, of P——, manufacturer of bird-cages, fenders, and brass stands for fire-places, arrived in America, without property, has brought up a large family, and is now a man of considerable wealth. Mr. ———, of ———, a piano-forte maker, has been similarly successful. I do not state these cases on the ground that there is now an opening in either of these callings, but merely as illustrative of the idea given at the commencement of this paragraph.

The merchant I do not conceive would be very successful, that being a profession so adapted to the native American habits, and is entirely preoccupied.

To the capitalist, as such, I hardly know what to say: America is the country of speculation, and therefore, as such, capital *might* be employed with singular advantage. On the whole, to such I can only recommend a perusal of the previous details.

Knowing that you feel interested in Mr. Birkbeck's settlement, I forward a plan of it, which was sent from Illinois to this country a short time before my arival in that territory, by a gentleman connected with Mr. Birkbeck.

Plan shewing the situation of Mr. Birkbeck's and Mr. Flower's first purchase in the Illinois territory.

Range X. Township II. East of 3d. Meridian.

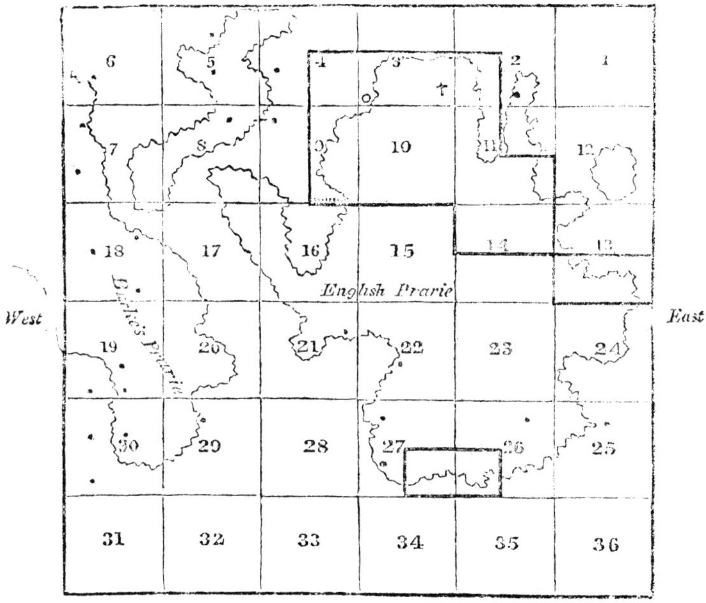

Note.—Every square in the above is one mile, or 640 acres, 36 miles forming a *township*; the squares are called *sections*.

REFERENCES, &c.

"English Prairie," in lat. 38° 30′ N. and long. 88° W. of London, is 4½ miles long, and 4 miles wide; it is high on the N. and E. sides, and lies on a ridge about equal distances (6 miles) from the Great and the Little Wabash.

The strong lines inclose Mr. Birkbeck's and Mr. Flower's purchases.

† Site, said to be that intended for Mr. Birkbeck's house.

...... Proposed line of cottages.

o A hunting cabin of Mr. Birkbeck's party.

. . . . . . Entries of American back woods' men, all but six of which are said to have been made between August and November 1817.

APPENDIX.

FOR THE INFORMATION OF EMIGRANTS.

CHOICE OF A VESSEL. — A ship is preferable to a brig, as the sea motion in the former will be less felt, and the accommodations are generally superior. The English ships in the American trade are not equal to those in other trades; whilst, on the contrary, the best American vessels are in the British trade; so that it is well to select an American ship, the *safe* age of which will be according to the quality of the timber and the building, and these can only be known by persons very conversant in those subjects. There are certain ships of established reputation, a few of which go to the port of London, and a greater number to Liverpool; among the former are the Electra, Captain Robinson, and the Tontine, Captain Turly, for Philadelphia; the Criterion, Captain Avery, and the Minerva Smyth (a very superior ship), Captain Allen, for New York; there is also the Venus of New York, the character of which is, I believe, respectable; but I cannot speak of her from personal knowledge. From the port of Liverpool there are a great number of first-rate ships for Philadelphia, Boston, and New York; among the latter is what are called the "Packet Line," which consists of the Pacific, (an old but good vessel,) Captain Williams; the Amity, Captain Stanton; the Courier, Captain Bowne; and the James Munroe, Captain Watkinson (Captain Watkinson is a careful and excellent seaman). One of these vessels sails *punctually* on the first of every month from Liverpool. The charge for passage is, in the cabin, 45 guineas, which includes wine, and, indeed, almost every luxury — in the steerage 9l. exclusive of every thing but water. The house of Crapper, Benson, and Co. at Liverpool, are the agents for these ships, which are first-rate in every respect, and all their commanders are men of great experience. There are also, quite equal to these, the Nestor, Captain Stirling; the Atlantic, Captain Matlock; and the Anne Maria, Captain Waite (of the latter vessel and captain, Mr. Flower, who recently went in her with a large party to the United States, speaks in the very highest terms): to these I would add, as respectable ships, the Ann, the Carolina Ann, and the Importer. There are several others of this class with whose names I am not familiar; but it would be judicious in every person to make minute enquiries as to the character of the ship and captain with which they propose engaging; for it should be known that there are some very indifferent American ships, which go to both Liverpool and London, and particularly the latter port. *A regular trader* is generally to be preferred to a chance ship. The prices (with the exception of the packet ships) will vary according to circumstances; for the cabin from 30 to 45, and for the steerage from 7 to 10 guineas. It should be remarked that even this is a subject of barter. A few ships sail from Bristol and Greenock for New York — the Fanny from the latter port is rather celebrated. A passage from Havre, in France, to America, is often to be obtained much cheaper than from this country. Should a large party engage the same vessel, they would act prudently to procure an extra boat, for in case of accident or shipwreck, the two ship-boats would not be found sufficient; and upon such melancholy occurrences the crew commonly escape, and the passengers are lost.

Cabin Passengers, though supplied by the Captain, would find a small private stock desirable. A plum cake, soda powders, a few good apples and oranges (the latter will keep if not previously bruised, and if each orange is carefully rolled in paper), preserves of several kinds, and cider, which will be found particularly pleasant at sea.

Steerage Passengers should provide for seventy, though they may not be out more than fifty days. They are compelled by law to take 80lbs. of meat. I should recommend a variety; say 30lbs. beef, 20 of ham, 20 of tongue, 10 of bacon: herrings are pleasant, and salt cod particularly so, when eaten with egg-sauce: 50lbs. bread, of the best biscuit, and loaves cut in slices and toasted: rusks will be found very pleasant in tea: 30 to 40lbs. of flour; a few pounds of oatmeal; ditto of rice; ditto of groats; ditto of arrow-root; 10 cheese; 100lbs. potatoes. Have a small net bag to boil them in: this will prevent confusion with the cook, and also their being exchanged for others of, perhaps, an inferior quality. 5lbs. coffee, *ground*, and kept corked in a bottle, for the purpose of excluding the atmospheric air: 1lb. tea; 14lbs. sugar: a small quantity of spirits, of wine, and bottled porter: the latter, mixed with an equal quantity of water, with sugar and nutmeg, will be found very agreeable. Have a definite understanding for the quantity of water per day. A filtering machine can be bought at 79. Titchfield-street, London, for 20s. Eggs to be kept in bran, and frequently turned. 10lbs. butter. Milk will keep, if boiled, and mixed with sugar, in the proportion of 2lbs. to the quart. If the articles enumerated under the head *Cabin Passengers* can be afforded, they would be found particularly pleasant. If there are females in the party, there should be some fowls. A few tin articles for the purposes of cooking,

&c. Sea sickness cannot be prevented by any thing with which I am acquainted, though it can be materially lessened by being as much as possible upon deck, and by eating little at a time, and frequently.

In choosing a birth, either in the cabin or steerage, the middle of the vessel, or as near to it as can be procured, is desirable, on account of the ship's motion being there less felt. Books will be an occasional, and but an occasional, relief to the monotony of a sea voyage. Those of a light and amusing character are the most suitable. Reading for more than half an hour at any one time produces the head-ache, and sensibly affects the eyes. *Medicines* are an important article of sea stores: they should be in pills, and taken frequently, with great exactness, at stated periods, and in as small quantities as can possibly produce the effect. Steerage passengers should have a specific agreement with the captain for the use of the place of convenience: this is an important consideration; and I have heard of great inconvenience experienced by such persons in being denied this. A flute, a violin, and a pack of cards, are pleasant companions.

Packing up. — A SELECTION should be made in a box by themselves of clothes intended to be worn at sea. Those of the most inferior kind will do as well as the best. A warm great coat will be found useful. The provision casks should be written on " Stores." Baggage must be entered at the Custom-house; and in procuring a *cocket*, care should be taken that the whole of the packages are enumerated: if this is neglected, an additional expence will be incurred.

Articles desirable to be taken out. — Clothing of every kind, except silks and silk pocket handkerchiefs. Females would do well to take no article of dress, *particular* in appearance. Men's trowsers should be of the *Wel-*

lington kind only. The American fashions differ in some things from ours; and any deviation from them is much remarked upon. Most convenient and unbreakable articles of domestic utensils. No cabinet furniture. A good stock of table-linen and bedding: whether feather-beds are desirable or not is, I believe, questionable. Carpeting, if it can be cut to suit other sized rooms; stationery of every kind; agricultural implements; musical and philosophical instruments.

United States' Duties on Importation upon the following Articles:

	Per Cent.
Side and Fire Arms - -	20
All articles manufactured of brass -	20
Buttons - - -	20
Bonnets - - - -	30
Bridles and Saddles - -	30
Books (blank) - - -	30
Cutlery - - -	20
All articles manufactured of cotton -	25
Millinery - - -	30
All articles manufactured of copper -	20
Ditto of pewter - -	20
Ditto of steel - - -	20
Ditto of tin - - -	20
Parasols and Umbrellas - -	30
Paper - - - -	30
Printing Types - - -	20
All articles manufactured of wool -	25
Ditto of wood - - -	30
Ditto of earthen and stone ware -	20
Ale and Beer in bottles, per gallon 8d.	
Ditto in casks - - - 5¼d.	
Shoes (leather), per pair - - 13d.	

Articles free of Duties :

Philosophical Apparatus, if specially imported by order, and for the use of any society, incorporated for philosophical or literary purposes, or for the encouragement of the fine arts, or by order and for the use of any seminary of learning.

Anatomical Preparations.

Animals imported for breed.

Wearing Apparel, and other personal baggage, in actual use.

Rate of Coins :

English Pound Sterling is 4 dollars, 44 cents.

Irish ditto, 4 dollars, 10 cents.

French Livre, $18\frac{1}{2}$ cents.

Dutch Florin, or Guilder, 40 cents.

Fees of Officers :

To the Collectors and Naval Officers,

Every port entry 2 dollars.

Permit to land goods 20 cents.

Every bond taken officially 40 cents.

Bill of health 20 cents.

(There is commonly a demand of two dollars made for this by the captain : this is, of course, an imposition.)

Passengers' Baggage, &c.

Entry is to be made by passengers of all clothes, tools or implements of trade, or profession, arriving in the United States to settle, which articles are exempted from duty. The form of such entry, and oath respecting the same, as follows:

Entry of baggage, wearing apparel, &c. imported by in the master, from New-York,

(Here the particulars to be inserted.)

District of
Port of

I, do solemnly, sincerely, and truly swear, (*or affirm,*) that the entry subscribed by me and hereto annexed, contains, to the best of my knowledge and belief, a just and true account of the contents of the several mentioned in the said entry, imported in the from and that they contain no goods, wares, or merchandise whatever, other than the wearing apparel and other personal baggage (*or if the case require*) and the tools of the trade of all which are the property of who has, or have arrived, who is, or are shortly expected to arrive in the United States: and are not directly or indirectly imported for any other person or persons, or intended for sale.

So help me God.

If the articles shall be entered by any other person than the owner, bond to be given in a sum equal to the amount of what the duties would be, if imported subject to duty; that the owner shall within one year verify such entry on oath, or the collector may direct such baggage to be examined; and if any article is contained therein, which ought to pay duty, entry must be made thereof; and if an entry is made as aforesaid, and upon examination thereof, any article is found therein subject to duty, (*not having been expressed at the time of making the entry,*) it is forfeited, and the person in whose baggage the same shall be found, forfeits and shall pay treble the value thereof.

Mechanics, intending to continue as such, would do well to remain in New York, Baltimore, or Philadelphia, until they become familiarised with the country. Persons designing to settle in the western States will save some expences by landing in Philadelphia. Those to whom a few pounds is not an object, will shorten their voyage two or three days by arriving at New York. The summer route from thence to Philadelphia is particularly pleasant, with the exception of 25 miles land-carriage, and sleeping one night on the road: the whole can be completed for about ten dollars. In winter, there are excellent stages (by far the best in America) from New York to Philadelphia: the fare is from eight to ten dollars, and the journey is completed in fourteen hours, —distance, 96 miles.

The route to the western country, by way of New Orleans, is attended with many disadvantages: it is much longer, and more dangerous, in consequence of a great deal of coasting, and the difficulties of the gulph of Florida. The voyage from the Balaize, at the junction of the Mississippi with the gulph of Mexico, to New Orleans, though but 100 miles, is always tedious, and sometimes vessels are three weeks in getting up that distance. The yellow fever is of annual occurrence at New Orleans. The steam-boats, though numerous, *cannot* proceed at stated periods, and a residence at New Orleans may be long, and *must be expensive;* and to take passage in a keel-boat *up* the stream, would be an almost endless undertaking.

The best mode, in my judgment, is to proceed from Philadelphia by way of Pittsburgh. Horseback is very preferable to the stage, particularly on the Allegany mountains. A poor family would have their baggage conveyed in the cheapest way by the regular stage-waggons,—themselves walking; and this they will find in crossing the mountains to be better than riding (except on horseback). They should take with them as good a stock of *eatables* as they can with convenience, the charges on the road being very extravagant. Those who have their own waggons should have them made as strong as possible, and their horses should be in good condition. Small articles of cutlery, and all the machinery necessary for repairs on the road, are of first necessity. When arrived at Pittsburgh, the cheapest and easiest mode of travelling is to float down the river; for which purpose there are boats of almost every variety, (steam-boats excepted,) from 2s. 3d. upwards, per hundred miles. Upon this mode of travelling I do not enlarge: half an hour's residence in Pittsburgh will convey more information than I could in twenty pages. Warm clothing should be taken, as there is sure to be some *severe* weather in every part of America. The articles required in floating down the river will be nearly as follows:—The "Pittsburgh Navigator," a small volume, and which may be had at Cramer and Spears; nails, hammer, hatchet, tinder-box, box for fire, gridiron, iron pot, coffee-pot, coffee-mill, tea-pot, plates, spoons, knives and forks, mugs, candles, coffee, tea, sugar, spirits, meat, potatoes, bread, pens and ink, paper, medicine, and a gun. If there is what is called "a good stage of water," that is, if the waters of the Ohio are high, which they always are in the spring and autumn, boats will be taken by the stream, without rowing, from three to four miles per hour. Except in cases of dense fog, they can be allowed to float at night in the Ohio. In the

Mississippi this would not be safe, the navigation of the latter river being both difficult and dangerous. Unless the waters of the Ohio are very high at its falls near Louisville, a pilot should be engaged to navigate the boat over them.

THE END.

☞ *The Author will take pleasure in attending to any communications on the subject of America, if letters are addressed to him (post-paid) at Messrs. Coates and Fearon's, Wine-Merchants,* 18. *Adam-Street, Adelphi.*